Terror Threat

INTERNATIONAL AND HOMEGROWN
TERRORISTS AND THEIR
THREAT TO CANADA

Terror Threat

INTERNATIONAL AND HOMEGROWN TERRORISTS AND THEIR THREAT TO CANADA

Dwight Hamilton
Kostas Rimsa

DUNDURN PRESS
TORONTO

Copy-editor: Andrea Waters
Designer: Erin Mallory
Printer: Transcontinental

Library and Archives Canada Cataloguing in Publication

Hamilton, Dwight, 1963-

Terror threat : international and homegrown terrorists and their threat to Canada / Dwight Hamilton, Kostas Rimsa.

ISBN 978-1-55002-736-5 (bound)
1. Terrorism--Canada. I. Rimsa, Kostas II. Title.

HV6433.C3H34 2007   303.6'250971   C2007-904656-8

Conseil des Arts du Canada   Canada Council for the Arts

Canadä

ONTARIO ARTS COUNCIL
CONSEIL DES ARTS DE L'ONTARIO

We acknowledge the support of the **Canada Council for the Arts** and the **Ontario Arts Council** for our publishing program. We also acknowledge the financial support of the **Government of Canada** through the **Book Publishing Industry Development Program** and **The Association for the Export of Canadian Books**, and the **Government of Ontario** through the **Ontario Book Publishers Tax Credit program** and the **Ontario Media Development Corporation**.

Care has been taken to trace the ownership of copyright material used in this book. The author and the publisher welcome any information enabling them to rectify any references or credits in subsequent editions.

J. Kirk Howard, President

Printed and bound in Canada
www.dundurn.com

Dundurn Press	Gazelle Book Services Limited	Dundurn Press
3 Church Street, Suite 500	White Cross Mills	2250 Military Road
Toronto, Ontario, Canada	High Town, Lancaster, England	Tonawanda, NY
M5E 1M2	LA1 4XS	U.S.A. 14150

"Keep neither a blunt knife
nor an ill-disciplined looseness of tongue."
— Epictetus

Acknowledgements

The authors are grateful for the expertise of Bruce Koffler as well as the support of the Ontario Arts Council for this project.

Preface

This book was written in an attempt to bring Canadians up to speed on most of the myriad aspects of terrorism. Six years after the events of September 11, 2001, the public's perception of the so-called war on terror is that it is a fiasco.

Consider the debate earlier this year when an Ottawa-based professor suggested that the minister of national defence and the chief of the defence staff should be tried in the Hague for complicity in war crimes. The professor felt he could rationalize his position, as combatants captured by Canadian troops in Afghanistan are handed over to the Afghans, who can be less than gentle at times with their alleged insurgents.

Just this June a coalition of Quebec-based peace groups calling itself Guerre à la Guerre ("War Against War") launched a letter campaign, mailing more than two thousand envelopes to soldiers, their spouses, their children, and anyone else who happened to reside near Valcartier, before its base deployed an overseas contingent. "Canada's role in Afghanistan is a trap. It means on-the-ground Canadian soldiers become 'cannon fodder' for the illogical and unjust policies of generals and politicians," the letter read. It also warned that troops would be involved with "complicity with the civilian deaths and other activities — like the transfer of prisoners to potential torture and death — that are tantamount to war crimes."

It would seem that nothing has changed in la Belle Province since the conscription crisis of 1917. Notwithstanding the fact that encouraging desertion among serving soldiers could be considered tantamount to an act of treason, sending nasty notes to those in uniform is an old Front de Libération du Québec (FLQ) trick (see page 22). But there is another issue here: all this banter over war crimes was a field day in the media, and the conflict can be used as priceless propaganda by Islamic terrorists and their fan clubs. In the ninja's world it is known as an attack on the "mind castle." Now Canada can be seen in the world's eyes as having a governmental regime that would make Idi Amin blush. As was said in *The Six Napoleons*: "The press, Watson, is a most valuable institution, if only you know how to use it." Even a top leader in the FLQ (and the author of its second manifesto) admitted to the CBC in 1990 that the media was instrumental in that terrorist group's efforts.

Actually, some would like us to believe that Canada will have a "maximum impact" FLQ déjà vu this year, as a communiqué apparently from that group circulated and said "strategic targets of importance" would be hit in Montreal, including bridges, railways, airports, gas stations, government offices, and shopping malls. "We will especially target traffic on main highways," the communiqué continued, "a combination of vehicles, letter bombs [and] remote-control explosive devices will be used and most of these devices are already in place."

While the message was seemingly directed to businesses that don't conform to Quebec's French-language law, it is nothing new. In December 1986, several outlets of a department store chain in Quebec were bombed with Molotov cocktails by a group purporting to be a new cell of the FLQ whose demand was to ban the retail store's English signage. The label was adopted because of its public relations value and illustrates a little-known feature of terrorism: well-known names being used by copycats for additional leverage in achieving their objectives.

The authors have attempted in this book to stick to a policy of not naming suspected terrorists awaiting trial; only those convicted of terrorism offences are identified. Although the suspects' names are already in the public domain, the writer of a book (as opposed to periodicals that have a relatively short shelf life) has an additional responsibility to attempt to ensure fairness, and no one undeserving should have their names lingering in a terror tome for years.

It would also take us years to explain the topic of terrorism in its entirety, hence the unique format of this work. In addition to three narrative chapters, we include a set of ten "intelligence files" that are stand-alone works covering specific issues, some more technical than others. Due to time and space constraints, cyber-terrorism and terrorist group financing are not covered, but the authors feel that these topics received adequate attention in our earlier work. Appendices include the federal government's list of banned terrorist organizations as well as an eclectic collection of documents written by terrorists themselves.

The authors would also like to point out that any adverse mention whatsoever in this book of individual members of any political, social, ethnic, religious, or national group is not intended to insinuate that all people of that group are terrorists or their supporters. In fact, actual terrorists represent only a small minority of dedicated and often fanatical members in most such groups. It is they and their actions that are the subject of our ongoing research.

Terrorism is a moving target in a world whose pace is ever increasing, and many events can easily render analysis highly problematic. In the meantime, readers who wish to stay abreast of this world can tune into CJOB Winnipeg's *The Nighthawk with Geoff Currier*, where I am frequently a guest commentator on international security issues. Our work is gaining a small but dedicated following, and we were sincerely flattered when *Inside Canadian Intelligence* was nominated for the Doubleday Military Book Club's Ribbon of Honor Award in 2006, as well as having the book stocked in the university libraries of Harvard, Yale, and Georgetown.

Lastly, we note the increasing interest in terrorism within Canadian academia, which is long overdue. Hopefully, this sector will mature given sufficient time and resources. In the early 1980s, when the authors worked together in intelligence and terrorism was barely considered a discipline, the Advanced Police Science program at Toronto's Humber College included the first academic course on terrorism in North America, and Mr. Rimsa was its instructor.

Dwight Hamilton
2007

1: Welcome to Our Jungle

"They seek to mutilate and destroy ..."

Many Canadians believe that terrorism occurs only on the remote-controlled screens of CNN, not in their own backyards. This is no surprise. Few today are old enough to remember the Front de Libération du Québec and other terrorists that have bombed, killed, and maimed in this country. Another reason for complacency is the mind game of denial. It is simply too horrendous for the common citizen to think of a 9/11 occurring in downtown Toronto, Montreal, or Vancouver and to carry on with their daily routines.

Another basis for this smug belief, however, is the pacific nature of modern Canadian society. "In the recent past we've had those who behaved as if democracy was a given," veteran foreign correspondent Peter Worthington once wrote. "Realities like intelligence, security, and an able and well-equipped military are not popular among the arms-into-ploughshare types."

True, very few citizens of Canada have ever been members of the military or other organizations that deal with such dangerous and distasteful problems on a regular basis. Why would they? We enjoy the second highest living standard on Earth, and one of the lowest rates of criminal activity in the developed world. Based in such a Garden of Eden, it's been pretty easy for Canadians to ignore terrorism over the years and to carry on in ignorant bliss.

The reality is that terrorism has been with Canada for many years, lurking, for the most part, just beneath the public's radar screen. How many have heard of an organization calling itself the Initiative de résistance internationaliste? Yet in August of last year an oil executive's car was firebombed in Loraine, Quebec, by the IRI for "financing an imperialist army that is committing barbarous acts in places such as Iraq." The group has also claimed responsibility for bombing a hydro tower near the American border in 2004.

Modern terrorism in Canada can be said to have begun in 1963, when the FLQ mounted a campaign that included more than four hundred crimes and culminated in the kidnapping of a British diplomat and the death of a Quebec government minister. It took an additional three years before this threat subsided and was replaced by a political party attempting to achieve the same goals by working within the system. This extremist battle continues within our federal Parliament to this very day.

During and shortly after the FLQ era, various Cuban terrorists were active in Canada in opposition to the communist regime of Fidel Castro, and the Cuban Consulate in Montreal was bombed more than once, as well as the Cuban Embassy in Ottawa. In those decades Croatian terrorism was also a problem. While its purpose was predominately to raise awareness for a democratic Croatia, which was in the grips of Marshall Tito's Yugoslavia at the time, it was a danger to our citizens. Threats against Yugoslavian consulates were common, and the Toronto one was bombed on November 25, 1965, as was the Yugoslavian Embassy in Ottawa two years later. Croatian terrorism has occurred in Canada as recently as April 1979, when a prominent pro-Yugoslav business was bombed in Toronto; Croatian separatists were arrested but were later released due to lack of evidence.

Between 1982 and 1986, a homegrown left-wing anarchist group called Direct Action was a key terrorist player in this country, and even though the five main members were arrested, their support structure and its mentorship has remained untouched to this day. The year 1982 also heralded the beginning of Armenian terrorism in Canada. Like the Cubans and Croatians, these "freedom fighters" wanted liberation; their goal was to free Turkish Armenia, and they conducted a campaign of assassination against Turkish diplomats here. A hostage taking culminated in the death of a security guard in 1985, and it would be a further five years until the violence ceased.

Beginning in the mid 1980s, Canada was plagued by terrorism from Sikh separatists, and the nation has still not recovered, as debates regarding the Air India inquiry prove two decades later. Until 9/11,

Canada held the dubious honour of having had the world's worst airline mass murder ever committed against its citizens.

Less dramatic, but no less important, is the fact that different terrorist groups have used Canada as a base of operations in support of their infrastructure over the years. According to the Canadian Security Intelligence Service (CSIS), there are between twenty and thirty terrorist organizations operating in Canada in any given year, and this has been the norm since the early 1970s. Yet it has taken more than twenty-five years for our government to outlaw the Liberation Tigers of Tamil Eelam (LTTE, or Tamil Tigers), despite the fact that most civilized countries had done so long ago.

Since 2001, Canada has faced perhaps its greatest terrorist threat from Al Qaeda and its umbrella organization, which was brought home to the public with the arrest of the alleged cell members of the Toronto 17 in June 2006. As you will see in the following chapters, the risk to Canada and its citizens — and not just to troops in Afghanistan — is very grave.

For a number of reasons, Canada is an attractive venue for Al Qaeda. Long borders and coastlines offer many points of entry that can facilitate movement to and from various sites around the world, particularly the United States. There are few travel restrictions in a democracy, and you can cross American border easily, especially if holding a Canadian passport. We are a wealthy nation and an excellent location in which to raise money for causes abroad. There are also many choice targets here; Al Qaeda could choose from a multitude of American-owned corporations, if they deemed it necessary. Canada is a good place to get financial aid, both private and public. Its citizens have good hearts and are easy to manipulate because they are trusting, and terrorists have no problems in abusing this friendship for their own ends.

Then there is the issue of political exiles accepted into Canada as refugees, who often have axes to grind back home. It's well known that 95 percent of our refugees are immediately allowed to stay here, and more than fifteen thousand have arrived since 9/11, including twenty-five hundred from terrorist sponsor states or countries affected by domestic terrorism. Claiming refugee status is a tried and true infiltration method of terrorist organizations.

A Canadian immigration lawyer who handles many cases from Iraq was recently quoted as saying, "I'm telling clients ... I don't want to hear about how you get here, but if you do, your chances of getting in are virtually 100 percent."

Another problem is the ease with which a foreigner can get a student visa. There are a growing number of such students today, often from countries that are in turmoil. The opportunity for terrorists to abuse this system is evident; look at 9/11 as an example.

Canada, with an eye for tolerance of different ethnic groups, has a population that an Al Qaeda terrorist can blend into with great ease, and large immigrant communities can provide a source of haven and support. These groups can include many people who bring bizarre political views to our shores and still have strong ties to the old country, which makes them ideal recruits for extremist activities.

But before we look at today's situation — and to better understand the nature of terrorism — let us examine a short history of each wave that has hit our home and native land.

FLQ

The FLQ was a homegrown quasi Marxist-Leninist group from Quebec that operated in loosely connected cells spanning at least two generations. Their main objective was to recast the province as a fully sovereign, exclusively francophone-controlled state within North America (see Appendix IV). Terrorists often have specialties in the types of tactics and methods they use, and the FLQ specialized in bombs. Their operations began with limited results, as often happens to such fledgling organizations, but they were not easily deterred from their cause.

In Montreal on February 23, 1963, a cell placed a bomb at the base of the CBC-TV antenna on Mount Royal and another near radio station CKGM, but both failed to go off. Their second action took place on March 8, 1963, by throwing Molotov cocktails into three armouries there. The terrorists started leaving the group's initials painted on walls to serve as a calling card for the authorities and the press.

Of course, compared to the Al Qaeda of today these operations were amateurish, but the group now had its feet wet and was soon blowing up Canadian National Railway tracks a few hours before a train carrying then Prime Minister John Diefenbaker was due to pass. The planting of bombs in Montreal at various places — including a Bank of Canada building, numerous Royal Canadian Legions, Central Station, the Royal Canadian Mounted Police (RCMP) headquarters, armouries, and other military locations — became a daily occurrence. Residencies of Montreal VIPs were bombed, including those of the mayor of Westmount and millionaire Peter Bronfman. Ominously, the Ministry of Labour was targeted several times, which should have set off warning bells that its minister might be a potential target. Four people were wounded in attacks on the Canada Club, the Reform Club, and the Renaissance Club, which were prestigious English-speaking businessmen's haunts. Westmount and Montreal city halls, post offices, Queen's Printer's offices, key bridges, and many businesses and banks were bombed as well.

These bombings created fear in most people, but they were greeted with a sense of support from many FLQ sympathizers. There were two that one of the authors personally remembers, however, that did not glean the support of anyone in Quebec. On September 23 and November 21, 1968, two liquor stores were targeted for bomb attacks in downtown Montreal. As the liquor board is a government corporation it would under normal circumstances be a legitimate terrorist target. But the FLQ misjudged Quebecers' love of fine spirits, and the terrorists were the butt of jokes and curses from both the English and French populations for some time. No further attempts to bomb liquor stores were made; department stores were fair game, though. For example, on November 24, 1968, the downtown Montreal Eaton's was targeted by two bombs on the same day. Many schools were also targeted by bombings or the threats of them.

Like many terrorist groups, the FLQ attempted to portray a Robin Hood or white knight image and would often involve themselves in local labour disputes, for example bombing the Westmount home of the president of Murray Hill, a taxi and limousine service, and two garages owned by Chambly Transport on Montreal's South Shore on the same day.

In addition to Montreal, there were numerous bombings in the Quebec City area and other parts of the province, as well as in Ottawa. There, a bomb exploded in a mailbox in front of the building of the U.S. Secretary of State on December 31, 1968, and several bombs placed in street-corner mailboxes were defused on January 16, 1969. In Quebec City, two bombs exploded in front of the famous Château Frontenac hotel on June 19, 1969. And while many military and defence-related facilities were targeted, two should be emphasized with respect to possible future terrorist incidents in Canada: the bombings of Montreal's Queen Mary Veterans' Hospital on May 28, 1970, and of National Defence Headquarters in downtown Ottawa on June 24, 1970. If the FLQ can target these places, Al Qaeda certainly can too. In addition to these attacks, six other bombings in Montreal stand out from the rest of the FLQ's actions:

- April 20, 1963: A bomb exploded at the Canadian Army recruiting centre downtown. The night watchman was killed in the first casualty of this dirty campaign. This marked the first step of the FLQ as a truly lethal organization.
- May 16, 1963: A bomb destroyed an oil tank at the Golden Eagle Refinery.
- May 17, 1963: In the affluent English-speaking section of Westmount, fifteen bombs were placed in street-corner mailboxes on the same day. Ten of them exploded, and Sergeant Major Walter Lejay of the Engineers was seriously wounded while he was attempting to disarm one.
- February 13, 1969: A bomb caused a massive explosion on the main floor of the Montreal Stock Exchange and twenty-seven people were wounded.
- March 7, 1969: A bomb was placed under the overpass of the Metropolitan Boulevard but was defused.
- July 30, 1969: The Cap Rouge company was targeted by Canada's first booby trap car bomb, which exploded before it could be disarmed.

When it comes to money, robbery is a common tactic of smaller terrorist groups, and this was the main form of FLQ financing. They began on April 30, 1963, with a Canadian Army payroll robbery; then, on September 26, 1963, a stickup at a Royal Bank netted the group nearly $7,000. On February 27, 1964, another holdup secured $9,000 from a Caisse Populaire. This was followed by an armed robbery at a Provincial Bank where $3,000 was stolen and yet another theft at a National Bank branch where $5,000 was taken on April 9, 1964. The FLQ then moved on to robbing cinemas, following a basic rule of terrorism by changing tactics and striking where not expected. On May 1, 1966, they hit the Cinéma Élysée and grabbed $2,400. This is only a sampling of robberies that the FLQ committed; between 1968 and 1970, at least twenty-five thefts of cash were attributed to them. Although most were carried out in Montreal, a good number were committed in rural areas as well. And while the amounts of stolen cash seem to be low, they were healthy sums in those days.

"Expropriation" is a term that has been used by terrorists in the past; it is another word for the theft of goods. It is used to legitimize through language criminal acts conducted by terrorists. Words are important in perception management, and all terrorist groups readily understand this fact. Their needs are plenty, leading to a diverse range of robberies. For a small group, it is more cost-effective to steal weapons and ammunition from the enemy than to purchase them on the black market. In many developed countries it is also difficult to get the firepower and explosives required in sufficient quantities. Theft is the answer.

The FLQ's efforts at stealing equipment and supplies began with a burglary of radio station CHEF in Granby, Quebec, on November 26, 1963. Radio equipment was stolen with the intent of setting up a clandestine broadcast station to support the group's propaganda efforts.

On January 30, 1964, a theft took place at the Fusiliers du Mont Royal armoury in Montreal, and $21,000 worth of military equipment was taken. Soon after, on February 20, 1964, various guns and ammunition valued at $21,000 were stolen from the armoury of the 62nd Regiment of the Royal Artillery in Shawinigan, Quebec.

An armed robbery of the International Firearms gun shop in Montreal took place on August 29, 1964. Several cases of weapons were stolen and two people were killed.

From April to June 1965, the theft of dynamite from various construction sites in Quebec took place, and FLQ responsibility was published in the group's underground newspaper *La Cognée* ("The Hatchet").

Sometimes the needs of terrorist groups are not as dramatic as weapons and explosives. On October 23, 1965, a burglary at the New Democratic Party office in Montreal netted the terrorists a mimeograph machine and office materials.

Even the Canadian Cadet Corps was not immune. On April 16, 1966, there was a theft of guns, ammunition, and other military equipment from the Collège Mont-Saint-Louis in Montreal.

To get the word out, the FLQ began publication of *La Cognée* in October 1963, and they even attempted to construct their own radio broadcast system. The group also sent communiqués to select radio stations and newspapers for reprinting. Naturally, acts of bombing, kidnapping, and murder also kept the FLQ in the public eye, in most cases gleaning support for their cause. So the newspaper was also used for other purposes. Issue number 46, published in November 1965, gave detailed instructions for such revolutionary techniques as provoking the police, avoiding arrest, and spreading false rumours. In April 1966, *La Cognée* published new instructions on bombing and sabotage, and information on making better bombs, robbing banks, and other terrorist tactics and weapons became regular features. These were meant to inspire others to form independent terrorist cells and commit acts in the name of the freedom of Quebec and the institution of a Marxist-Leninist government.

Threats and hoaxes were a common and inexpensive means of terrorism for the FLQ. Of them all, though, there is one that strikes close to home for the authors. Through their infiltrators and supporters, the group managed to get the names and addresses of all the counterterrorist joint task force members in the Montreal area, and they sent death threats directly to their homes and families.

The beginning of the end for the FLQ occurred on October 5, 1970, when British diplomat James Cross was kidnapped from his home in Westmount. Five days later a different FLQ cell independently kidnapped Pierre Laporte, the Quebec minister of labour, from his home in St. Lambert. Various elements of the Canadian military moved to Ottawa to secure federal government installations and guard officials at 1:15 p.m. on October 12. Three days later, military aid to the civil power was requested by the Quebec provincial government, and a company of infantry was inserted by helicopter in downtown Montreal, the first of many province-wide deployments. In addition, certain regulations under the *War Measures Act* were later invoked on October 16, one of which allowed police to detain suspects for eleven days without charge, as opposed to forty-eight hours under the existing provisions of the Canadian Criminal Code (see Appendix V). This has proven to be a very contentious point in Canadian history.

John Turner, the federal justice minister at the time, later explained the rationale for implementing the act this way: "The action the government took was drastic. I have no intention, nor has the government, of evading or attempting to minimize that fact. It was a drastic measure because it was precipitated by persons with an utter contempt for the rights of others. It was a measure brought on by persons with an utter contempt for the democratic process. They seek to mutilate and destroy our social institutions, including that of representative government."

On October 18, Laporte's body was found in the trunk of a car parked at the St. Hubert airbase. He had been strangled. With this murder, the FLQ lost some support, but not all. After intelligence found where the Liberation Cell was holding James Cross, Operation Ragout secured a one-block perimeter in Montreal North, so the government could negotiate for the diplomat's liberation.

Believe it or not, after the October Crisis it took an additional two years to roll up the FLQ's support infrastructure. Meanwhile, some of the active cell members languished under the Cuban sun, where they had been exiled in return for Cross's life.

Direct Action

Also known in the media as the Squamish Five, Direct Action was a domestic leftist anarchist group that was small in size, as it was not given the chance to grow. When security forces dismantled it, the group consisted of a military cell operating between Vancouver and Toronto, with support cells in Vancouver, Winnipeg, Toronto, and Montreal. Their method of operation was sophisticated, developing along the lines of the Italian terrorist group Prima Linea ("First Line" or "Front Line"). Like them, many Direct Action operatives tried to have normal jobs during the day and conduct terrorist activities in their free time, although the bassist for the hardcore punk band the Subhumans quit that gig before joining up. Its members also tried not to have anything in their homes that could incriminate them, putting together their bombs only when required.

A Direct Action cell member once worked in the support arm of the Red Army Faction (RAF) in Germany, and the group was also allied to the Revolutionary Cells of Germany and other terrorists of the time. Direct Action propaganda was distributed via certain bookstores in every major city across the country, placed in the magazine racks amongst legitimate publications. One had to know what to look for and where, but the material was in the open and anyone could buy it.

In the Prima Linea network, all cells worked independently of each other. Operatives gleaned targets from the propaganda material, which gave non-specific instructions such as "Hit NATO and the Military Industrial Complex." The propaganda also did not state how the terrorist act was to be committed; that depended on the sophistication achieved by a particular cell. Since cells were self-taught, some could commit only simple acts of vandalism or arson, but more sophisticated ones could use improvised explosive devices, while others moved on to stolen explosives. The terrorist act could be a bombing, an assassination, or a hostage taking, as the type of act was never defined in the material. In addition, the leadership that created the propaganda never actually knew any of the cell members, and vice versa, which provided a high level of security and deniability. Although Direct Action never achieved Prima Linea's level of sophistication, it was on the right path.

Direct Action began its operations in 1982 when offices of British Columbia's environment ministry were vandalized. In May of that year, the group bombed the Cheekeye-Dunsmuir Hydro Power Station on Vancouver Island, and the explosion was so powerful that the facility was almost completely destroyed. Then on October 14, the Toronto plant of Litton Industries, which manufactured guidance systems for American cruise missiles, was bombed. The blast was so loud it was heard kilometres away by one of the authors, who was with a counterterrorism class at Humber College at the time. A van loaded with forty-five kilograms of dynamite was used and caused considerable property damage in addition to wounding ten people (see Appendix III). In Vancouver on November 22, the group firebombed three pornographic video stores and claimed responsibility as the Wimmin's Fire Brigade. In another twist, the group threatened to poison South African wine sold in British Columbia and succeeded in having the products pulled from store shelves across Canada in 1986.

Only five people from Direct Action were ever arrested and charged with any criminal activities. No one from the direct support arm of approximately forty members was charged due to the difficulty of collecting evidence in those days. In addition to the Litton bombing, the operatives arrested on January 20, 1983, were also charged with conspiracy to sabotage aircraft, radar equipment, and fuel storage tanks at CFB Cold Lake in Alberta; the sabotage of a Canadian Coast Guard icebreaker under construction in Vancouver; and the robbery of a Brink's armoured car. The toughest time handed out was a life sentence to one member who ended up serving seven years. At a Canadian university where that member was recently reading from her memoirs, the coordinator of the school's Public Interest Research Group said, "In the wake of September 11 and the crackdown on public dissent, anti-globalization activists are at a crucial point in time. Many are concerned that their activities can be deemed as 'terrorist' particularly under Bill C-36, which is now law. I think hearing [her] experiences first-hand will be very insightful for all."

Direct Action's exploits have also been featured in a movie and in a television documentary, in which a reporter remarked, "There are important lessons to be learned in the aftermath of September 11. Here too a group of determined political activists working in secret decided to get in on the action."

Armenian Terrorism

Armenians suffered the first genocide of the twentieth century at the hands of the Turks; a million died in 1915 during a death march that has remained largely unknown in the West. Canadian filmmaker Atom Egoyan's *Ararat*, released only a few years ago, is one of the few mainstream treatments of the subject. At the time of Armenian terrorism, their homeland included areas in Turkey and the former Soviet Union.

An independent Armenian state now exists; its birth was not by terrorist action, however, but by the collapse of Communism. Before that, two main terrorist groups were active in Canada: the Armenian Secret Army for the Liberation of Armenia (ASALA) and the Justice Commandos of Armenian Genocide (JCAG). ASALA was a Marxist-Leninist group whose purposes were the liberation of occupied territories from Turkish control and unity with the Soviet Union. They were supported by the Soviets, Syria, and the Popular Front for the Liberation of Palestine (PFLP), a key terrorist group of the time. Formed in January 1975, they used tactics that included obtaining as much media exposure as possible, with bombing and assassination as key tools. A newspaper published in Beirut was a key propaganda tool. They were financed by sponsor states, as well as by drug trafficking, extortion, and donations from the Armenian diaspora. The group's targets were mostly Turkish embassies, diplomats, and government offices in various countries, and cells were located in Toronto, Montreal, Los Angeles, and New York City as well as across Europe. In Canada, they maintained ties with certain Palestinian Liberation Organization (PLO) terrorist groups and with the Irish Republican Army (IRA).

JCAG was nationalist in its political philosophy and financed by the diaspora, but it did have the support of the PFLP and the Lebanese Phalangists. Founded in October 1975, its objective was a free, independent, and united Armenia. Headquartered in Paris and organized in two- to three-person cells, JCAG used bombings, assassinations, and embassy hostage takings of generally Turkish targets to further their cause. Every JCAG attack was followed up with a communiqué, demonstrating the group's appreciation of the value of propaganda.

Armenian terrorism began in Canada in January 1982 when a bomb exploded in a stairwell at the Turkish consulate in Toronto. Other bombings included two incidents at the Air Canada freight offices at Los Angeles International Airport and one at a Swiss Air office in Montreal. Numerous bomb threats were made to the Turkish Embassy in Ottawa, Canadian embassies overseas, the CBC, and the Toronto and Montreal subway systems, which grabbed the attention of the entire country.

Headlines were also made at about seven in the morning on March 12, 1985, when three JCAG operatives jumped out of a rented U-haul truck and attacked the Turkish Embassy in Ottawa, killing a security guard on the spot and using explosives to gain entrance to the building. After holding several people at gunpoint, they surrendered to police four hours later without killing any more.

But terrorists don't always surrender. On April 8, 1982, Kemelettin Kani Gungor, a Turkish commercial attaché in Ottawa, was shot twice by a lone gunman as he was entering his vehicle in the outdoor covered parking lot of his apartment building and was left severely paralyzed. Three Armenians were arrested in Toronto two years later and convicted for conspiracy in his attempted murder, but the actual shooter has never been caught. In another case, Colonel Al Attila Altikat, a Turkish military attaché based in Ottawa, was assassinated on his way to work on August 27, 1982. A lone JCAG gunman approached his vehicle while it was stopped at a traffic light and emptied ten rounds from a 9mm Browning Hi-Power into him. Despite police sealing the city with roadblocks, the assassin has never been found.

Sikh Extremism

Sikh separatists desire an independent homeland they call Khalistan in the Kashmir area of northern India. Today, it is the Indian state of Punjab. For Sikh terrorists who have supported that goal, Canada has been used as a place to hide, acquire financial support and weapons, and plan assassinations and bombings in India as well as here. Babbar Khalsa, Babbar Khalsa International, the Khalistan Liberation Force, the Khalistan Commando Force, and the International Sikh Youth Federation are the major Sikh terrorist organizations.

Acts of extremist violence have taken place in Toronto, Winnipeg, Vancouver, and Ottawa. Ujjal Dosanjh, a current federal member of Parliament and former premier of British Columbia, was attacked in February 1985. On May 25, 1986, four Vancouver-area Sikhs were charged with the attempted murder of Malkiad Singh Sidhu, a minister in India's Punjab government. Sidhu was ambushed and shot on an isolated logging road on Vancouver Island. All four were later convicted. On June 14, 1986, seven Canadian Sikh extremists were arrested after police raids in Hamilton and Brampton, Ontario, as well as in British Columbia, and charged with conspiracy to commit terrorist acts in India, including a plot to blow up the Indian Parliament buildings. On November 29, 1986, six Canadian Sikhs were arrested in Pakistan and charged with attacking an Indian diplomat near Lahore.

Canadian journalists have not been immune from the danger either. Kim Bolan, who has reported extensively on Sikh extremism over the years, was told, "You die like Gandhi woman," and had a bullet fly by her house in July 1998. In addition, the publisher of the *Indo-Canadian Times*, Tara Singh Hayer, who had been left a paraplegic after an attack a decade before, was murdered in November of that year.

But these acts pale in comparison to the events of June 23, 1985. First, a bomb exploded at Toyko's Narita Airport that was in luggage removed from Canadian Pacific Air Flight 003. Two Japanese baggage handlers were killed, and it was just plain luck that the bomb did not explode on the aircraft while airborne. But less than an hour later, Air India Flight 182 from Toronto was destroyed by another suitcase bomb off the coast of Ireland, and that strike killed 329 people, including many Canadian citizens.

Most Canadians who live outside British Columbia think the Air India bombing was a lone incident, or that it has more to do with India than Canada. What many people are not aware of is that less than a year after that tragedy, five Montreal-area Sikh terrorists were arrested and charged with conspiracy to place a bomb on another Air India aircraft out of New York. The most tragic aspect of the case is that none of the crime's masterminds have been convicted after all these years. Until the events of 9/11, the Air India bombing was the worst airborne terrorist attack in the world's history, and a Canadian federal inquiry into the disaster is still ongoing.

Al Qaeda

It's been reported that the Al Qaeda network may have had a presence in Canada as early as 1992, when the blind cleric Sheik Omar Abdel Rahman, one of the masterminds behind the first attack on the World Trade Center, was sighted at certain mosques here. But it would be another seven years before a Montreal-based member of Armed Islamic Group (GIA), Ahmed Ressam, known as the millennium bomber, made headlines around the world when he crossed the Canadian border en route to blast Los Angeles International Airport into the next one thousand years. He is now in an American prison. After an intensive investigation in which some GIA members were caught in France, French magistrate Jean-Louis Bruguière convicted twenty-four members of the Montreal cell (some in absentia) in September 2001, and its reported leader, Fateh Kamel, has since served his sentence and returned to Canada. As of 2007, another is still fighting extradition to France on forgery charges after a Canadian judge found there was not enough evidence to conclude that he belonged to the cell. Bruguière has reportedly accused Canada of "not taking the threat of terrorism seriously."

Still, the public was largely unfamiliar with Al Qaeda and Osama bin Laden until the strikes against the United States on September 11, 2001, after which they both became household names. Before Pakistani security forces killed him in 2003, Ahmed Khadr, a.k.a. Al Kanadi ("the Canadian"), was reportedly a money man for Al Qaeda and a close friend of bin Laden himself. One of his sons was wounded in a fatal gun battle, one is awaiting trial at Guantanamo Bay Naval Base (Gitmo), and another is fighting extradition to the United States so he won't end up in that dock as well. After attending training camps in Afghanistan, yet another of Ahmed's sons rejected *jihad* ("holy war") and worked as a mole for the CIA while at Gitmo, as well as signing a movie deal that's worth half a million U.S. dollars.

Five citizens from Algeria, Egypt, Morocco, and Syria are currently held under the auspices of National Security Certificates, issued by Citizenship and Immigration Canada. They are suspected of having ties to Al Qaeda, the Algerian Armed Islamic Group, the Egyptian Islamic Jihad, and the Vanguards of Conquest. Four have been released on bail under strict conditions. One of those released thinks his conditions are too restrictive and remarked to a reporter, "There is no big difference between the jail and outside." In addition, at least nine suspected Canadian terrorists were abroad as of 2005, either incarcerated or at large. They are thought to be mixed up with Al Qaeda, Hezbollah, and the Usbat Al Ansar groups.

After two years of undercover investigation here at home, about four hundred heavily armed officers from an RCMP joint task force made one of the largest sweeps of alleged terrorists in North America on the night of June 2, 2006. Although they were initially dubbed the Toronto 17 by the press, an eighteenth man was later arrested, and the British also took a man into custody in connection with the case. Four of the suspects from the Toronto area are boys under the age of eighteen.

What the suspects code-named Operation Badr included several plans, one using suicide truck bombs against such targets as the Toronto Stock Exchange, CSIS headquarters, and the CBC building in that city. In addition, it is alleged that one team considered storming Parliament Hill in Ottawa to behead several hostages — including the prime minister. (The original Battle of Badr, fought just outside Medina in A.D. 624, was considered a key turning point for the Muslim Prophet Muhammad's fortunes.)

The Crown claims some members had trained in terrorist tactics at a remote rural location near Washago in the dead of winter, and others bought what they believed to have been three metric tonnes of ammonium nitrate fertilizer (a common ingredient in making explosives) during an elaborate sting operation. In later developments, the press reported that a member of the local Muslim community had been a mole for security forces in the case, which apparently then caused the man to go public with his identity. A second mole, whose identity is still secret, went into hiding under the Witness Protection Program. A publication ban was quickly imposed by the courts on evidence presented at bail hearings and the trial, but some media outlets are challenging this blanket prohibition. The case is predicted to be one of the most complex in the history of Canadian criminal law, as it involves about 2 million pages of government documents. According to some reports, it could be years before a trial date is even set.

Some things may be developing at a less-than-glacial pace, however. A couple of months after the arrests, the moderate co-founder of a prominent Muslim-Canadian organization (who had been interviewed with one of the authors on television just days after the incident) resigned from his position. "I am doing this because I fear for my life and the safety of my family," he told reporters. "I've had enough, I've spent too much time dodging the bullet."

More Terror

Terrorist support activities in Canada are too numerous to recount here. The IRA, PFLP, Hamas, and Hezbollah have been active here for many years, collecting donations to fund their operations. In fact, the alleged former head of the PFLP's Canadian wing just lost a bid not to be deported based on the premise that his involvement in the organization was a form of freedom of expression guaranteed under our constitution.

The Tamil Tigers have been notorious for years for their extortion of the Tamil community here, in addition to the manufacture and sale of forged passports. The IRA has used Canada for R & R and to purchase weapons (including Stinger missiles) and support equipment like model aircraft controllers that could be used as remote bomb detonation devices. The IRA has also used certain bars in Toronto, Calgary, Edmonton, and other cities as fronts for the collection of donations; one of the authors once lived just across the street from one. Providing a safe haven for terrorists in Canada is another important activity, as the case of a suspect in the 1996 Al Khobar attack in Saudi Arabia shows. According to the charges, the man drove the Datsun scout car before the bombing and later fled the country for Canada. He was arrested by the RCMP in the winter of 1997 and later wound up in American hands by his own volition. As well, two men who are allegedly members of the Basque Fatherland and Liberty (ETA) were arrested in Vancouver and in Quebec City in June 2007. What were they doing here?

And according to a 2003 CSIS Annual Report, certain elements of single-issue groups found within the environmental, animal rights, anti-globalization, and white supremacist movements still pose a direct threat to Canada. Animal rights criminal activities have included mailing pipe bombs and letters containing razor blades (allegedly tainted with poisonous substances) to scientists, taxidermists, and hunting outfitters. In addition, fur-bearing animals have been released from commercial premises and poisoned turkeys have been threatened in supermarkets during major holidays in support of the animal rights movement. "Ecotage" is the term used by environmentalists for their terrorist acts. Spiking trees, damaging equipment, and spraying noxious substances in public buildings are tactics employed by these groups, and close links exist among them and animal rights extremists from around the world.

The Ku Klux Klan has been affiliated with several groups in Canada, including the American-based Aryan Nation, which set up camp in Alberta on August 5, 1986. On the opposite side of the racial coin, Canadians have also been targeted by supporters of the African National Congress (ANC), which threatened to poison South African wines shipped to Canada. The American Militia Movement, while not established in Canada, has endeavored to expand northward: a cache of weapons and equipment belonging to a group was discovered in British Columbia.

Then there was the bizarre case of an individual terrorist who hijacked a bus from Montreal and forced it onto Parliament Hill on April 7, 1989, holding hostage all on board. The hijacker demanded Syrian forces withdraw from Lebanon and release a number of Lebanese prisoners. The incident turned into a bit of a fiasco when police lost track of the bus at one point, but the RCMP's director of criminal intelligence subsequently referred to the incident as an example of "excellent cooperation" among law enforcement agencies. Another freelance terrorist bombed Montreal's Central Station on September 3, 1984, protesting Pope John Paul II's visit to Canada that year.

Finally, when looking at international terrorism, the Peruvian Sendero Luminoso ("Shining Path") bombed the Canadian Embassy in Lima in 1991, and one must not forget that terrorist groups in Peru, Turkey, Colombia, and other countries have kidnapped many Canadians for ransom over the years. Currently, there are thirty-four terrorist groups that are outlawed in Canada (see Appendix I).

Aftermath

Many believe that terrorism does not work, much like the idea that crime does not pay. This is mistaken — it can. In some cases where terrorists have overthrown their enemies they have become the leaders of their countries. Others, like Che Guevara, became world icons as revolutionaries (even though he was hunted down like a dog in his final days without any support from friends or a country).

In the case of the FLQ kidnappers, they eventually came back to Canada and served some prison time, but none remain in jail. Some former members of the FLQ even ended up working for Quebec's civil service. Rheal Mathieu, imprisoned in 1967 for bombings that killed two people, even went back to his old ways and received a six-month jail term in 2001 for attempting to firebomb Second Cup coffee shops in Montreal because their signs were not in French. Before his sentencing, Mathieu told the court that his acquittal on related bombing plot charges was "a good thing."

One could also argue that since the October Crisis, the federal government has poured millions more in funding into Quebec than it might have had there not been a wave of terrorism in the 1960s. In addition to the imposition of coast-to-coast bilingual language policies, the social status of Quebecers has improved considerably and quickly. Indeed, in the last forty years it's been a pretty good idea to be from that province if you want to be prime minister of Canada for more than about a year. So these days, even conservatives from Alberta are toying with constitutional concepts like "nations within nations."

C'est la vie.

2: Basic

*"The ability to hack off a tribal leader's limb
just to intimidate the rest of the village ..."*

Terrorism has existed since mankind first organized into small bands or tribal groups. Only the means of conducting it have changed — and, perhaps, the level of brutality.

To be able to understand terrorism and the current threat from Al Qaeda and their umbrella group, one must understand some of the basic concepts. To define a terrorist or terrorism is very difficult. In fact, most countries in the world cannot agree on a single definition — one man's terrorist is another man's freedom fighter. As a result, we will provide you with our personal interpretation of one.

Political terrorism is a technique that may be defined as a violent criminal act designed to create fear in a community, or a segment of a community, for political purposes. In other words, it is violence or the threat of violence to achieve a political end by invoking fear. For example, 9/11 was meant to inspire fear in all Americans by striking at different targets in different locations and inflicting casualties on a massive scale. The violence was aimed at a broad audience of Americans. At the other extreme, terrorizing a specific group, would be the threatening letters sent to the home addresses of Montreal police officers during the October Crisis.

Terrorism is also message by deed: attacks have been referred to by revolutionary movements in the past as "armed propaganda." One of its purposes is to overthrow a target government, but it can be used to invoke political, economic, and social change short of an overthrow. In addition, it is a low-risk activity. This does not mean that terrorists may not place themselves at high risk at the time of operations, but most operations are conducted with the loss of only a few compared to the casualties and damage inflicted. In the 9/11 attacks, fewer than twenty suicide terrorists killed about three thousand people; to the rest of the Al Qaeda network, the operation was low risk. There is also little risk in detonating roadside remote-controlled bombs, a tactic currently in use in Iraq and Afghanistan. Few of the people who detonate the charges are ever caught at the scene of the crime. And to make matters even better for the bad guys, terrorism is cost-effective. To assassinate someone may cost only the price of one bullet. Larger operations like 9/11 may cost just several hundred thousand dollars, yet inflict billions in damage.

During the Second World War, the Soviets alone lost 10 million dead. While terrorism kills relatively few people compared to conflicts like this, it does so with great impact. You can see the uproar in the Canadian media every time just one of our soldiers is killed in Afghanistan, even if in a traffic accident. The entire strategic direction of the West's counterterrorist agenda is questioned. This is exactly what the terrorists want to happen. As we are knowledgeable in unconventional warfare, the authors can state that whether due to the lack of understanding of terrorism by our political and media leaders or due to the use of such incidents for personal political gain, this reaction has a very negative effect on our operations overseas, as the enemy is encouraged to keep striking at Canadian targets. They are attempting to get what they want by coercing us into specific action or inaction, so they cannot be stopped in accomplishing their goals. If we bring our troops home from Afghanistan, Al Qaeda will be able to establish better bases for operations against us, and the war will continue — only this time they will concentrate on targets here.

The only way to conduct a counterterrorist campaign is to have the government and the public united in the actions required to ensure victory by security forces. Any controversy or even open government debate creates a window of opportunity that is always exploited. This is a war no less serious than a conventional one, and we should treat it as such.

Most people do not understand that the use of terrorism is often preceded by a declaration of war by the terrorist group. It was true for the Red Army Faction (Baader-Meinhoff Group) in Germany, the Brigada Rosa ("Red Brigades") in Italy, and other European groups. It is so today for Al Qaeda and its terrorist allies and affiliates, who formally declared war on the United States and its allies. What is foreign to most who are unfamiliar with unconventional warfare is that a group, rather than a nation-state, can declare war. In many groups of the past, the individuals considered themselves to be soldiers in a revolutionary war; in fact, many groups use rank structures, especially in wars of national liberation. But since they sometimes do not wear identifying markings and/or are not part of a legitimate nation-state, terrorists are not afforded any protection from the Geneva Conventions as POWs under international law. The Geneva Conventions apply only to signatories, which must be nation-states. Therefore, the only type of law that can be applied to terrorists is the criminal code. As a technique, terrorism is employed directly against civilians, or against military forces in a way that results in much civilian collateral damage. Conventional warfare is (technically) directed against military targets, although there have been exceptions in the past.

A terrorist need not be a trained soldier. Any man, woman, or child can make a conscious decision to employ violence for a political cause. In his book *Revolutionary Catechism*, Sergey Nechaev wrote, "The revolutionary is a dedicated man. He has no personal inclinations, no business affairs, no emotions, no attachments, no property, and no name, everything in him is subordinate toward a single thought, and a single passion." This is no exaggeration, and it gives you the insight required to understand a true terrorist: one who is is prepared to die for his or her cause because of extremely strong beliefs. Soldiers are prepared to die for their countries; police officers, firefighters, and paramedics are prepared to die in defence of helpless victims; mothers are prepared to die for their children. Terrorists are prepared to die for their cause.

Are terrorists that much different from us? In terms of strong motivation, they are not. Where the terrorist differs from the soldier is in actions: the ability to hack off a tribal leader's limb just to intimidate the rest of the village, the targeting of women and children with bombs in an open-air bazaar, and so on. Canadian soldiers are governed by the Queen's Regulations and Orders and by the Geneva Conventions, and have the duty and responsibility to refuse an unlawful command. Terrorists are usually unrestricted by our laws or moral standards. But there are rules. Often terrorists groups apply brutal penalties for breaches in discipline. Religious terrorists follow their own interpretations of faith in God. The difference is that terrorists do not apply the same rule of law or moral standard to their enemies; the main attitude instilled in them over time is that the goal justifies any means. So are freedom fighters also terrorists? They may or may not be depending on the tactics they use; terrorism is just one of many options in unconventional warfare.

Julius Caesar was a victim of terrorism. What happened on the Ides of March was definitely a political assassination. The Hebrew Sicarii, who would assassinate Romans, soldiers, and administrators in crowded marketplaces by shoving a short sword into them, were terrorists. So was the famous Assassin sect of the Middle East, which used religious beliefs to extort power and money from their neighbours until Mongol hordes, with their own form of terrorism, put an end to their empire. But it was during the French Revolution that the term "terrorist" was first used, by Robespierre. Ironically, there was originally pride in claiming to be one. Hundreds of different groups have followed over the centuries; some still exist today but have long since morphed into criminal organizations such as the Chinese Tong and Italian Mafia, both of which were initially organized as freedom-fighting entities.

Napoleon's invasion of Spain in 1807 marked the appearance of the French term "*guerrilla*" (meaning "small war") in response to the tactics used by the Spanish. This warfare was defined by Napoleon as the tactic of fighting small, limited engagements when conditions favoured the irregulars. It's a form of warfare, not a type of war. A weaker force assumes the tactical offensive in selective forms and at specified times and places of its own choosing. Guerrilla warfare has been used in every kind of environment by groups from everywhere on the political spectrum. It is used when it is impossible to conduct conventional warfare or in conjunction with a conventional campaign. The term "guerrilla warfare" is often confused with "terrorism," which is also a stage in the process of an attempted overthrow of a government. Terrorism follows the first stage, preparation (which includes organization, training, recruitment, group development, and the use of propaganda), and precedes the third stage, government repression. These steps are then repeated until enough recruits are available for guerrilla/insurgent warfare and eventually conventional war, which leads to a general uprising against the government.

If terrorism has existed for centuries, why has there been a dramatic increase in the tactic's use in the last half-century? First, many empires collapsed after the Second World War as the British, French, Dutch, and Germans were all too impoverished to maintain a hold on their former colonies. The world then had several new, struggling states, some with valuable natural resources, all with many grievances, and none with guaranteed political stability. The simultaneous development of the Soviet Union and the United States as superpowers then led to a proliferation of terrorist groups, which were generally supported as proxies to gain access to natural resources and strategic geography. As weapons of mass destruction in the hands of the superpowers acted as deterrents and did not allow the two enemies to engage in conventional warfare, unconventional warfare was used. Weaker countries learned through the superpowers how to wield this efficient political weapon, and the growth of government support for terrorism grew. We now refer to them as terrorist sponsor states.

This geopolitical situation, combined with the availability of advanced weapons technology and improved travel and communications for ordinary people, has made today's environment a more deadly threat to the average person than ever before. It's worth looking at the different types of terrorism currently in use to understand how widely interpretations can range.

War terrorism describes terrorist acts within a conventional war and the hardships suffered by the civilian population because of war. For example, the term can be used to describe the bombing of London by the Germans in the Second World War, the bombing of Berlin, Dresden, and other cities by the Allies in retaliation, and the strikes on Hiroshima and Nagasaki. War terrorism can also refer to the violence inflicted by military forces under total war or scorched earth polices, and the suffering inflicted on ordinary civilians by such strategies.

Establishment terrorism is used by governments (usually dictatorships) against their own people to maintain political power. Examples can be readily found by looking at the starvation of 7 to 10 million Ukrainians in the 1930s under the grip of Stalin and the mass deportations of Ukrainians, Lithuanians, Latvians, Estonians, and Poles to Siberia in the 1940s. One basis of the current Chechen conflict lies in the fact that nearly the entire Chechen population (after being conquered by the Czars) was deported to Siberia by the Soviets at about the same time. In a culture where feuding and revenge are the norm, it is no wonder that the Chechens seek revenge on the Russians. The excesses of the Soviet KGB and other intelligence organizations throughout the world are another example of establishment terrorism.

Insurgent terrorism covers many subcategories. The first concerns those groups using terrorism for a nationalist or ethnic cause, such as the FLQ, IRA, Tamil Tigers, and the Chechens (who can be seen as having an additional twist of religious ideology thrown into their cause as well). The Jewish Sicarii, Irgun, and Haganah are also examples. The second is radical/revolutionary groups, such as Germany's Red Army Faction or Italy's Red Brigades. The third is known as radical/reactionary, covering groups such as the Nicaraguan Contras. The fourth consists of exile groups, such as the Cuban Omega 7, that operate outside of their former country. The fifth, social issue terrorism, includes groups like the Animal Liberation Front and environmentalist terrorist organizations. The sixth is psychotic terrorism, in which a terrorist acts on his own for the righting of some imagined political injustice. The best example would be that of the soldier that shot his way into the Quebec Legislature and took hostages in the 1980s. The seventh category is the individual terrorist who acts on his own but in support of some popular cause or group. The eighth is criminal terrorism exacted by organized crime or criminals on the street. The ninth includes religious-based groups such as the current Palestinian Islamic Jihad, Hezbollah, and the Al-Aqsa Martyrs' Brigade, although these have a nationalist twist. Then, with Al Qaeda, there is religious-based terrorism in its purer form.

Transnational or international terrorism occurs when a group starts operations in different parts of the world and recruits different citizens from around the world; Al Qaeda is a prime example.

There can be no terrorism without a cause, real or imaginary, and sometimes a mix of the two. Causes can be direct or permissive. Direct causes are centred on grievances and may be based on the geographic location of a minority ethnic group like the Kurds in Iraq, the Armenians in Turkey, or the Basques in Spain. Economics may be added as a direct cause. While the FLQ wanted ethnic separation, one justification for their acts (from their perspective) was that the French populace of Quebec was financially repressed, with the English being the owners and them being the workers. Sometimes direct causes can be strictly social or political, like the claim of the American group Weather Underground that the targeted nation-state is a "World Evil." In other cases, a direct cause is based on the right of equality or on idealism related to a political theory (like Marxist-Leninism, adhered to by groups such as the Red Brigades).

Permissive causes can include target availability, how numerous targets are, and the advances in several technologies. Advances in weapons technology allow terrorists to use plastic explosives, fully automatic rifles, grenades, rocket launchers, and shoulder-fired surface-to-air missiles. Advances in aircraft technology have made international travel far easier. Advances in media technology allow the target audience to watch terrorist events live and later see them replayed over and over, from anywhere in the world. As terrorism is propaganda by deed, this has been a boon for recruitment. But the most important permissive cause may be public toleration, ranging from supporting the goal of the terrorist to displaying indifference over the conflict. This allows terrorists to carry on and expand without reprisal.

Since the mid 1980s there has been a shift from left-wing terrorism to right-wing, and ethnic and religious extremism have increased in importance. Communism, which includes Trotskyite, Marxist, Marxist-Leninist, and Maoist sects, was very popular in the past, and a number of left-wing movements continue to exist, such as the Turkish Revolutionary People's Liberation Party-Front, the Peruvian Shining Path, and the Naxalites of India. Their importance is on the wane, however.

Often, the ideology of a terrorist group is influenced by whether it is based in a rural or urban area; their tactics are then followed as part of doctrine. For example, the Shining Path is predominately a rural terrorist group and follows the doctrines of Mao Tse-tung. The Red Brigades and Red Army Faction were strictly urban groups and followed a more Marxist-Leninist approach. In the case of the Marxist Tupamaros of Latin America, although it was predominately an urban terrorist group, it attempted to maintain a limited rural campaign to spread security forces thin. If either a rural or urban group is successful in its campaign to become a mass movement, it will eventually encompass both styles of tactics.

Today, along with American militia groups, Great Britain's Combat-18 and various skinhead associations (the latter being especially prevalent in Germany) form the core of the right-wing extremist movement. But religion is the strongest ideology of all. This makes Al Qaeda and its umbrella organization an extremely difficult threat to suppress, especially given the basic principles of terrorism.

First, terrorism has a cyclical nature. After a period of time security forces will kill and capture a number of the terrorists to the point that it will affect their direct action operations. The group will then reduce the number of operations and concentrate on recruitment, training, reorganization, planning, and preparation. Then it will start all over again. If you do not destroy the political support arm as well as the military arm, terrorism will keep occurring in cycles.

Second, terrorism spreads through internal splits. These splits are often based on ideology, disagreements over tactics, or, if a terrorist group has never killed before, the death of its first victim. Once the first person has been murdered, does it matter if you embark on a campaign of assassination? The split usually means not the end of fighting, but the formation of more terrorist groups, each with relatively the same agenda, but using different tactics. Often, one of the groups becomes progressively more violent. The ETA break-off group, the ETA Military Front (ETA-M), is more militant than its predecessor. The Belgian Revolutionary Front for Proletarian Action was a splinter group of Combating Communist Cells. In 1968, Ahmed Jibril broke off from the PFLP and formed the Popular Front for the Liberation of Palestine — General Command (PFLP-GC). In 1969, Nayef Hawatmeh broke off from the PFLP and formed the Democratic Front for the Liberation of Palestine (PDFLP) because the PFLP was not radical enough. Black June Organization leader Abu Nidal formed his group in 1973 when he broke with Yasser Arafat's group Fatah, part of the PLO, because they were not radical enough. This does not happen only in the Middle East or Europe; it is a worldwide phenomenon. The Pan Africanist Congress of South Africa formed because the African National Congress was not violent enough. In Angola, National Union for the Independence of Angola was formed in 1964 after a split from the Front for the National Liberation of Angola. In South America, the Peruvian Shining Path was a break-off group from the Bandera Roja ("Red Flag").

Third, terrorist groups morph due to long campaigns. The Weather Underground existed for decades in one form or another. There were break-off groups as well, such as the May 19 Coalition, active from the mid 1980s to the 1990s. After over a decade of underground war, many Weather Underground members were ready to settle down, and did, but Cuban intelligence and financial support continued for each new group that formed.

Fourth, terrorist groups merge. Sooner or later, groups are hit hard by security forces. Often the weak remnants join stronger groups, or two weak groups will unite. In Italy, the Armed Communist Unit merged with the Red Brigades after being hit hard by police infiltration. The

Armed Proletarian Nuclei merged with the Red Brigades in 1979. In Germany, the 2 June Movement merged with the Red Army Faction. Previously, the Tupamaros West Berlin group, which had originated in the counterculture anarchist group the Hash Rebels, had merged with the 2 June Movement. In the U.S., the Chicano Liberation Front disbanded in 1971 after a bomb killed an operative, and the remnants joined the New World Liberation Front. When the Emiliano Zapata Unit disbanded, its remnants joined the New World Liberation Front or the Front for the Liberation of Chicanos, operating in the Bay Area of San Francisco. In Latin America, the People's Revolutionary Army accepted Tupamaros and Miristas into their ranks. In Venezuela, the Fuerzas Armadas de Liberación Nacional merged with the Leftist Revolutionary Movement (MIR) in 1969, which splintered into three terrorist groups within a year: Zero Point, the People's Revolutionary Army, and the Red Flag.

But attrition due to law enforcement is not the only reason for a merger. Giangiacomo Feltrinelli, an Italian multi-millionaire who earned much of his money by holding the exclusive publishing rights to *War and Peace* in the West, was also the leader of a terrorist group called the Partisan Action Groups (GAP). After he died in Milan on March 15, 1972, when a bomb he was planting exploded prematurely, the group united with the Red Brigades, bringing money, weapons, training, connections, safe houses, and much more to their cause. At that time GAP consisted of about fifty terrorists, including a support network — about the size of Canada's Direct Action.

Terrorists know that bigger is usually better, and sometimes new groups are formed from the merger of smaller ones. Action Directe of France was formed by the merger of NAPAP and GARI. In 1964, George Habash and Wadi Haddad launched the infamous Palestinian PFLP when three small terrorist groups joined together: the Heroes of the Return, the Palestinian Liberation Force, and the Young Men of Revenge. The reason given for the union was that there was strength in numbers. After a time, terrorist groups operating in the same country or with the same ideology will often join under an umbrella group. This way, each retains its own name and can conduct its own operations, but joint operations are conducted under the umbrella name. The Guatemalan National Revolutionary Unity was such an entity. It consisted of the Guerrilla Army of the Poor, the Rebel Armed Forces, the Organization of the People in Arms, and the Guatemalan Labor Party, which was the political support arm. Other umbrellas in Latin America included the

Peruvian Revolutionary Front and the Marti National Liberation Front, whose membership consisted of five different groups.

Although these were all national umbrellas, in Europe the continent-wide Political Military Front was created in the mid 1980s and counted the Portuguese FP 25, the French Action Directe, the Belgian Combating Communist Cells, the German Red Army Faction and Revolutionary Cells, and the Italian Red Brigades in its ranks.

Until 1974, the PLO was a terrorist umbrella group that consisted exclusively of members who professed violence as the only way of dealing with Israel. According to some, it still is, because within its ranks it retains entities that have rejected peace as means of achieving their political objectives. These are known as the Rejection Front and include the PFLP, PFLP-GC, remnants of the former Abu Nidal Organization, the PDFP, and some other smaller organizations. Today, the PLO has a three-hundred-person Palestinian National Congress that is directed by a smaller body of Palestinian leaders, who are all from these groups. But the PLO also includes government ministries like health and education. Actually, this was the case even before 1974, when Yasser Arafat's Fatah, the largest of all members at the time, rejected violence. The fact is that an umbrella group represents the unification of different organizations to conduct not only joint terrorist operations but also political ones. In the case of the PLO, it was a mini government in exile, which eventually became legalized in the West Bank and Gaza.

Fifth, terrorism follows the principle of generations. Terrorism has a cyclical nature due to crackdowns by security forces. However, in some cases the whole group appears to have been arrested or killed, and yet actions continue. The reason for this is that often the arrests are merely the tip of the iceberg. Terrorists are generally replaced in two ways. First, people from the support network who have been specially prepared take the place of the fallen. Second, even if the military arm is destroyed, as long as the political arm continues to exist, new recruits are found for both the military and support arms without difficulty. Sometimes, remnants of the original group can reinforce and provide leadership for these new recruits.

The new group is called a generation. There were four generations of the Red Army Faction and six of the Red Brigades. A good rule to follow is that a generation will last from five to eight years before its end. In the case of the RAF, a generation consisted of only 30 to 40 armed action unit members and 200 to 250 direct support branch members. A ratio of one active terrorist to five to seven direct support members is the norm. That is all it takes to have a government spend billions of additional dollars on internal security. And with each generation, terrorist groups become more violent.

The first generation of the RAF (1969–74) was not especially skilled, but the second (1974–76) was a fairly professional and deadly group, whose leader was Siegfried Haag, the former lawyer of the RAF's first generation. The group's third generation (1976–79) cared little for public support, which increased the violence level even more; the leader at that time was Bridget Mohnhaupt. The fourth generation (1979–93) was at the peak of international terrorist group cooperation. Targets were expanded to encompass NATO military and military industrial complex facilities, and it was this generation of the RAF that was deeply into espionage on behalf of the Warsaw Pact.

The legacy of the Red Brigades was similar The first generation (1969–72) distributed leaflets, set fire to corporate cars, initiated strike actions, and beat up managers. The second (1972–74) conducted knee-capping, expropriations, and bombings, and they organized themselves into a formal cell structure. The third (1974–76) conducted assassinations and kidnapping. The fourth (1976–81) raised the number of assassinations and kidnappings to a new level. The fifth (1981–85) took an international direction, expanding their operations to strikes against NATO and the military industrial complex. The sixth (1985–94), although smaller, was better trained and organized into ten-person cells, and members were younger and more ruthless. Full international cooperation with other terrorist groups was achieved during this time.

Democracies are extremely difficult to protect due to the prevalence of permissive causes of terrorism, such as toleration and indifference. Compounding the problem are the intrinsic cyclical lulls between terrorist activities, which can make it appear to the public that peace is at hand. But that is the nature of the beast. The principles of generations, merger, and spread are some of the reasons why the U.S. has stated that any war on terror will be a very lengthy one. Al Qaeda will be even more violent in time, with nuclear, biological, or chemical (NBC) weapons becoming a stronger option for them. There will also be mergers of groups around the world as counterterrorist operations take effect — Al Qaeda has already formed an umbrella organization, and it will grow in the future. Take our word for it.

3: Beyond Basic

INTELLIGENCE FILE 001/2007 – COMPLEX TERRORISM –

INTRODUCTION

In 1605, an angry man named Guy Fawkes planned to blow up the British Parliament with thirty-six barrels of charcoal, sulfur, and saltpeter; he went down in history as the explosives expert of the Gunpowder Plot after the scheme was discovered. This was the first time in history that a concept now referred to by many researchers as complex terrorism was attempted. The first notable modern incident took place in 1969, when neo-Fascists bombed the railway station in Bologna, Italy, killing sixteen people and wounding hundreds more.

But it was a series of attacks in the early 1980s that really ushered in today's era of complex terrorism when a mostly Shiite Islamic jihad coalition (composed of Amal, led by Nabhi Berri; the Al Dawa, led by Sheik Fadlallah; Hezbollah, led by Abbas Mussari; and the Suicide Brigade, led by Imam Hussein) struck Western interests, using suicide bombers and trucks filled with explosives. In Lebanon, 45 people were killed when they hit the U.S. Embassy and its living annex. On October 25, 1983, they hit the U.S. Marine barracks there, killing 241, and the French military contingent headquarters, killing 58. The Israeli headquarters in Tyre was also hit, as well as the American and French Embassies in Kuwait, killing 5 and wounding 87. The strike against the Americans in Beirut resulted in the largest explosion on earth since Hiroshima.

DEFINITION

Complex terrorism is similar to the martial arts of aikido or jiu-jitsu. It uses the strengths and weaknesses of the target itself to cause more damage than would otherwise be possible. Little money or expertise is required to conduct operations, and it can cause huge financial losses with either minimum or maximum loss of life. Terrorists can select targets according to a required result. This type of terrorism does not necessarily require suicide attacks, but they make the action more spectacular and add to its propaganda value. The concept has also been known as technological terrorism, because it often uses advances in relatively crude weapons technology to target the high technology of an infrastructure: the key is the target itself and its susceptibility to collateral damage. We will define the concept as using the technologies of the weapon in concert with the target itself to create a force multiplier in order to gain the greatest damage and/or highest casualties possible with the lowest probability of being apprehended, using low-level technology and at relatively low cost without distinction between political, military, economic, or civilian targets.

The difficulty in defining this type of terrorism and describing the concepts involved led Western governments to ignore warnings from intelligence analysts back in the early 1980s, when the Americans were driven out of Beirut. Another reason warnings were ignored was the belief by politicians — and, indeed, many intelligence analysts — that if a group of terrorists were to commit such acts of violence, the public outrage, even from those supporting the cause, would be so sharply against them they would lose support; thus, they theorized, they would not dare to experiment with such a technique as complex terrorism in the first place. It was presumed that terrorists would be rational — or, to put in better context, that they would have the same logic that we do in Western society. This belief was a fallacy, because all cultures across the world have differences in logic based on the experiences of the region they live in. You cannot apply your own moral principles and template of behaviour to others. Those that have lived and operated in different parts of the world know this to be true. The objective analysis of events is not the only factor that should be considered by an intelligence analyst.

It appears that many analysts, especially in North America, forgot one of the basic rules of terrorism: groups grow more violent over time, due to their growing frustration and callousness. Also overlooked was the psychological effect of groupthink on the individual terrorist living in the underground environment of their chosen vocation.

With the exception of the United States, Israel and Sri Lanka have suffered the most from this tactic of terror. On August 21, 1995, a suicide bomber in a bus killed five and injured fifty-two others in Jerusalem. In January 1996, there were four suicide bombing attacks in Israel, killing sixty-three and injuring hundreds in revenge for the assassination of the Hamas leader Ayash. Actually, these types of attacks have been a way of life in Israel since about that time. The country has also been targeted outside its borders. Remember the 1994 Jewish community centre truck bomb in Buenos Aires? It killed ninety-six people and wounded hundreds.

Sri Lanka has been living with complex terrorism for about the same amount of time as Israel. The Tamil Tigers, known in Canada only for their support activities, have used this concept as well as suicide bombers since the early 1980s, targeting the civilian downtown centre of Colombo, the national airport, and the political leaders of Sri Lanka. All of these attacks killed and injured hundreds at a time. In 2007, the group even smuggled ten unassembled Czech-manufactured light aircraft into Sri Lanka and put them together piece by piece. Capable of flying at 250 kilometres per hour, these planes have bombed Colombo twice so far, and the government is considering buying some Soviet MiG-29s in response. This is a tactical first in terrorism and demonstrates how a technological advance can aid such an organization much more than it can aid those who counter them.

Here in North America, the World Trade Center, a symbol of American global economic power, was first attacked on February 26, 1993. The event brought the threat of complex terrorism to the public's attention, as it occurred on this side of the Atlantic. The attack left six people dead and one thousand injured. The bomb, which was a mixture of fertilizer, nitric acid, and sulfuric acid, was laced with anthrax and left behind a one-hundred-by-two-hundred-foot crater that cost $650 million to repair. The reaction was confusion and fear, mixed with a desire for revenge. Tomahawk missiles into the Sudan and Afghanistan were the response — unfortunately, to no effect. The Oklahoma City bombing just two years later proved that complex terrorism was possible from homegrown extremist groups, and the attack on the Khobar Towers in Saudi Arabia on June 25, 1996, also targeted Americans. Then came the attacks on the U.S. Embassies in Nairobi, Kenya, and Dar es Salaam, Tanzania, on August 7, 1998, which claimed 301 lives and wounded more than 5,000. Next, the USS *Cole* was attacked in Yemen on October 12, 2000, killing seventeen sailors. Unfortunately, most Americans were still oblivious to the threat they faced. This ended abruptly on September 11, 2001, and those strikes have been the pinnacle of complex terrorism to date. But it can and will get worse. The current trend in terrorism is a mixture of conventional and complex tactics in support of each other.

It may be argued by some that the following does not necessarily fall under the classification of complex terrorism, but rather under an examination of weapons or conventional tactics. Fair enough. The definition of this concept is still in the development stage for many intelligence analysts, but it can include the following:

- Use of conventional/unconventional explosives to inflict mass casualties. Complex terrorism in our definition includes attacks that cause very high loss of life to a civilian population.
- Use of conventional/unconventional explosives detonated at multiple targets to inflict mass casualties or damage. This also includes the use of multiple smaller bombs targeting one selected infrastructure.
- Use of unconventional military weapons to inflict an unusually high kill count: These types of attacks use military technology to inflict a huge loss of life.
- Terrorist-improvised nuclear, biological, or chemical weapons. Facilities could be attacked by terrorists and diseases or toxins released, but most likely these strikes would include the development of a biological weapon that could target large events such as sporting matches, concerts, or rallies. Other targets could also be selected in any city's downtown core.

Higher levels of damage and/or casualties can be expected with complex terrorism: Al Qaeda has no regard for bad press in the world's media and no regard for the fact that a terrorist sponsor state will suffer. The group considers all people in the target nation as the enemy: there is no such thing as collateral damage. There is also disregard for the strong counterterrorist actions that will be taken against the group itself. In the past revolutionary or insurgent groups attempted to initiate change; today religious terrorism demands retribution for supposed harm done. No longer is the tactic simply armed propaganda meant to grab the attention of the target audience; there is no need for national support from within the countries. As a result, target states' ability to use negotiation as an effective political tool has been lost. And as the public becomes more and more saturated with exposure to attacks, terrorists need more spectacular tactics to get the media attention they require. The psychological effect of a large strike is also much greater today, as the media has developed to the point of giving the public live coverage from anywhere in the world.

Will this trend continue? Al Qaeda certainly has the financial and technical ability to commit complex terrorism attacks on a continual basis, and their leadership is better educated than most in the past. The fall of Soviet Union created a vacuum, leaving the U.S. as the only superpower, and it represents the culture of the West. The possible availability to terrorists of Russian know-how and nuclear material increased at about that time, which gave them the means to acquire vast amounts of information required to conduct complex operations, even with NBC weapons.

The prognosis is pretty dark. There are many soft targets in the developed countries of Europe and North America, making defence difficult, and the availability of suicide "martyrs" make certain operations more viable than in the past. With the current feelings of hatred for the West in many places around the world, complex attacks will also not affect Al Qaeda's base of political support. As it is an internationally based organization that had years to develop without restriction, support in a specific country is not crucial.

The successful trend of using complex terrorism over the past twenty years has encouraged more use. In our current international climate, violence is increasing and democratic freedom of movement and access to information make for easier target selection and access. Is it so difficult to believe that a terrorist group may have reached a stage of frustration and feel a sense of impotence great enough that it will pursue any means to achieve its objectives?

THE PRINCIPLE OF THRESHOLD EVENTS

This relates to the level of violence used in a terrorist attack. Once a threshold event takes place, an invisible psychological line has been crossed, and once a series of similar events takes place, the line disappears completely, allowing similar, but not necessarily identical, events to take place. It is important to realize that such an event need not be committed by the same terrorist group: the line can be crossed by one group, making it easier for a different one to cross it as well.

On March 20, 1995, twelve people were killed and fifty-seven hundred were injured in a sarin nerve gas attack on a crowded subway station in the centre of Tokyo, Japan. A similar attack occurred nearly simultaneously in the Yokohama subway system. The Aum Shinrikyo ("Supreme Truth"), an apocalyptic religious cult, was blamed for the attacks. This was the first use of a chemical nerve agent in a terrorist attack that caused mass casualties, and has been widely viewed by most intelligence experts as the point of no return regarding the use of chemical weapons. The reaction of the world to this incident was blasé at best. There were the standard condemnations and the perpetrators were rounded up, but no strategic actions to fight the potential for mass chemical attacks were taken by Western governments.

But by taking a closer look at the Aum Shinrikyo, one is better able to understand the Al Qaeda mentality and the direction the group is likely to take in the future. The Aum cult produced various chemical and biological agents in quantity. It manufactured ricin, anthrax, LSD, sodium pentathol ("truth serum"), and sarin, with a production goal of seventy tonnes. The gas was successfully tested on sheep in Australia, where the Aum had certain business ventures. Cyanide and mustard gas were produced in large quantities, as well as other toxins like VX nerve agent, Q fever, phosgene, and CS and CN gases. The cult even travelled to Zaire in an attempt to obtain the Ebola virus.

The Aum Shinrikyo was founded in 1987 by a solitary man, Shoko Asahara. The religious belief taught was a mixture of various Eastern religions, with the Hindu god Shiva, the Destroyer, as its deity. The chief belief was that Armageddon would happen shortly and only the merciful and godly would survive. Cult members lived for "X Day," when the group would take over Japan by the wide use of sarin. They planned to begin by killing government members at the first session of a new parliament using sarin. The personnel recruited by the Aum were often of very high calibre. Among its members were a cardiovascular surgeon, a particle physics graduate, two applied physics graduates, and an electronics engineer. The group recruited alienated scientists, sometimes sending them to study in the U.S. It was a multi-million-dollar enterprise: in 1990, the entrance fee to join was $8,000. Like Al Qaeda, the Aum had money.

By 1990, the group was already culturing *Clostridium botulinum*, the efforts being led by a molecular biologist from Kyoto University Viral Research Center. In April of that year, the Aum tried to use a modified exhaust pipe filled with botulinus toxin in Tokyo as a test. It was unsuccessful, but they didn't give up.

In 1993, a Russian recipe for the mass production of sarin and blueprints for AK-74 assault rifles were obtained, and forty-five cult members were trained by former KGB Alpha Team members within a year. On June 9, 1993, the Aum again tried a vehicle-mounted aerosol attack at the imperial wedding of Prince Naruhito, this time using anthrax. The same month, members tried for four days to spread anthrax from a Tokyo rooftop but failed as the particles were not the right size for proper dispersion. The Aum then acquired a blimp, which is a good way of distributing nuclear, chemical, or biological agents, as well as two remote-controlled mini drone helicopters that are used to photograph volcanoes. These can fly for ninety minutes at a time and can carry a payload of eight kilograms, enough sarin to kill a small town. Light fixed-wing and helicopter pilot certificates were obtained by two Aum members in Opalocka, Florida, on October 31, 1993. Florida flight schools seem to be popular among international terrorists.

From 1987 to 1995, between $10 and $15 million was invested by the group in sarin production equipment alone. The main laboratory was completed in October 1993. The terrorists also bought large quantities of an antidote to sarin, through agricultural suppliers. The Aum had laboratories for NBC research at their Mount Fuji headquarters and had purchased a ranch in Australia that had a uranium mine, for which they paid the government $110,000 in mineral rights before shipping the radioactive material back to Japan in suitcases. In addition to manufacturing handguns and rifles, the group produced the explosives TNT and RDX in quantity. There also was a laser weapons research facility with a rail gun that fired a 20mm shell by electromagnetic force at over 218 metres per second.

In March 1994, a former KGB colonel sold a suitcase-sized nerve gas detector to the cult. For those who think the Aum was a problem only for the Japanese, it will come as a surprise that by the end of 1994 there were thirty thousand members in Russia; they had even recruited physicists from Moscow State University. By this time, the group had its own trained military units (including a commando section) as well as an intelligence organization.

On June 27, 1994, more than eighteen kilograms of sarin was released from a truck using an aerosol spray in a residential area of Matsumoto in order to kill three judges who would be ruling against the cult in a court case. The cult finally hit pay dirt by killing 7 people and injuring more than 150, many of whom were permanently damaged. Police initially blamed one of the area's residents, until they received documents from disgruntled cult members a year later. On September 20, the Aum tried to kill a journalist who spoke out against the cult using a First World War substance called phosgene that swells lung tissue and kills by asphyxiation. The Aum injected the gas through the mail slot of her apartment, but miraculously she survived.

By this time, recruits numbered in the tens of thousands around the world. In addition to land investments, Aum-owned businesses by 1995 consisted of three core firms, with thirty-seven corporations, twenty-one front companies, and thirteen associate firms organized by followers. Aum members even ran for election in local government. The cult also began murdering or attempting to murder cult opponents, both internal and external. Japanese National Police Agency chemists were soon detecting sarin on the outside of the perimeter of the main Aum compound, and the police placed an undercover operative into the cult. She was quickly murdered. Wiretaps were then placed on phones.

On March 15, 1995, three suitcases were placed at Kasumigaseki subway station with botulinus toxin inside. Eventually, they were turned in to the lost and found. All were in working condition, but the person detailed to arm the suitcases had a guilty conscience, and they failed to detonate. Unfortunately, Japan's luck was due to change.

On March 20, five Aum members with bags of sarin boarded different trains at opposite ends of the Tokyo subway system, which would converge at Kasumigaseki station, located in the city's business centre, at 8:00 A.M. A police raid on the group's main compound was slated for the next day, and it was no coincidence that police headquarters was in the immediate vicinity and due for a shift change at 8:30 A.M. Many police officers should have been on the subway trains. Vinyl bags holding the contents separate were pierced by sharpened umbrella tips. Sarin, an extremely deadly agent invented by the Nazis, is colourless, odourless, and destroys the nervous system. Victims collapsed in the trains and on the platforms of stations. They were also blinded. The smell of the gas (only 30 percent of the mixture was sarin) was reported in fifteen subway stations. Police found it difficult to locate the sources of the gas, because they did not know what to look for. Amazingly, only 12 people were killed, but the attack wounded more than 5,500. If it were not for the impurities in the sarin, the death toll could have been much worse than 9/11.

Police responded by raiding the Aum compound two days later with a thousand officers in riot gear. Widespread arrests were made. About a week later, Takaji Kunimatsu, chief of the National Police Agency and head of the Aum investigation, was about to be driven to work when an assassin pumped four rounds from a .357 Magnum into his back. This finally sparked an international investigation in six different countries. On May 16, 1995, Shoko Asahara was arrested, and by the end of that year about 350 members had been detained by the police. It should be noted that from April to June 1995, several copycat attacks using cyanide and phosgene were made in Japan by others. Copycat attacks also occurred in Australia in February 1997, when two chlorine bombs were discovered in crowded shopping centres.

Today, Asahara and about a dozen other Aum members are awaiting execution. The cult is still active, however, despite knowledge of the attacks. In 2000 the group changed its name to Aleph (the first letter of the Hebrew alphabet) and currently has seven main locations in Japan and twenty smaller branches where members practise meditation. The remnants of the group are currently watched over by Japan's Public Security Investigation Agency, with about fifty agents assigned to the task.

Al Qaeda is as rich as the Aum. It also has many of the same weapons desires as the group. Any psychological invisible line has already disappeared, so democracies must be ready for any level of threat. The Aum had enough sarin to kill 4.2 million people.

COMPLEX TERRORISM IN CANADA

Canada has been the target of at least four strikes that could be classified as complex terrorism. The fourth was the Air India disaster, while the first three were courtesy of the FLQ. (It is interesting to note that the FLQ were among the first modern terrorist groups to use multiple bombs). On May 16, 1963, a bomb destroyed an oil tank at the Golden Eagle Refinery in Montreal, and fifteen bombs were placed in street-corner mailboxes in Westmount the following day. Ten of these exploded, and one person was seriously injured. On January 16, 1969, several bombs were placed in street-corner mailboxes in Ottawa, but were defused before they could be detonated.

Canada has also figured prominently in some complex attacks that might have occurred, had they not been discovered by law enforcement. Not too many know that on May 30, 1986, five Montreal-area Sikhs were arrested and charged with conspiracy to place a bomb on another Air India flight departing from New York City. Two of the suspects were found guilty and sentenced to life imprisonment. On December 14, 1999, Ahmed Ressam, who had entered Canada under a false name in 1993, was arrested as he tried to cross from British Columbia to blow up Los Angeles International Airport. Ressam belonged to a Montreal-based cell of the Armed Islamic Group.

INTELLIGENCE COMMENTS

The ignorance of complex terrorism found in the public and, more importantly, in many politicians has been a detriment to counterterrorist efforts in of all the Western nations. Denial leads to the belief that Al Qaeda can be treated as if it were a conventional terrorist group — pull out of Afghanistan and the problem will go away. This is a quaint concept. Unfortunately, Al Qaeda is not a traditional terrorist group, and they will not go away and leave us alone until they have achieved their desired objectives, explained in detail in Chapter 6.

Conventional attacks by Al Qaeda should be neither discounted nor forgotten, but complex terrorism remains the highest threat from this group, especially in regards to hazardous chemicals and homemade bombs. Our urban centres and oil and gas infrastructures are key targets.

It is unlikely that Al Qaeda can build a nuclear bomb at the present time, but the possible targeting of a nuclear plant on 9/11 suggests the group could cause a meltdown that could be almost as catastrophic. A ground attack on a nuclear power plant in North America, Great Britain, France, or Germany would likely not be effective, but it might be successful in other coalition states that have lower levels of security. It is likely that Al Qaeda has the resources for one or more radiological dispersal devices (RDDs), more commonly known as dirty bombs, and cells in Belgium, Denmark, France, Germany, Italy, Great Britain, and Spain have been apprehended planning chemical attacks.

A constant level of complex terrorism has been reached in Western Europe and North America due to Al Qaeda and their allied network. This threat requires targeted nations to engage in an unprecedented counterterrorism campaign that includes the destruction or intimidation of sponsor states, the elimination of funding for terrorists, and a public relations effort in order to gain support for the coalition states and to impede terrorist operations. In addition, our security forces must infiltrate the political and social front groups and terrorist support infrastructures in order to disrupt operations through the collection and analysis of intelligence.

Different groups have at times used complex terrorism sporadically as a means to an end, but since the early 1980s Israel has been targeted consistently by Hamas and the Islamic Jihad, and Sri Lanka has had the Tamil Tigers on their hands every day. The West has generally ignored these campaigns, however, which shows a lack of understanding of the threshold event principle. The Japanese Security Bureau did not anticipate any strikes either, even though a lot of evidence was reported of suspicious activity by the Aum in the early days. This example proves just how far a terrorist group, especially a religious one, can proceed with NBC weapons construction.

The copycat attacks in Japan using cyanide, phosgene, and pepper spray and the two chlorine bombs activated in crowded Australian shopping centres prove the threshold principle, and show that similar acts are perpetrated by terrorists other than those in the initiating group. Al Qaeda and its network currently use a mix of complex and conventional tactics, but it should be emphasized that the network is the first to constantly use complex terrorism at a higher level than Hamas or the Tamil Tigers.

4: Home Front

INTELLIGENCE FILE 002/2007 – COMPLEX TARGETS AND – METHODS OF ATTACK

INTRODUCTION

No one supplies more fossil fuels to the United States than Canada. As a result, it was reported just this February that the Al Qaeda organization in the Arabian Peninsula issued a plea to its admirers to hit Canada's oil and gas infrastructure. "We should strike petroleum interests in all areas which supply the United States," with the intent to "choke the U.S. economy," they said. Attackers were told to give Canadian oil fields, pipelines, loading platforms, and carriers first priority, followed by similar targets in Mexico and Venezuela.

According to a 2002 Associated Press study that tallied the infrastructure of the United States, that country includes about 600,000 bridges, 170,000 water systems, 2,800 power plants (104 of them nuclear), 305,000 kilometres of interstate natural gas pipelines, 75,000 dams, and 463 skyscrapers that are at least five hundred feet tall. All of these are potential targets for complex terrorism attacks. To understand where Canada is, you can get a rough estimate by taking into consideration that we have about one-tenth the population of the United States. Divide the above figures and those provided within this briefing by ten and you will have an approximate number of potential targets in Canada.

INFRASTRUCTURE TARGETS

Infrastructures are networks that are tied to the point of synergy. Critical infrastructures are those that if destroyed or damaged would interrupt the operation of other infrastructures. Some are more important than others, and some are tied more closely together: without energy, all machinery could stop, and there may be no electricity; if it's oil and gas infrastructure, you may not be able to drive anywhere, or gasoline will have to be rationed. Infrastructures can be local, provincial, regional, or national in scope. There are many types of critical infrastructure, and many targets within those types would be suitable for a complex terrorism attack. Terrorists may choose to target the energy or financial infrastructures, or the critical infrastructures of government, telecommunications, and other industries.

CRITICAL NODES

The places where networks connect are called nodes. Critical nodes are those that if destroyed or damaged would cause failure or partial failure of the infrastructure.

The World Trade Center was a financial/economic node as well as a symbolic target, being one of the world's tallest buildings. However, it can be argued that it was not a really critical node, because if it had been, the financial effect on the country's economy would have been considerably greater. While it is a critical node, the Pentagon received limited damage in military terms on 9/11. The terrorists accomplished little in a practical sense with their attack. However, the Pentagon is also a symbolic target, and that was where Al Qaeda's real success lay.

To gain maximum effect and benefit, terrorist groups like Al Qaeda will in the future select critical nodes; this does not mean that symbolic targets will be ignored altogether, but rather that dual-purpose targets may be selected.

ROLE OF TECHNOLOGY

Without the use of technology there would be no guarantee of a successful attack on any infrastructure. A terrorist needs explosives to cut a pipeline effectively and quickly. A terrorist needs to hijack one plane (a piece of very high technology) to be able to crash it into a stock exchange building and another to crash into the reserve facility in order to have any real effect on the financial infrastructure of a country. A terrorist requires automatic weapons to kill tourists so that the economy of the target country will be affected. A plane can also be blown up by the use of technology, for example, by plastic or liquid explosives, or with a SA-7, SA-18, or Stinger missile.

TYPES OF CRITICAL INFRASTRUCTURE

DAMS
Dams are important not only for the electricity that they generally provide but also to prevent flooding of the area concerned. In 1972, Buffalo Creek Dam in West Virginia broke and twenty-nine kilometres of a valley were flooded in fifteen minutes. More than one hundred people were killed and four thousand were left homeless. Approximately 80 percent of the survivors suffered from post-traumatic stress disorder. Sometimes it does not take very sophisticated technology to destroy advanced machinery. On March 28, 1978, three generators were sabotaged at Grand Coulee Dam using a crowbar. At the time, these generators were among the largest in the world.

POWER GRIDS
The ice storm of 1998 left more than a million people in Quebec, Ontario, and parts of the northeastern United States without electricity. Several centimetres of ice had formed on power lines and hydro towers from the incredible amount of freezing rain. The ice toppled several towers, and it took several weeks before many got their power restored.

The North American electrical blackout on August 23, 2003,

had a profound effect on millions of people in addition to costing a huge amount of money for American and Canadian industry and government. A major portion of the continent's electrical grid collapsed like a row of dominoes. In some cases, the fall of each part of the grid led to a draw of too much power on its adjacent parts, causing sequential collapse. In other cases the problem was the opposite: the closing of lines to an adjacent system caused too much power to be available in one area, leading to the shutdown of power plants there. In each case a safety mechanism or switch between each area should have kicked in to stop the falling of the next domino. Only some worked.

In addition to an internal grid, Ontario is connected to the United States grid, to the Quebec grid, and to a western grid. If terrorists, through infiltration, blackmail, or bribery, could affect the critical nodes of the power grid of the Toronto area, for example, they could paralyze the city for weeks, if not longer. Devastating blackouts of the past include the one in 1965 in the northeastern United States, which affected New York City and a total of 30 million people. On July 14, 1977, New York faced another blackout where there was widespread rape, looting, and vandalism during the hours of darkness, causing millions of dollars in damages and immense human suffering. More than 280 million litres of sewage poured into the city's waters because the water treatment plants could not operate.

The August 2003 blackout — a blackout that lasted in most areas for only a few hours during daylight — affected hundreds of thousands of businesses and the lives of about 50 million people. New York City alone lost over $1 billion. In the retail sector, the loss of sales tax revenue was $40 million. Blackouts also affect the ability to respond to emergencies such as fire or injury, and the affected area in this case included New York City, Boston, Detroit, Cleveland, Toronto, and Ottawa. About 1.5 million people were left without water in Cleveland for more than twenty-four hours, and there were more than four hundred cancelled flights. About three hundred people even camped out in the New York Stock Exchange building.

It takes thirty-six hours to restart a nuclear power plant on average, and twenty-two out of about one hundred power plants that had to be shut down in this case were nuclear. Many other systems short-circuited, causing smaller power failures that then affected industry, the financial sector, and transportation. Telephone switching stations were also affected.

According to a 1985 report by the Center for Strategic and International Studies at Georgetown University, simultaneous attacks on three transformers in the national electric grid system could take out the northeastern United States for two to three weeks. Today, information on them is readily available from libraries, trade journals, state, provincial, or federal energy agencies, or directly from public utility companies. There are 328,000 kilometres of transmission lines served by four regional grids, including Western Interconnection, Eastern Interconnection, and the grids operated by the Electricity Reliability Council of Texas and the Province of Quebec. These sectors contain five thousand power plants fuelled by natural gas, nuclear energy, oil, and coal.

Transmission lines, power plants, and substations are common terrorist targets all around the world. In 1978 in El Salvador, 80 percent of the electricity to the entire country was interrupted for a week. Between September and December 1981, there were twenty-one bombings of the Puerto Rico Electric Power Authority. The left-wing Chilean terrorist group MIR also knocked out 80 percent of the electrical power in Chile for three days by near-simultaneous multiple bombings. On April 29, 1993, terrorists blasted a power pylon in the southern Philippines, plunging ten provinces into darkness. There are also other means to disrupt transmission lines: balloons with chaff could be used, for example. Chaff could also be used against electrical substations using homemade mortars.

NUCLEAR-RELATED

These targets include nuclear power plants, nuclear research facilities, waste and material storage facilities, nuclear weapons, nuclear-powered ships and submarines, and ships transporting nuclear materials. There are many types of radioactive material that could be used for an RDD, which poses the greatest threat from terrorists. Cobalt-60, used in cancer therapy, can be used to contaminate an area if the right amount is available. Radium can also be used, as can cesium-137, iodine-131, strontium-90, plutonium, uranium-235, depleted uranium, and uranium powder. Even unprocessed uranium ore could be used for an effective scare, to induce panic or to emphasize a potential nuclear threat. Such a device could be built from scratch, or a tank holding radioactive waste could be blown up, producing the same result.

If an RDD is properly deployed, casualties over a period of fifteen to thirty years can be expected. The number of casualties will usually depend on the amounts of material inhaled more than on physical contact, as people affected will be likely be decontaminated quickly. Radioactive particles can be swallowed, inhaled, or absorbed through the skin, and the effects are cumulative: once exposed, a second, smaller dose can kill. For example, the inhalation of 12,000 micrograms of plutonium causes death in sixty days, and 1,900 micrograms means death in a year. About 700 micrograms causes death in three years, and 260 micrograms means that cancer will develop in time.

The availability of the nuclear materials required for an RDD is greater than many can imagine. Nuclear materials are used frequently in medicine, and amounts can be found in almost every hospital across Canada as well as at certain medical instrument production facilities. To put this into perspective, 14 million patients undergo medical treatment using nuclear material every year in the U.S., and there are four thousand hospitals from which low-grade radioactive material can be stolen.

NATURAL GAS

There are more than 450,000 kilometres of gas pipeline in North America. Exposed and unprotected gas pipelines stretch for hundreds of kilometres — some run through urban areas and present deadly potential for a terrorist attack. Our largest is the Trans-Canada Pipeline, which stretches for 42,000 kilometres, but there are others, such as the Mackenzie Valley line, which alone is worth about $5 billion. Just a simple leak of natural gas in Toronto on October 4, 2002, caused the evacuation of several square blocks in the downtown core.

If a distribution gas line in the financial district of Toronto were to be targeted with explosives, the devastation, both physical and financial, could be immense. The Ghrirba Synagogue was the target of a suicide terrorist attack on April 11, 2002, on the Tunisian Island of Djerba; a natural gas truck was used as a bomb, purposely parked against a wall of the synagogue. Fifteen people were killed, including twelve German tourists. The economy of the island was also affected by the attack.

Another similar incident took place in Milan, Italy, in late March 2004, when a man wired seventy propane tanks in his car for an attempted suicide attack, but the bomb exploded prematurely on the way. Between July and October 1995, France was hurled into a GIA bombing campaign based on devices made out of gas camping canisters and nails. On June 19, 2004, Quetta, Pakistan, was the location of an attack by unidentified terrorists who fired fifteen rockets at that country's largest natural gas field (the Sui), seriously wounding a paramilitary soldier. No damage was reported to the installation, but the message from the terrorists made its point. Less than two years later, Pakistan signed an agreement with these same terrorists allowing them border crossing rights without interference in Afghanistan to fight our troops there. The natural gas fields in northern Afghanistan have also been targeted by Taliban terrorists in the last few years.

In addition, the FBI once thwarted a plot by a U.S. militia group to blow up a 90-million-litre propane storage facility outside Sacramento, California. In April 1997, four Ku Klux Klan members were arrested by the FBI in Texas; they planned to blow up a natural gas refinery there and use the incident as a diversion for an armoured car robbery. In Mexico City a liquefied natural gas explosion killed 452 people and injured 4,248. Some facilities are in populated areas and would kill thousands and injure many more.

Liquefied natural gas terminals that load or unload supertankers are key complex terrorism targets. New York City has two main facilities of this type, and the surrounding area is heavily populated. The German RAF once bombed a U.S. vehicle depot that held liquid gas. If the terrorists had been fully successful, the damage could have been severe to both material and people. Containers and pipelines can also be targeted by thermite bombs, a terrorist favourite in the past. A Canadian Pacific Railway accident on February 21, 2003, near Belleville, Ontario, initiated an evacuation of more than five hundred people. Four propane cars exploded out of six, fortunately not damaging two cars of ammonia at the site. Keep in mind that this could have happened in a more populated area.

OIL INFRASTRUCTURE

In the last seven years, the proven oil reserves of Canada have increased from about 5 to 180 billion barrels due to the increased technology now available for the retrieval of the oil sands at Fort McMurray in Alberta. That's more than Iran, Iraq, and Kuwait. Next to Saudi Arabia, we have more oil than anyone else, and 10 percent of what America uses is Canadian. Perhaps as a result, an Al Qaeda–friendly group stated this year, "We should strike petroleum interests in all areas which supply the United States, and not only in the Middle East, because the target is to stop its imports or decrease it by all means."

In the Middle East, the oil industry is in the crosshairs. At the present time only Saudi Arabia can pump more oil, as all other producers are at their limits. So an attack against Saudi oil could cripple not only the American but also the world economy. Al Qaeda is aware of this, as can be seen in captured documents in Afghanistan, and threats from Al Qaeda against Saudi oil have been common. The West also stands accused by Al Qaeda of stealing Muslim treasures at paltry prices; Al Qaeda states that the oil business is the biggest theft ever witnessed by mankind. Keep in mind that terrorists can hurt the U.S. and Europe without even going there, and the recent rise in oil prices is partially due to the need for increased security. The Saudi arm of Al Qaeda has claimed responsibility for an attempted suicide attack on the world's largest oil processing facility at Abqaiq in Saudi Arabia's eastern province in February 2006.

Pipelines

In 2006, an Internet blog associated with Al Qaeda instructed Canadian and American jihadists to attack an Alaskan oil pipeline. Saudi Arabia narrowly avoided an Al Qaeda attack on a major pipeline and oil terminal complex in 2005. More than twenty arrests were made in conjunction with the case. The Rastanura Oil Terminal and Refinery and its pipeline system are the most important oil facilities in the Persian Gulf — the terminal transfers 5 million barrels every day to supertankers. By using a mini submarine or boat packed with explosives, terrorists could eliminate this.

There have been more than three hundred attacks against the Iraqi pipeline system since the fall of Baghdad in April 2003. The 950-kilometre-long pipeline leading from the Kirkuk oil fields into northern Turkey pumps 800,000 barrels per day, and the entire route has been shut down repeatedly. The militia belonging to Shiite Muslim cleric Moqtada al-Sadr has also repeatedly attacked the pipelines leading to Basra on the Persian Gulf. On August 17, 2003, the giant oil pipeline in Northern Iraq near Baiji was blown. This halted oil exports to Turkey only days after they had resumed after another such explosion.

Al Qaeda could also strike in North America, where there are more than 400,000 kilometres of oil pipelines. The Trans-Alaskan line is 1,250 kilometres long and has eight pumping stations that make ideal terrorist targets; this line alone carries 17 percent of American oil. In addition, there is the Inter Pipeline Fund, one of Canada's largest petroleum transportation businesses, which consists of 5,000 kilometres of pipeline and 1.2 million barrels of storage space.

Terrorist organizations are experienced in the sabotage of pipelines. On October 18, 1998, the Ejército de Liberación Nacional (ELN) planted a bomb that exploded on the Ocensa pipeline in Antioquia, Colombia, killing seventy-one people and injuring at least one hundred others. The pipeline is jointly owned by the Colombia State Oil Company Ecopetrol and a consortium that includes American, French, British, and Canadian companies. As well, on December 11, 1984, a NATO fuel pipeline was bombed in six places in Belgium.

Terminals

On April 24, 2004, suicide bombers in a dhow (a type of boat commonly used in the Middle East) and two speedboats attempted to destroy Iraq's two main oil transfer terminals in Basra, but failed. The attack killed three U.S. sailors. The U.S. Navy and Coast Guard now have a 2.8-kilometre restricted zone around the terminal on the seaside and have thirty warships on patrol to guard against another such attack.

GOPLATs

Other possible targets of terrorist attack are gas and oil platforms (GOPLATs) out at sea. In the U.S., companies have provided private SWAT teams to protect the rigs in the Gulf of Mexico and other domestic locations. The question is whether these teams could get there on time to prevent destruction. Iraqi land-based oil rigs have been attacked by terrorists, but attacking GOPLATs takes know-how with respect to oil field operations to be able to place the explosives effectively.

Tankers

Oil tankers have been attacked in the past. On October 6, 2002, an Al Qaeda suicide squad using a small boat loaded with explosives targeted the French oil supertanker *Limburg* in the Gulf of Aden, loaded with four hundred thousand barrels of Saudi crude oil. The technique used had been previously refined by the Tamil Tigers and was similar to the 2000 attack on the USS *Cole*. In 2005, Moroccan terrorists allied to Al Qaeda were arrested for plotting to do the same to ships passing through the Strait of Gibraltar.

In 2006, the London-based International Maritime Bureau reported an increase in the number of tugboats hijacked in the Strait of Malacca.

The bureau stated that the tugs could be packed with explosives and target passing ships. One-quarter of the world's trade and 80 percent of Japanese oil flow through this single strait. This concerned the U.S. so much that it offered military assistance to the Malaysian government. The aid offered was rumoured to be in the form of U.S. Marines in speedboats. Malaysia stated that it would send out its own patrols. Prime areas where oil tankers can be attacked are in the Straits of Hormuz, Gibraltar, and Malacca as well as in the Gulf of Aden.

Refineries
Oil refineries can be found in Canada, Saudi Arabia, the U.S., and many other countries targeted by Al Qaeda. Texas alone has twenty-five refineries producing over one-quarter of American capacity and has already received FBI warnings about Al Qaeda. By crashing a hijacked plane into the Abqaiq Refinery in Saudi Arabia, Al Qaeda could stop the flow of 7 million barrels of oil a day. Al Qaeda did attempt to destroy a portion of an oil refinery in Saudi Arabia in 2006. The truck bomb never reached its target because of a system of concentric security rings around the facility. Refineries are an old staple for terrorists. On June 1, 1980, the African National Congress bombed strategic oil-from-coal plants in South Africa, causing $7 million worth of damage. On May 14, 1984, the ANC attacked another oil refinery; this time four ANC terrorists were killed.

Fuel Tank Farms
In 1973, two terrorists of the Japanese Red Army and two others from the PFLP blew storage tanks of a Shell Oil facility in Singapore using plastic explosives. Frogmen from the Contras conducted sabotage on October 14, 1984, against oil installations on the Pacific coast of Nicaragua. In addition, the Contras conducted an attack using small planes on September 8, 1984 (targeting the oil storage facility at Managua Airport) and another using speedboats on October 10, 1984 (targeting a port-side fuel depot). The FBI once thwarted an attempt by the Ku Klux Klan to blow up a refinery in Bridgeport, Texas, the location of the Strategic Petroleum Reserves of the U.S.

Fuel Trucks
The IRA has used fuel trucks as mobile bombs. In February 1977, a 7,500-litre fuel tanker with a bomb suspended inside the tank at the

end of a fishing line was left for police to disarm in the middle of the commercial centre of Belfast. There are fifty thousand gas tankers bound for service stations every day in the U.S. alone, presenting plenty of opportunity for terrorists.

Foreign Oil Workers
In May 2006, Al Qaeda terrorists stormed an oil company office in the Red Sea port of Yanbu in Saudi Arabia, gunning down six foreign workers. Four weeks later they attacked another oil office in Jhobar, holding hostages and killing twenty-two foreign workers.

Gas Stations
On May 15, 2003, Al Qaeda bombed nineteen Shell and two Caltex gas stations in Karachi, Pakistan. In January 1974, the gas lines at gas stations in Berlin, Germany, were severed by the 2 June Movement. If plastic explosives had been used, the devastation would have been immense.

INDUSTRIAL INFRASTRUCTURE
Chemical Plants
An assessment published in 1999 by the U.S. Agency for Toxic Substances and Disease Registry found that chemical plant security was fair to poor. The study also found that background checks of employees were not done, railway cars carrying cyanide compounds, chlorine, and liquefied petroleum gas were parked near residential areas, and truck shipments often went through cities despite prohibitions.

After 9/11, the FBI contacted twenty-seven thousand American corporate security managers to place them on the highest state of alert, as there are well over fifteen thousand facilities in the U.S. that handle hazardous chemicals. Today, chemical plants pose a great danger to their surrounding areas. Our cities have grown, and the outskirts where such plants were built have often turned into a mix of residential and commercial real estate where once there were only open fields. According to risk management plans filed with the U.S. Environmental Protection Agency several hundred plants have estimated that worst-case releases could spread toxic vapour clouds that would travel over twenty-five kilometres, and more than two thousand plants stated that worst-case incidents would affect a population of one hundred thousand people or more. Nearly half of these risk management plans were once posted to the public by the agency on its website. Although they were removed after 9/11, they may have been already accessed by terrorists.

The 1984 Union Carbide plant leak in Bhopal, India, proves the level of destruction that a terrorist attack on a chemical plant can have. The leak of methyl isocyanide killed more than three thousand and injured more than two hundred thousand. Almost as many people are permanently disabled today as were killed. It is still the worst industrial accident in history. A survey by the American Chemistry Council surveyed 982 plants in 2001 and found that over 30 percent had not identified areas subject to potential sabotage and that 25 percent had not conducted criminal background checks of employees and contractors.

There are thirty-five thousand distinct hazardous agents produced worldwide for legitimate industry.

In September 2001, in Toulouse, France, an unsolved explosion killed twenty-nine people and injured more than three thousand. French investigators believe the explosion was an accident but are continuing an investigation of a Tunisian man called Hassan Jandoubi, who died in the blast. He was reportedly seen earlier shouting at plant truck drivers who displayed an American flag after 9/11. A successful terrorist attack on a chemical plant may be as simple as firing a rocket-propelled grenade into machinery from a car at the side of the road. A new twist to drive-by shootings.

Trains with Hazardous Chemicals
Each tanker train car can contain 125,000 litres of liquid: that's a lot of chemical and would make a fine target for a complex terrorism application. To compound this threat, often such cars pass through cities. When built, the railroads for the most part went around cities and towns, but years of prosperity and city growth have encompassed not only the railway lines but also the industry that these lines supported. In 1979, a train derailment in Mississauga, Ontario — where it was feared toxic gases might leak from the overturned and burning tanker cars — led to the evacuation of over two hundred thousand people; police, who had to give the evacuation order by going door to door, had long exposure to potential risks in the smoke cloud. No accurate records were kept at that time (such as who was exposed and for how long), and no follow-up investigation as to health effects was done.

Chemical Trucks

In the United States there are 770,000 hazardous material shipments a day; 50,000 of them are gas tankers with loads from 34,800 to 43,500 litres of fuel, about the same as a Boeing 747 airliner. Some of these trucks are destined for Canada. Nabil Al-Marabh, an alleged associate of Osama bin Laden, had attended a driving school in Dearborn, Michigan, to obtain a commercial driving license and then procured a permit to haul hazardous material. During a raid of his residence in Detroit, the FBI found two Arab immigrants, Karim Koubriti and Ahmen Hannan, had also attended a Detroit-area truck driving school. U.S. Attorney General John Ashcroft stated that the two are believed to have had advance knowledge of the 9/11 attacks.

Annual losses due to cargo theft are in the $10–12 billion range in U.S. and several billion in Canada. There is also a possibility of a terrorist sneaking a hazardous material truck across the Canadian or Mexican borders into the United States. Not all trucking companies have panic buttons, emergency communications, or GPS tracking transponders — let alone do real security checks on the drivers of such vehicles.

Ships Containing Chemicals

Chemicals come in all forms; some are liquid, others are solid. Ships, because of the hazard and expense of air transport, often carry many of them.

TRANSPORT INFRASTRUCTURE

Over 10 million containers come into this country every year. If terrorists interfere and slow that commerce the cost would be tremendous. Airports, highways, and waterways are the transport infrastructure's conduits. Many choke points for transportation infrastructure exist, and this information is not hidden in a democracy.

Subways

On December 3, 1996, a bomb exploded aboard a Paris subway train as it arrived at the Port Royal station, killing two French nationals, a Moroccan, and a Canadian, and injuring eighty-six others. No one claimed responsibility for the attack, but Algerian extremists were suspected; this was only one attack of many against the Paris subway over a period of a year. No further reminder is necessary with respect to the Aum's 1995 Tokyo subway strike.

Traffic Control Centres
Every major city requires computerized control centres for traffic control. Two or three bombs at the appropriate locations and the gridlock would not only affect the personal lives of everyone who lives there but also bring business to a standstill. If you have experienced a power blackout in a downtown area before, you know what we mean.

Overpasses
A well-placed bomb at a choke point may be used in a terrorist attack, or a series of truck bombs at highway overpasses could be used, similar to the attempt made by the FLQ in 1960s Montreal.

Bridges
Bridges have been common targets of insurgents and terrorists for decades because they are choke points. In 1978 specific bridges were targeted for sabotage by terrorists in El Salvador; they successfully cut the country in half, and it took months to fully re-establish road communications.

Tunnels
The targeting of the Holland Tunnel in New York City by Al Qaeda is a good example of this potential type of terrorist strike. The Taliban also have extensive experience with tunnel sabotage in Afghanistan. In the past, the *mujahideen* successfully closed down the tunnel on the main north-south highway leading from Kabul. Tunnels of various sizes can be found in many large Canadian cities.

Buses and their Terminals
Bus terminals (especially in developing countries) are important nodes in transportation infrastructure. Bombs are the most common way to attack these hubs, but bus terminals would make perfect targets for complex terrorism attacks employing an RDD or improvised chemical or biological weapons. The spread of disease from any transportation centre is simple and quick.

Although costly in suicide bombers they have to use, the Palestinian Islamic Jihad, Hamas, and the Palestinian Martyr Brigades have all targeted buses. Other countries where terrorist bus attacks are common are Pakistan and India, so Al Qaeda is very aware of all the ins and outs of the tactics involved.

Trains and their Terminals
Union Station in Toronto is on the Al Qaeda hit list according to captured Al Qaeda documents in Afghanistan. More than a million people pass through this station each day; it is a hub or critical node for the city's subway system, its passenger and commuter trains, and some of its buses. As always, terrorism is a practical application, and success is predicated on the use of common sense (like timing). The rush-hour train bombings in Madrid and London attest to this fact.

Railway Bridges
In the United States there is what is called the Strategic Corridor Network, which is composed of three crucial bridges. There is the railway bridge over the Potomac in Washington D.C., another in Cincinnati, Ohio, and a third whose identity is not widely publicized. Canada has bridges over such defiles as well, including certain railway tracks and passes in British Columbia's Rocky Mountains, that could be targeted.

Airports
The name Ressam automatically comes to mind. Also known as the millennium bomber, the GIA member was arrested at the Canada/ U.S. border in 1999 before he could target Los Angeles International Airport.

Passenger Aircraft
In addition to the Air India bombing, one should also not forget Pan Am Flight 103 over Lockerbie, Scotland, which killed 278 people. As well, Mohamed Atta, the tactical leader of the 9/11 World Trade Center bombing, originally planned to initiate simultaneous explosions on twelve American passenger aircraft while they were over the Pacific in an operation code-named Project Bjonka.

Air Traffic Control Centres
There are twenty air traffic control centres in United States, as well as backup locations. Just forty bombs could do a nasty job of destroying the air transport infrastructure, and some very serious accidents could take place. Although there are military backups to even the civilian backup locations, it would take considerable time to get things back to normal, and time is money.

Canals
The Panama Canal or the Suez Canal would be closed for quite some time if Al Qaeda were to sink just one boat in either one of them; there is also the possibility of destroying the locks on these canals. The St. Lawrence Seaway consists of the Soo Locks (with four controlled by the U.S.), the eight Welland Locks and the Welland Canal (controlled by Canada), and the St. Lawrence Locks (two controlled by the U.S. and five by Canada). In addition there are the Trent-Severn Waterway and the Rideau Canal, which, although not used for commerce, are used extensively for tourism in the summer months.

Harbours
Harbours can be the terrorist target of NBC weapons or bomb attacks. The objective may be the harbour itself, the facilities located inside of it, or another ship docked with a cargo of hazardous material.

Passenger Ocean Liners
Luxury ocean liners have been targeted at least twice by terrorists, once in Latin American waters back in the 1960s and then again in the Mediterranean Sea in 1985, when the Palestinian PLF took hostages on the Italian cruise ship *Achille Lauro*. These ships would also be ideal targets for a biological attack.

Ferries
Ferries have been common targets for terrorist attacks in places like the Philippines, which is the home of Al Qaeda associate the Abu Sayaaf Group. Canada has many large ferries that could be bombed, targeted for chemical or biological attack, or taken over to create a hostage situation. They operate in British Columbia, Prince Edward Island, Nova Scotia, Newfoundland, and Ontario.

CITY INFRASTRUCTURE
Water Filtration
There have been attempts in the past to contaminate the water supply of different North American cities. An Al Qaeda cell in Rome, Italy, was also planning to strike against that city's water supply, so this type of strike in Canada is potentially very real. Canadians may be surprised that many water filtration plants still use chlorine shipped in ninety-tonne railcars; if released, the chlorine could kill people as far as five kilometres away.

From Walkerton, Ontario, we also have a good example of what can happen when a town's water supply becomes contaminated.

Aqueducts and Sewage
The aqueducts that traverse California for over eight hundred kilometres would also make attractive and devastating targets for bio-terrorists. There are also similar aqueducts in countries like Italy and Switzerland. Most people have already seen what can happen to sewage facilities if power goes out, but these facilities could also be the direct targets of a terrorist attack. The repercussions could be enormous with respect to the spread of disease, let alone the havoc it would cause.

Local Power Grids
The local power grid is mentioned here only to emphasize the fact that terrorists could select one city as a target for different types of multiple attacks that would render it uninhabitable.

ECONOMIC INFRASTRUCTURE
Financial Institutions
Every stock exchange has a backup; even if NASDAQ was destroyed operations would switch to locations in Connecticut and Maryland. The restart of trading takes only a few hours, and ample contingency planning is in place. Even so, there are many different large financial institutions for terrorists to choose from in Canada or the United States.

Shopping Malls and Retail Stores
Bombs placed inside or outside a store are common. Any such terrorist attacks will affect shopping in the district targeted, especially if it is a protracted campaign of bombings. On August 1, 1998, a 225-kilogram car bomb planted by the Real IRA exploded outside a shoe store in Banbridge, North Ireland, injuring 35 people and damaging at least 200 homes. Two weeks later they planted another one that exploded outside a local courthouse in the central shopping district of Omagh, killing 29 and injuring more than 330 others. There are also other ways to target retailers. On July 17, 1986, the Canadian chain Miracle Food Mart removed all its fruit from South Africa in about two hundred stores based on a threat received from the domestic Canadian terrorist group Direct Action.

The Tourist Ambush
On November 17, 1997, Al-Gama'at al-Islamiyya gunmen shot and killed fifty-eight tourists and four Egyptians and wounded twenty-six others at the Hatshepsut Temple in the Valley of the Kings near Luxor. Thirty-four Swiss, eight Japanese, five Germans, four Britons, one Frenchman, one Colombian, a dual Bulgarian/British citizen, and four unidentified people were among the dead. Twelve Swiss, two Japanese, two Germans, one Frenchman, and nine Egyptians were among the wounded.

This type of incident has happened several times over the past ten years in Egypt. The purpose is to disrupt the local economy and to get the attention of the governments of all those dead tourists. The latter would naturally put pressure on the Egyptian government to keep foreign citizens safe within Egypt, and this makes for bad blood between the affected countries. When Hamas, the Palestinian Islamic Jihad, or the Martyr Brigades strike Israel using a suicide attack they also affect the Israeli economy, which, like Egypt's, depends very heavily on tourism.

AGRICULTURAL INFRASTRUCTURE
Dykes, Levees, and the Food Supply
Flooding would kill or injure many, in addition to causing economic hardship for the affected region. Grain storage facilities can be the targets of contamination, either chemical or biological. This could have extensive economic ramifications if contamination could be accomplished at key nodes. Biological weapons have also been used against crops and farm animals.

IT INFRASTRUCTURE
Rerouting passenger trains, changing the pressure on a gas pipeline, and causing oil refinery explosions through the use of computers are just some of the projects being worked on by Al Qaeda, according to captured documents and the results of interrogations. Other plans include the possible disruption of air traffic control and creating power blackouts and even affecting the flow of sewage. Conventional computer cracking tactics can also be used to leave "time bombs" that support other operations to be carried out at a specified time in the future. Key computing centres can always be bombed, as they have been in the past by other terrorist groups like the Weather Underground as early as the late 1960s.

Telecommunication Centres

In spring 1975 a fire in the New York City Telephone Exchange disrupted service for up to a week in some parts of that city, and no emergency services were available for several days. In what caused a serious telecommunications problem across the entire island of Puerto Rico, terrorists once cut a fibre optic line serving the governor's building, a major hotel, and other public buildings to protest plans to sell the main phone company.

FEDERAL AND PROVINCIAL GOVERNMENT INFRASTRUCTURE

Direct Action targeted the British Columbia environment ministry, and the FLQ targeted several federal and Quebec provincial ministries in 1960s and 1970s. It is alleged that the Toronto 17 cell was considering targeting the Parliament buildings along with ones occupied by Crown corporations like the CBC. National and regional Emergency Management Centres also present significant opportunities for terrorists.

MILITARY INFRASTRUCTURE

No need to go into detail here. Targeting the military was a favourite sport for the FLQ, and one of the alleged targets of the Toronto 17 group was a Canadian Forces base, the identity of which has not yet been disclosed to the public.

5: New Dark Age

INTELLIGENCE FILE 003/2007 — NUCLEAR, BIOLOGICAL, — AND CHEMICAL WEAPONS

NUCLEAR WEAPONS

It might shock the sensibilities of some to learn that Canada helped build the bomb. In the days of the Manhattan Project, uranium ore from Great Bear Lake and a refinery in Port Hope, Ontario, was a key factor in manufacturing the world's first nuclear weapons.

Nuclear, biological, or chemical material can be dispersed into the air, water, or a surface, and in most cases of such threats, details have not been revealed to the public by the authorities for fear of panic. Since 1993, there have been more than 175 known cases of trafficking in nuclear material and 201 cases of trafficking in low-grade radioactive substances from medical, industrial, and research sources across the world. Today there are 483 nuclear power reactors, 651 research reactors, and 250 fuel-cycle plants worldwide, all of which are possible targets for terrorist attack. There are more than 100 nuclear power plants in the U.S. alone, many of them close to the Canadian border when the wind and weather are taken into account.

While it is possible for suicide terrorists to use a commercial aircraft to breach the containment dome of a nuclear power plant and set off an unshielded meltdown, in most cases success is unlikely. Nevertheless, the psychological effect would be devastating for people living close to such facilities. If a meltdown could be caused, there would be many quick deaths and cases of early sickness due to radiation poisoning. Victims left alive would likely suffer thyroid problems over the next thirty years, and their offspring would have genetic defects for the next century and a half. The radioactive contamination could cover thousands of square kilometres; the 1979 Three Mile Island incident forced about two hundred thousand people to be evacuated.

The possibility of terrorists obtaining one of the thirty to fifty nuclear weapons that Pakistan has is unlikely now, but the political situation there may change in time, making this a serious possibility. Attacking nuclear silos or road-based nuclear weapons is also a theoretical possibility, but such sites are heavily guarded. Also unlikely at this time is the chance of terrorists building a nuclear bomb of their own. Their prime difficulty is obtaining the nuclear material required; according to International Atomic Energy Association it takes twenty-five kilograms of highly enriched uranium or eight kilograms of plutonium to make an atomic bomb. But there have been numerous attempts to steal such material from different types of facilities: Karen Silkwood took plutonium out of an American plant and intentionally poisoned herself. This is the reason that since 9/11, nuclear facilities in Great Britain and the U.S. have been at the amber or yellow security threat level. Unfortunately, this has not been the case in many other facilities around the world.

The risk of nuclear proliferation to terrorists from Russia remains grave due to that country's economic troubles. In such a desperate environment, scientists can be bribed more easily to assist, especially if the scheme is run as a "black flag" operation, where the person making the approach misrepresents themselves. There is a constant risk of nuclear material smuggling for profit in other countries as well. The smuggling network that included Pakistan, China, North Korea, Libya, and Iran may have assisted Al Qaeda in gaining expertise and possibly more in regards to nuclear terrorism. In addition, China was identified as the source for nuclear weapon designs found in Libya that were received via Pakistan in February 2004. Some still included the original Chinese text and gave step-by-step instructions for assembling an implosion-type nuclear bomb that could fit atop a large ballistic missile. There were also technical instructions for manufacturing components for the device. Iran and North Korea also remain strong possible suppliers for a future Al Qaeda nuclear attack: both have weapon designs and highly enriched uranium. And both remain enemies of the West, especially the U.S.

Finally, there is the possibility that terrorists could build and detonate a radiological dispersal device (dirty bomb). Unfortunately, there are tens of thousands of locations in North America using radiation sources for medicine, industry, research, and agriculture that can yield low-grade nuclear material for these types of bombs. In November 1995, Chechen freedom fighters placed a thirty-pound container of cesium in Izmailovski Park in Moscow, and some intelligence services believe that Al Qaeda has already obtained black-market cesium-137 and cobalt-60. Robert Stodilka, head of the Research and Development Wing of the Department of National Defence, stated that Canada would need several days, if not weeks, to respond to a dirty bomb attack. Drastic measures would have to be taken by our government, including use of the Canadian military in a massive domestic incident. As early as 1983, Brian Jenkins of the Rand Institute felt that if NBC weapons were used in a domestic terrorist attack, the U.S. government would have to respond using draconian measures: the population would demand it.

For a terrorist group, any type of nuclear attack would incur greater implementation risk than other types of operations and would require additional security, but the payoff would be more than worth it. There is no doubt that these weapons are on Al Qaeda's agenda: plans on missile design and the manufacture of thermonuclear devices were found in four different safe houses in Kabul.

BIOLOGICAL WEAPONS

Biological warfare has been with us for centuries in conventional conflicts. In 400 B.C., the Spartans catapulted diseased corpses over fortification walls in the hope of infecting the defenders, as did the Mongols six hundred years later. Plague-ridden carcasses were also thrown over the walls during the Siege of Feodosiya in 1346.

The mix of biological weapons and terrorism is also not new. As early as the 1950s, the Mau Mau insurgents in Kenya used plant toxins to kill farm animals. A pellet fired from a device apparently fitted to an umbrella killed Georgi Markov, a Bulgarian defector and BBC Radio journalist, in 1978. The pellet, made up of 90 percent platinum and 10 percent iridium, contained the deadly toxin ricin. This is a classic example of establishment terrorism, as the KGB and the Bulgarian KDS were said to be involved. In another case, the Red Army Faction threatened in 1984 to poison the water supply of twenty German towns if RAF prisoners were not released. A laboratory housed in a large bathroom was discovered in Paris producing *Clostridium botulinum*. A town of twelve thousand people about 125 kilometres from Portland was the target of a U.S. domestic terrorist group in 1984. Their plan was also to contaminate the water supply. But these examples are just the tip of the iceberg.

There are over fifty countries today that can be suppliers, conduits, or potential proliferates of biological weapons, or that have the necessary equipment and know-how to build them. Current unclassified reports indicate that ten to twelve countries are pursuing biological weapons programs. The Convention on the Prohibition of the Development, Production and Stockpiling of Bacteriological and Toxin Weapons and on their Destruction is the key international agreement to stop the spread of biological warfare. As of July 1998, only 122 nations had ratified it. Unfortunately, there is no verification system as part of this or any other convention related to the subject.

According to the American Society of Microbiology, there are over 350 academic institutions in the United States alone that work with pathogenic microrganisms and toxins that could be used in biological weapons development. This gives you some indication of the number of facilities worldwide, many of which are in economically depressed countries. The anthrax attacks in the United States shortly after 9/11 are good examples of current unconventional biological weapons use. But there are many others as well. Right-wing militia members have been caught with anthrax in Las Vegas, Nevada. Also in the United States, a disgruntled lab employee took the toxin *Shigella dysenteriae* and contaminated muffins and doughnuts in a hospital staff lounge, causing twelve people to fall ill.

Closer to home, two Canadians using a Mississauga-based front company called ICM were caught buying botulinum and tetanus cultures illegally from the United States in the mid 1980s. Both toxins were transported across the border at Buffalo, New York, after being purchased from American Type Culture Collection in Maryland. Only the tetanus was recovered. There is also the recent case of an Egyptian man who was carrying a package of anthrax in a suitcase destined to be received by a contact in Canada. Irbrahim Saved Soliman was given a suitcase in Cairo, but curiosity must have gotten the better of him as he is now dead and all evidence is in the hands of the Brazilian police. The ship on which Soliman was travelling was to deliver bauxite to Quebec.

To give you an idea of a biological weapon's lethality, sixty-six people died when anthrax spores were released from a biowarfare plant in Sverdlovsk, Russia, in 1979. The U.S. State Department ordered all embassies to obtain and store three days' supply of the antibiotic ciprofloxacin as a response. Biological weapons can be dispersed by many unconventional means such as from a crop-dusting plane over a packed stadium or into the ventilation system of a high-rise office. Just one fluid ounce of anthrax dispersed in enclosed building for one hour would cause mass casualties. A two- to three-hour exposure in an enclosed stadium could cause up to seventy thousand casualties. Aerosol dissemination by means of a smoke generator during a city's rush hour could also produce horrific results.

Al Qaeda has had a long-standing interest in unconventional biological weapons. Many a captured terrorist has admitted to training in this area or knowing of such training taking place. Mohamed Atta, one of the leaders of the 9/11 attacks, once purchased a cream called Acid Mantle for redness on his hands that resembled irritation caused by detergent or bleach. Detergent happens to break up clumps of anthrax spores into smaller, deadlier particles. The pharmacy he visited was in Delray Beach, just a few kilometres from the first post-9/11 anthrax attack. More importantly, he and other terrorists had used the Internet to research the purchase of crop-dusting planes in the United States.

CHEMICAL WEAPONS

In conventional warfare, chemical weapons have been used for centuries. As early as the 424 B.C. siege of Delium during Peloponnesian War, the Greeks used sulfur fumes against their foe. Current unclassified reports from U.S. intelligence indicate that between twenty-two and twenty-four countries are pursuing chemical weapons programs. Some have been identified as terrorist sponsor states or states with strong terrorist ties. As discussed in the previous file, the threshold event involving use of chemical weapons by a terrorist group has already taken place, when twelve were killed and more than fifty-seven hundred injured in a sarin nerve gas attack on the Kasumigaseki subway station in the centre of Tokyo, Japan. The die has been cast.

Chemical warfare is ubiquitous in terrorism. In April 1975, the German RAF stole fifty-three litres of mustard gas from a West German army bunker and threatened the cities of Bonn and Stuttgart. Since the beginning of the 1970s, the U.S. domestic terrorist group Symbionese Liberation Army used cyanide bullets to target the police, and terrorists have poisoned grapes from Chile with cyanide. In fact, when it comes to chemical warfare, food is a favourite for terrorists. In the Philippines, poison was once discovered in Dole pineapples. In Uganda in 1977, threats to poison the country's tea and coffee crop were made by rebel factions during Idi Amin's reign of terror. In Great Britain in the 1980s, the Animal Liberation Front injected mercury into turkeys at Christmastime and threatened to spike Mars candy bars with rat poison, costing the company that makes them $4.5 million. The Tamil Tigers reported that Sri Lankan tea was laced with potassium cyanide in 1982, and despite the fact that no contamination was found, the threat affected the country's entire economy.

In Canada during the 1980s, wine from South Africa was threatened several times by the sympathizers and supporters of the ANC and Direct Action, resulting in massive recalls. Medicine can be tainted too. While it turned out to be a criminal case, one should not forget that seven people died in Chicago when Tylenol was replaced with cyanide in several retail stores in 1982. Because of this and a similar incident involving Perrier in Paris, we can see the legacy of product tampering in the form of specially secured containers to this day.

Water reservoirs have also been a tempting target for terrorists over the years. Although it would not have been viable, a letter from Australia addressed to a radio station in Detroit contained a threat to dump nerve gas into that city's water supply. Four members of the Republic of Africa Movement were once arrested in a plot to poison the water in Philadelphia. Even swimming pools are not immune; some were once flooded with a powerful herbicide in San Jose, California.

In a different twist, a white supremacist from Texas was sentenced to eleven years in prison on May 4, 2004, for stockpiling weapons and the components of a cyanide "bomb." When sodium cyanide is mixed with hydrochloric, acetic, and nitric acids the combination can produce an extremely lethal vapour. In this case, the terrorist had enough material to kill everyone in a three-thousand-square-metre building (the equivalent of a large store).

Chemical weapons have also figured prominently in political assassinations by establishment terrorists. The Soviet KGB had a two-barrel weapon that shot prussic acid contained in glass ampoules that would break on a fine grating in the barrel once fired, and a Ukrainian defector was once killed by this method in Europe. It is also strongly rumoured that the KGB killed Pakistani President Zia ul-Haq in 1988, while flying in a C-130 Hercules aircraft sabotaged by a still mysterious gas. The plane crashed, killing all aboard, and it is thought that the pilots were possibly knocked out by fentanyl, the same gas used in by Russian security forces in the 2004 Moscow theatre siege. Zia ul-Haq was a strong supporter of the mujahideen that were fighting the Soviet occupation the time. More recently, a Saudi-born Chechen commander, Ibn-ul Khattah, was assassinated with a poison letter by the Russian counter-intelligence FSB in the spring of 2002.

Here in the West, the CIA revealed to a U.S. Senate Intelligence Committee a bio-inoculator electric gun that silently fires tiny poison darts that dissolve, leaving little trace. The weapon had a twelve-metre range and could employ various poisons. Hamas leader Khaled Meshal was injected with a toxin on the street in Amman, Jordan, in the fall of 1997. The Jordanian agents later captured the assassin and traded him to Mossad (Israeli intelligence) for the antidote. In one of the most blatant examples of establishment terrorism, four thousand Kurdish civilians were killed during a nerve gas attack against Halabja in northern Iraq, as Saddam Hussein put down a Kurdish revolt against his rule in March 1988.

Chemical accidents are good indicators of the possible results of a potential terrorist strike. Sometimes not very much of a toxic substance is required to produce alarming results, as was proven in 1968 when about four thousand sheep were killed by a small leak of VX nerve gas that escaped from a facility near Dugway Proving Ground in Utah. One also cannot forget the 1984 Union Carbide insecticide plant leak of toxic gas in Bhopal, India. With no wind to disperse the gas, the worst industrial accident in history killed about 2,500 and injured another 125,000. But there have been other cases closer to home. In July 2001, a sixty-car train carrying hydrochloric acid was derailed on the outskirts of Baltimore, Maryland, causing the evacuation of several blocks of that city. Then there was the 1979 train derailment in Mississauga, Ontario, where hundreds of thousands were evacuated from their homes. And about five hundred residents were evacuated on February 21, 2003, after another derailment of cars filled with hazardous chemicals near Belleville, Ontario.

These last incidents are mentioned because they are good examples of potential terrorist targets. Chemical plants are obvious, but railway lines often pass through residential areas because of city growth. There are also other targets where terrorists could use existing chemicals to their advantage. After certain security measures were taken in the wake of 9/11, dozens of people were charged in the United States with trying to obtain fraudulent licences to drive tanker trucks. You can imagine the damage just one rig could cause if it contained certain substances.

Chemical warfare fits terrorism like a glove. Millennium bomber Ahmed Ressam testified at his trial in New York that he participated in experiments at a training camp in Afghanistan using cyanide gas pumped into an office building's ventilation system. During the sentencing of the defendants in the first bombing of the World Trade Center in 1993, the judge spoke of the planned use of cyanide in that operation. The plotters hoped that one tower would topple and then gas released in the explosion would affect those in second tower. More recently, the *Washington Post* reported on December 12, 2002, that VX gas might have been smuggled by way of Turkey from Iraq to Al Qaeda in either October or November of that year. Later, unnamed American officials suggested that it was not VX but another chemical used in making biological and chemical weapons.

Also of note is that on January 10, 2004, Danish troops north of Basra, Iraq, found three dozen 120mm mortar rounds that contained blistering agent warheads. Such old ordinance was buried a decade ago, and its type could still be found in Afghanistan by Canadian troops, as the Soviets used chemical agents during their occupation.

On November 23, 2006, former Russian FSB officer Alexander Litvinenko was poisoned by ingesting polonium-210, a nuclear isotope that's exceptionally hard to procure in the required amount and would cost several million dollars to boot. On his deathbed he assigned blame to Russian President Vladimir Putin, about whom he had written two scathing books. Scotland Yard is still investigating, but has been severely restricted by Russian authorities. An example of establishment terrorism? Believe it or not, a movie of this real-world espionage drama is apparently in the works — and Johnny Depp is its star.

An RDD is the easiest nuclear device to build and is the most likely to be used by Al Qaeda or any other terrorist. On two occasions in April 1974, a domestic American group sprayed railway compartment cars with radioactive iodine-131 in Austin, Texas. Six people were medically affected. Iodine-131 was also used in the mid 1970s by Palestinian terrorists to contaminate a train in Austria. In 1996, three people who were part of a militia group acquired five canisters of radioactive radium to target county sheriffs, among others. Their intent was to poison these officials before taking over a county government in Long Island, New York. These are some examples of the simplest forms of attack that have transpired to date, based on a relatively small quantity of nuclear material available to the terrorists.

The fall of the Soviet Union facilitated easier nuclear material smuggling, and most stolen or smuggled material is suitable for an RDD. According to intelligence sources, Al Qaeda has probably not been able to obtain enough plutonium or highly enriched uranium to build a nuclear bomb, but it may have collected enough source material for an RDD.

Attempts to sabotage nuclear facilities have been made before by other terrorist groups with limited success. Meltdown is also possible but requires expertise and a large number of suicide attackers due the safety measures in place. It is within Al Qaeda's capabilities, however, and this is the second most likely style of attack. An armed attack on a nuclear power plant might not be effective in the United States, France, Great Britain, Germany, or Canada but might be successful in other coalition states that have lower levels of security. The psychological effect on our civilian population would be enormous even if the strike failed, however. For a six-month period in the mid 1970s, a Dr. Klause R. Traube had frequent contact with German terrorists. The RAF gained access to blueprints for all the nuclear plants in that country. Terrorists can also infiltrate nuclear facilities and research institutes or blackmail people that work at them.

Due to the extremely heavy security involved, the purchase or theft of nuclear devices by terrorists is very unlikely, and this includes stealing "suitcase nukes" from military facilities. Assassinations with the use of nuclear material are also possible, although unlikely.

But the threat of some sort of nuclear terrorism is very real. In 2002, British Customs and Port Authorities installed equipment at several ports, including Dover, Hull, Portsmouth, and Southampton, to detect radioactive materials. This was in direct response to their intelligence on Al Qaeda's capabilities. Known as remote radiological detection devices, they are concealed in crash barriers, traffic lights, and other locations around and within the facilities. Meanwhile, Sentinel II explosives detectors have been sold to different nuclear plants in Canada, including Chalk River north of Ottawa, as well as the CN Tower in Toronto. Based on ion detection technology, the device uses a puff of air to dislodge particles from a person and detect if he or she has handled explosives in the past several days. They're also worth $1 million each.

Knowledge of how a nuclear bomb is built is probably in the possession of Al Qaeda already. If a terrorist group has enough money, discipline, patience, and luck, they will be successful in building a nuclear device in time. This could take decades or just a few years, depending on the availability of suitable material. We can only hope that a homemade nuclear device will be a dud, due to the amount of material required for testing purposes. Unfortunately, Al Qaeda is not the only extremist group that may be capable of some direct action in the nuclear field. American militia groups have been found in possession of not only hazardous chemicals and dangerous biological cultures but also nuclear materials. And their philosophy is often based on the Bible's apocalyptic Book of Revelations and an obscure novel entitled *The Turner Diaries*, which is not likely to be made into a Disney film anytime soon.

The manufacture of certain biological weapons is relatively easy and inexpensive, and the expertise is readily available. Iran and North Korea both have probable biological warfare programs and pose a large potential source of toxic cultures. Al Qaeda stockpiles were not found in quantity, but the interest in developing biological weapons was definitely proven in Afghanistan. Enough was obtained for experimentation by probably both Al Qaeda and the Taliban, as NBC warfare was an area of close cooperation between these groups.

Biological warfare is different from chemical in a key way: how it can spread. A terrorist can be infected with a biological agent and knowingly or unknowingly follow a set route to infect as many people as possible. Several terrorists on a series of airline flights could infect an entire country in a matter of one day; in fact, to infect the major cities in the

U.S. it would take only twenty-five terrorists using this technique, a few more than participated in the 9/11 attacks.

It's a given that any epidemic in the United States could easily come to Canada. If a virus such as smallpox were introduced into our population, there would be a severe problem, as the victims require total isolation. Few hospitals have such facilities even in cities like Toronto, Montreal, or Vancouver, and those wards would overflow fast. A state of emergency would have to be declared, and military involvement would be required. As there would be no time to receive additional equipment, the army would have to go in as is.

Chemical weapons are relatively easy and cheap to produce. The personnel with skills to develop them can be found at any university and many commercial institutions throughout the world. The substances required could be easily obtained by theft or illicit purchase from these establishments, and this makes a chemical weapon the easiest NBC type to develop. Suicide attacks at chemical plants or involving tanker trucks, rail cars, or storage facilities are well within the capabilities of Al Qaeda.

Even mere threats of chemical contamination are effective in terrorism. Canadian corporations started to receive warnings of chemical or biological tampering with products from South Africa as early as 1983, and most were pulled from stores within a few years. In 1986, Canada stopped buying Sri Lankan tea due to the risk of cyanide poisoning by the terrorist group Eelam Revolutionary Organization of Students. Imported fruit from Chile and Israel has also been affected over the years, as terrorists once threatened to poison Israeli Jaffa oranges and Chilean grapes. Canada also went through the Perrier and Tylenol scares, even though these occurred in other countries.

The accumulated experience of an attempted attack in Paris and the successful strikes on Madrid, London, and especially Tokyo that involved commuter trains or subways has been duly noted by Al Qaeda, you can be sure. Cells in Belgium, Denmark, France, Germany, Italy, Great Britain, and Spain have been apprehended planning chemical attacks. The only reason they were even detected was because the cells maintained too much contact with one another in a non-surreptitious manner.

So far, Canada has suffered only financially from chemical weapons terrorism, but this could soon change. The RCMP arrest of an Ottawa software developer in connection with some London raids in April 2004 suggests that chemical warfare is being plotted right here, right now; some initial British reports indicated that some of the planned attacks included chemical weapons. It was also reported by Canadian media that a witness cooperating with authorities is a former CEGEP student from Quebec who claims in her statement that she ran money for the cell. After meeting with the suspect over a dozen times, she apparently wired the funds via the Western Union outlet in Ottawa's Rideau Centre. "He said it had to be a woman because sisters don't get caught — brothers get caught if they send money."

6: All for Allah

INTELLIGENCE FILE 004/2007
— AL QAEDA —
BACKGROUNDER

INTRODUCTION

Earlier this year, a bearded twenty-four-year-old computer-savvy man of Pakistani origin got off a bus in Kabul and just "stuck out" of the crowd. Afghan authorities arrested him on suspicion of attending a terrorist training camp in the hotbed border region of Warziristan and plotting a suicide bombing. Just months before, he had been living in Calgary with his father, a medical doctor who had trained in Karachi.

In days gone by, freshly minted and radically chic Canadian university grads might hike across Europe with a red maple leaf on their backpacks to "find themselves." Now some may be finding Islamic fundamentalism, and they have a choice of overseas venues like Afghanistan and Somalia in which to practise it. How did we all get here?

Every major war leaves loose ends. The First World War left us the legacies of fascism and communism. The Second World War and the Cold War left us wars of national liberation and ideological terrorism. Through natural transformation we now have a type of terrorism that is a mix of religion and ideology, nationalism, and regionalism. The Al Qaeda network contains different types of Islamic terrorist groups.

Some are more revolutionary against the state in which they have historically resided, such as the Egyptian Islamic Jihad. Others have more ideological overtones, ranging from utopian to almost apocalyptic in nature. Nevertheless, they all have the same general goals and have decided to fly the Al Qaeda flag under its organized umbrella group.

BASIC FACILITATORS

In the eyes of many, the United States has always been perceived as a grave threat to Islam. This is not only because of its military power and its support for authoritarian regimes in different Muslim regions, but also because of an American cultural invasion of songs, movies, and ideas that are foreign to many Muslims. To them, it is Western narcissism.

With the Iranian Revolution in 1979, the world saw the re-emergence of a religious nation-state. It gave many the idea that a controlled Muslim country was not only viable but actually might be an improvement on the authoritarian Middle Eastern regimes currently in power. There is widespread perception in the Islamic world that secular Muslim governments treat their people poorly. The seizure of hostages from the U.S. Embassy in Iran and the subsequent inability of the United States to influence the regime by economic embargo and military means showed many extremists that the U.S. was not invincible and that Muslims could stand up against a world power and win.

The war between Iraq and Iran saw the growth and development of a cult of suicide on the Iranian side. Martyrdom and a call to jihad became recognized as strong tactics in a war, and this led to the 1983 suicide bombings that included the U.S. Marine barracks in Beirut. These strikes accomplished the desired goal of forcing France and the U.S. to leave Lebanon, proving that terrorism — especially suicide terrorism — was an effective tactic that could be used against the West. These incidents then influenced Hezbollah to adopt suicide tactics against Israel targets in Lebanon. It took until the year 2000, but the Israeli Defense Force finally pulled out of southern Lebanon as well.

The invasion of Afghanistan by Soviet military forces in late December 1979 also played a key role in the events of today. By 1984, Abdullah Azzam had created Maktab Alkhidmat lil Mujahidin Al-Arab (MAK), an organization to funnel Arab aid to Afghans fighting the

Soviets, which included Osama bin Laden in its ranks. Even though the United States and Great Britain were still playing key roles in support of the mujahideen, once the Soviets withdrew their conventional military forces, both countries bowed out entirely in 1989.

Unfortunately, the mujahideen were not yet in control of the country and a Soviet puppet regime had been left behind. This regime kept receiving copious amounts of aid from the Soviets until 1993, when it was finally beaten in battle. Many mujahideen never forgave the U.S. and Great Britain for abandoning the fight for the freedom of Afghanistan before it was time to do so. Among those that felt this way were Osama bin Laden and his followers in MAK. In addition, the U.S. and the West remained key supporters of Israel and its domination over the Palestinian population, many of whom are of the Muslim faith.

The assassination of Egyptian President Anwar al-Sadat on October 6, 1981, had proven that direct strikes against the authoritarian leadership of Arab states were possible. Many of those who had been accused of this killing would become active leaders of the Egyptian Islamic Jihad, and eventually of Al Qaeda. Sadat's desire to accommodate Israel in a solution to bring peace to the Middle East sealed his fate, and the Israel-Palestine conflict continues to this day to be a key reason for hatred of not only the United States but all Western nations, including Canada.

Muslims were seen to be oppressed not only by Israel and by their own authoritarian regimes but also in places like Chechnya, Tajikistan, Kazakhstan, and Kyrgyzstan, which were controlled by bureaucrats from Russia or former Soviet Republics. In addition, persecution of Muslims was seen in the Philippines and in places like Bosnia, Kosovo, and the rest of the former Yugoslavia, where a campaign of genocide was being conducted in the 1990s. Other countries, such as India, Malaysia, and Indonesia, were also on the list of regimes that oppress Muslims.

Military bases in terrorist sponsor states, first in the Sudan and then under the protection of the Taliban in Afghanistan, allowed ten peaceful years for the preparation and training of Al Qaeda operatives. Recruits also gained battlefield experience in the wars of Bosnia, Kosovo, Chechnya, the Philippines, and other places as far away as China.

There are also internal religious factors that made the current situation possible for Al Qaeda. Religious rulings known as *fatwas* made the call for holy war simple. Recruitment by example, including suicide (or, as they insist, "martyrdom") operations, is automatic. The *hawala* system of banking allows terrorist financing operations to flourish. The system of Islamic religious schools known as *madrassas*, and the political takeover by extremist Wahhabist mullahs of many mosques, made it easy to preach the idea of an Islamic caliphate (a Muslim government ruled by a caliph) and bring new recruits to the cause. Religious scholars known as *ulamas* were also motivated to endorse the jihad.

SHORT HISTORY

Al Qaeda's founder, Abdullah Azzam, was a Palestinian/Jordanian ideologue and a member of the Jordanian Muslim Brotherhood. MAK (also known as the Afghan Service Bureau Front) was set up with the assistance of Osama bin Laden after Azzam met with him in Peshawar, Pakistan, in about 1983. MAK's mission was to funnel Arab aid to fight the Soviets in Afghanistan.

In time, MAK disbursed donations of $200 million that had been collected from around the world using different means. Saudi Arabia also provided financing to MAK through twenty-odd non-governmental organizations (NGOs) that were especially set up as front groups for that purpose. Bin Laden also added some of his own fortune, conservatively estimated at $25 to $30 million at that time. Therefore, Azzam, bin Laden, and MAK (with thirty offices in the United States) had credibility.

At the time of the Soviet occupation, Azzam assumed the title of Emir and bin Laden had the rank of Deputy Emir. MAK was divided into two main directions: relief for refugees and military operations. Azzam was preoccupied predominately with refugee relief, and bin Laden became the leader of the Foreign Brigade (the mujahideen who were recruited to fight the Soviets by MAK) as well as chief recruiter and overseer of all the training camps and guest houses. In short, bin Laden became the military commander and director of MAK.

Bin Laden's religious convictions deepened during this time. War always changes people to one degree or another, and bin Laden had changed. He was a true leader and actually participated in several battles with his troops from 1987 on. These actions greatly raised the esteem for the man, and a myth of invincibility developed around him as a military commander. While specifics of MAK operations cannot be determined (no records were kept until 1989), it is estimated that at the time there were 25,000 to 50,000 foreigners and 175,000 to 250,000 Afghans fighting the Soviet troops. The MAK leadership had contact with Saudi and Pakistani intelligence to receive information and arrange for weapons, and assistance was also received from the Muslim Brotherhood. In addition, the Americans and the British used the cover of both the CIA and MI6 to keep up an air of plausible deniability in providing weapons and equipment to the mujahideen, who were fighting a rival superpower.

The idea of a caliphate and a terrorist organization was brought up by Azzam in 1987, and he founded Al Qaeda (meaning "The Base") the next year. Azzam developed these ideas further over the next two years. When the Soviet military withdrew from Afghanistan in February 1989, MAK continued its fight against the Soviet puppet regime of Muhamad Najibullah that was left behind. Some sources have stated that there was tension between bin Laden and Azzam at the time, and bin Laden moved first to Khost, Afghanistan, and then to Peshawar, Pakistan, where he began setting up guest houses and camps. It is said that at this time a part of MAK broke off and went with him in a formal split. On November 24, 1989, Azzam was killed by a twenty-kilogram remote-controlled TNT bomb. Some point the finger at bin Laden, but whether or not he was responsible, he was now entirely in charge of MAK and Al Qaeda.

Extremely irritated by the fact that the U.S. and Great Britain had abandoned their policy of support to the mujahideen, bin Laden moved to Saudi Arabia. It would still take several years before Kabul fell, and possibly the needless deaths of hundreds of thousands of mujahideen. This is something bin Laden would not forget. But he now had more pressing concerns: on August 2, 1990, the mainly secular Saddam Hussein of Iraq invaded Kuwait, which was historically a part of Iraq. Kuwait also borders Saudi Arabia, which includes Islam's two most significant pieces of geography: Mecca and Medina. Bin Laden offered more than five thousand experienced mujahideen to the Saudi government to repel the invaders, but they ignored him. To add insult to injury, the Saudis brought in a coalition of Western infidels to defend Islamic sacred soil. Bin Laden's hatred of the West — and for Arab governments that are seen to support its aims — was now white-hot.

In February 1991, bin Laden declared members of the Saudi government to be *jahiliyya*, or false Muslims that had to be overthrown. This point of view did not impress the Saudi authorities, and when bin Laden learned of his imminent arrest, he departed for Pakistan on April 12, 1991. The terrorist cells he established in Saudi Arabia remained behind, however. Soon after bin Laden's arrival in Pakistan, a delegation from Sudan's National Islamic Front and its leader, Dr. Hasan Al-Turabi, invited him to live in that country. The "doctor" had come to power there in a June 1989 coup and believed in the spread of Islam. From 1989 to 1991, anywhere between one and five thousand Arabs who had fought in Afghanistan had moved to Sudan, and bin Laden was fully established there by September 15, 1991. Bin Laden agreed to train the National Islamic Front to fight against the Christian Sudanese People's Liberation Army, based in southern Somalia.

Bin Laden would get some help too. A 1991 military coup in Algeria and the extreme security measures that followed forced many members of the GIA (a terrorist group of Algerian veterans of the Afghan War) to Sudan, where they found shelter with the government and Al Qaeda. At least twenty-three Al Qaeda camps were built in Sudan and equipped at the group's own expense; the two largest were operating as early as May 1990 and were close to Port Sudan and north of Khartoum. By 1994 there were five thousand Al Qaeda terrorists training in Sudan.

Despite the fact that bin Laden was livid about the postwar infighting of the mujahideen, he kept busy in other ways. By February 1993, Al Qaeda had given its support to warlord General Muhammad Aided's militia in neighbouring Somalia; bin Laden–owned ships from the Port of Sudan brought guns, and three thousand mujahideen from Yemen were also flown in.

Back in Sudan, Al Qaeda established contact with twenty Islamic terrorist groups there and started providing them with weapons, financing, and training. Bin Laden also set up thirty companies in Sudan with at least two thousand employees, and his construction firms operating in Sudan built highways, dams, and an airport. Sudan paid him back with market monopolies in several products that were granted by government decree.

The country was also used as a base to support terrorism in Saudi Arabia, and it was during this time that bin Laden created a database of mujahideen as a list of potential Al Qaeda recruits. Meanwhile, Ayman al-Zawahiri, a business partner of bin Laden's based in Geneva, Switzerland, began recruiting, raising funds, and setting up cells in Europe. Then the Americans had a Black Hawk helicopter shot down in September 1993, of which much has been written. The upshot is that with the withdrawal of UN troops from Somalia the following March, both Aidid and bin Laden were seen as men capable of defeating the U.S. and its lackey, the UN.

Other Islamic extremists were impressed. In December 1993, the mufti of Bosnia asked for aid at a Pan African International Conference in Khartoum and received weapons, funds, and five thousand mujahideen from Al Qaeda. Contact with the Abu Sayyaf Group in Manila was also formally established that year, and bin Laden met with its leader. Al Qaeda cells formed in the Philippines at that time continue to operate to this day. By 1995, bin Laden would also have mujahideen waiting in Tajikistan, Chechnya, Bosnia, and Kashmir.

In February 1994, bin Laden was finally stripped of his Saudi citizenship. It is also rumoured that Saudi intelligence mounted an assassination attempt against him that same month. Not surprisingly, this invoked his wrath, which manifested itself in attacks on the Saudi National Guard headquarters in Riyadh on November 13, 1995, and an attack on the Khobar Towers military facility in Dhahran in June 1996, which killed nineteen American military personnel and wounded several hundred in the area. In addition, bin Laden's old friend al-Zawahiri was implicated in an attempted assassination of Egyptian President Hosni Mubarak in Addis Ababa on June 26, 1995. This incident led to the UN Security Council formally accusing Sudan of supporting terrorism and imposing limited sanctions on January 31, 1996.

Tipped off by the Sudanese government, bin Laden fled to Afghanistan after the U.S. attempted his extradition in May 1996. This was mostly now Taliban country, partially secured courtesy of Pakistani intelligence, which also felt that the U.S. had abandoned Afghanistan and the volatile regions of northern Pakistan after the Soviets retreated in 1989. Taliban membership was initially taken from Afghan refugees who grew up in Pakistan; the term means "seekers of knowledge," as most Taliban members were young students at that time. Back in a safe haven, bin Laden formally declared war on Israel and the U.S. on August 23, 1996. A fatwa was passed allowing Muslims to kill Americans, including civilians. Although it was ignored by the American administration, to many Muslims, this order unfortunately justifies Al Qaeda's attacks.

Kabul fell on September 26, 1996, and the Taliban took power backed not only by Pakistan but also by states such as Saudi Arabia and the United Arab Emirates. But control of Kabul does not translate to a full grip on Afghanistan. The Northern Alliance, the key remaining enemy of the Taliban, was (and still is) backed by the Russians, so 055 Brigade was formed with strength of two thousand foreign mujahideen to fight them. During this time, American cruise missile attacks on Afghanistan and Sudan made bin Laden even more popular in the Islamic world. But his revenge had just begun. In the spirit of jihad, two U.S. embassies in Africa were attacked in 1998, the USS *Cole* was attacked in 2000, and the American mainland was hit in 2001.

AL QAEDA BELIEFS

Two categories of beliefs are held by Al Qaeda. The beliefs in the first category are a part of the current trend in thinking across the world, but they can also be exploited by the terrorists for their own propaganda purposes. The other category is more exclusive to Al Qaeda and their supporters (although those may number in the millions). These two categories can assist in gaining a fuller understanding of Al Qaeda's mindset and the serious threat they truly pose. We will not elaborate on the reasons for these beliefs, nor the actions of those that inspired the beliefs in others. In intelligence, the prime responsibility is to give the leadership insight into the mind of the enemy, as well to outline their capabilities and the possible direction of future actions.

WORLD TRENDS
Religious fundamentalists of all persuasions believe that they are currently under some degree of threat. It is believed that modern secular society is trying to wipe out true faith and religious values. It is very important to keep in mind that not all fundamentalists turn to violence, however. Those who do tend to emphasize the more belligerent passages in their religious texts rather than the compassionate ones. But it should be realized that many people of different denominations do not approve of multiple mothers on a birth certificate. Some say it's time to slow down, sociologically speaking. This is a world trend for all deep religious believers, which includes members of Al Qaeda and those who aspire to be involved with them.

Al Qaeda aside, the United States of America is hated by other Muslims who don't support the terrorist group's methods, as well as by a great many non-Muslims. The strong American support of Israel is seen as proof that the U.S. is not concerned about Muslims, Palestinians, or Arabs. American interventions in Iraq and Afghanistan are seen as proof of the country's desire to use its military power against sovereign nations without just cause. In Islamic countries the U.S. is often seen as an aggressor that hates all Muslims. Other Western countries are automatically included in this hatred because that we often back the U.S. with regard to its policies on Israel and Iraq and/or Afghanistan. It is also believed that if the Americans withdrew their support from Israel, the state would not survive independently.

American or Western culture and ideas are seen as subverting the minds and bodies of the youth in developing countries, entailing the loss of centuries-old traditions and their identities as separate cultures.

AL QAEDA–SPECIFIC

Osama bin Laden intrinsically grasped Arab and Greater Islam's common displeasure with Israel and the West — more specifically, the United States. The cause of Al Qaeda is considered a noble goal because it is one of jihad. Islam is bin Laden's practical tool, and he is seen by many as having pioneered the idea of the modern jihad. A call to jihad is accepted readily by the poor of Islam, requires no permission from their parents, and needs only one book to be read — the Koran.

According to the Koran, jihad can be offensive and voluntary or defensive and obligatory. Bin Laden and Al Qaeda view their jihad as defensive and therefore compulsory for all Muslims. Islamic fundamentalists believe the duty of jihad was neglected by Egyptian President Sadat, and that the fatwa issued for his assassination was justified. According to Al Qaeda, key reasons to join the jihad include helping to prevent non-believers from dominating Islam and protecting oppressed Muslims around the world. Any Muslim may fulfill a personal "call of Allah" and follow in the footsteps of predecessors such as the son of Muhammad. In addition, by accepting jihad you will not have to fear Hell, which explains the high percentage of suicide attacks.

Key to spreading Al Qaeda's word to the masses are madrasssas. These religious schools found throughout parts of Asia and the Middle East also provide a source of economic aid to terrorist groups, in addition to helping facilitate a "Hearts & Minds" campaign. Mosques matter too. According to a January 1999 Islamic Council of America report, out of three thousand mosques in the United States, 80 percent were controlled by extremists at the time. If that was (and continues to be) true, the system can easily spread the radicalism required for perpetual recruitment to Al Qaeda's ranks.

OSAMA BIN LADEN'S OBJECTIVES

Bin Laden's aims can be presented in different ways based on analyses of different statements made by Al Qaeda in the past. The following is a compilation of interpretations ranging from the most conservative to the most extreme, which should lead to important insights into the purpose of Al Qaeda.

- Eliminate the American presence in Saudi Arabia.
- Erase the American presence throughout the Middle East.
- Stifle the American cultural influences in Islamic countries.
- Stop the American oppression of Muslims, including within the United States.
- Stop Israeli and American cooperation in the oppression of the Palestinian people.
- Eliminate the Israeli threat.
- Shift more economic power toward the oil-exporting nations of the Middle East.
- Cleanse Muslim governments by overthrow if need be, including those of Saudi Arabia, Indonesia, Jordan, Syria, Pakistan, and more than twenty-five other countries.
- Take over Pakistan and its nuclear arsenal.
- Create caliphates to be joined together at a later date by unifying all Muslim states under Al Qaeda control.
- Continue the spread of Islam by expansion with the goal of eventually forming a worldwide caliphate.

The current goal seems to be establishing a pan-Islamic caliphate throughout the world by working with allied Muslim extremist groups to overthrow regimes it deems non-Islamic and expelling Westerners from Muslim-governed countries. Gazing into a crystal ball, the world could soon see a deadly combination of Middle Eastern oil money, manpower from a population base that has been growing much faster than the West's for some years now, Pakistani and/or Iranian nuclear weapons capability in the hands of Al Qaeda, and a zealous intent of spreading the word of Islam to non-believers. Not a pretty picture.

SIGNIFICANT INCIDENTS WITH AL QAEDA

It is important to emphasize that the Al Qaeda network is the first in history to use complex terrorism on a constant basis. This is because it was accepted by the group's most important target audience: potential supporters and recruits. This was crucial in carrying on with more strikes; the way the West reacts is of little consequence to bin Laden. To build his caliphate he needs recruits. To get recruits Al Qaeda must conduct more and more spectacular attacks. Terrorism is propaganda by deed, after all. There have been a number of noteworthy plots and attacks by Al Qaeda.

Al Qaeda was definitely behind the 1993 World Trade Center bombing, in which fifty-six people were killed and more than five thousand were wounded. On December 9, 1994, Ramzi Yousef, one of the masterminds of that bombing, boarded a Philippine Airlines flight from Manila to Cebu, requesting seat 26 in economy class. Yousef left the plane in Cebu, but on its return flight two hours later a bomb under seat 26 exploded. Luckily the aircraft was able to make an emergency landing with only one passenger killed. Yousef was plotting to bomb twelve American airliners simultaneously, and the incident was a dry run for the planned mass murder.

Sheik Rahman and seven others were arrested in 1995 planning to blow up the Lincoln Tunnel, FBI headquarters, the Holland Tunnel, and the United Nations. An incredible 795 kilograms of diesel oil and fertilizer were intended for use on each target.

In November 1995 and June 1996, American military facilities in Saudi Arabia were bombed.

The Egyptian Embassy in Islamabad, Pakistan, was targeted by a car bomb that killed fifteen people and wounded fifty-nine on November 11, 1995.

On November 13, 1995, a truck bomb exploded in Riyadh at a Saudi National Guard communications centre. Seven were killed and many more injured.

In Algiers on February 11, 1996, a car bomb in one of the main squares killed seventeen and wounded ninety-three others.

On August 7, 1998, the U.S. Embassies in Nairobi, Kenya, and Dar es Salaam, Tanzania, were bombed, killing 301 individuals and injuring more than 5,000. That day marked the eighth anniversary of the arrival of American troops in Saudi Arabia. Ineffective American retaliation came in the form of cruise missile attacks on residences and training camps in Afghanistan on August 20, 1998.

On January 3, 2000, an attempted strike against the American warship USS *Sullivan* was made in Yemen by an explosive-laden suicide boat. The craft sank because of its poor condition and the weight of explosives involved. But on October 12, 2000, an Al Qaeda cell from Kuala Lumpur was successful in bombing the USS *Cole* in Yemen's Port of Aden with a boat full of "martyrs." Seventeen American sailors died and another thirty-nine were seriously wounded.

Nine Christian churches were bombed in Indonesia on Christmas Eve in 2000, killing 14 parishioners and wounding 119 others. The bombs were wrapped as Christmas gifts. In a related incident on December 30, 2000, five bombs exploded in Manila, killing 13 and wounding more than 100. The bombs exploded almost simultaneously on a train, on a bus, on a park bench near the U.S. Embassy, in an airport warehouse, and outside a luxury hotel. On New Year's Day in 2001, another bomb in Manila killed 22 and wounded 120. The mastermind behind the series of church bombings, Omar Al-Faruq, admitted planning other simultaneous attacks throughout Southeast Asia using truck bombs.

Four Al Qaeda terrorists (including a Sudanese national) were arrested in India in June 2001 over a car bomb plot to bomb the U.S. Embassies in India and Bangladesh.

In the deadliest Al Qaeda attack to date, the World Trade Center was destroyed and the Pentagon damaged by jumbo jets flown kamikaze style. United Airlines Flight 93, which crashed into a field in Pennsylvania, may have intended to target one of the five nuclear power plants nearby. These attacks cost the U.S. more than three thousand lives. The skyjackers used global positioning satellite (GPS) devices purchased a day before the attack to know their location after they had control of the aircraft. As is standard operating procedure with terrorists, there's no point in carrying incriminating evidence until the last possible moment.

In December 2001, a Sudanese-based Al Qaeda cell fired a surface-to-air missile at an American aircraft at the Prince Sultan military base in Saudi Arabia.

Al Qaeda associate Richard Colvin Reid attempted to ignite a bomb in his shoes on a transatlantic flight from Paris to Miami on December 23, 2001. Each sneaker had four ounces of pentaerythritol tetra nitrate and triacetone triperoxide hidden in it. The latter substance is used by Hamas and the Palestinian Islamic Jihad as an initiating explosive.

The Ghrirba Synagogue on the Tunisian island of Djerba was partially destroyed on April 11, 2002, when a natural gas truck was detonated along its wall by suicide bombers in retaliation for Israeli actions against the Palestinian people. Fifteen people were killed, mostly German tourists. During the investigation it was discovered that a phone call had been placed to a Michael Christian G., a Polish-German dual citizen who had converted to Islam. He is possibly a Caucasian control officer for Al Qaeda.

Half a tonne of explosives were discovered packed in a car only three hundred metres from the U.S. Embassy in Kabul on July 30, 2002. This find was just by chance because of a traffic accident and a car chase that ensued thereafter.

On October 6, 2002, the French oil tanker *Limburg* was attacked by Al Qaeda off the coast of Yemen in the Gulf of Aden. The crew saw a high-speed boat approaching from the starboard side before the explosion. The vessel was carrying 63 million litres of crude oil.

At Kuta Beach in Bali, Indonesia, 188 people were killed and more than 300 injured in bombing of the Sari and Padi discos. Many tourists were present, and ninety Australians were killed. This attack was a joint Al Qaeda–Jemaah Islamiyyah operation, in retaliation for the Australians sending elements of their SAS regiment to Afghanistan.

On November 28, 2002, ten Kenyans and three Israelis died in a vehicle bomb attack at the Paradise Hotel, north of Mombassa, Kenya. At approximately the same time, two surface-to-air missiles were fired at an Israeli Arkia airliner taking passengers to Tel Aviv. These missiles luckily missed their target.

Simultaneous bombings on four commuter trains in Madrid, Spain, on March 11, 2004, killed 191 people and wounded 2,050 more. This was a deliberate attempt by Islamic terrorists inspired by Al Qaeda to influence that country's elections to force the withdrawal of Spanish troops from Iraq. It was successful — terrorism works.

At the height of the morning rush hour on July 7, 2005, three bombs exploded within fifty seconds of one another on subway trains deep in London's Underground. A fourth bomb blasted apart a double-decker bus about an hour later. These attacks killed fifty-six people and wounded about seven hundred more. Once again, Islamic terrorists inspired by Al Qaeda but not necessarily in touch with its operatives look to be the culprits. In a second attack on London just two weeks later, four suicide backpack bombers hit three subway trains and a double-decker bus at noon. As most of the devices malfunctioned, only one injury was reported. As with the first London strike, it was Al Qaeda–inspired.

On July 11, 2006, seven bombs aboard commuter trains blew up within eleven minutes of each other in Mumbai (formerly known as Bombay) in India. This strike killed 209 people and wounded another 714. It is alleged by Indian authorities that members of the Lashkar-e-Toiba group and the Student Islamic Movement of India were responsible.

An alleged plot to blow up multiple aircraft en route from London to New York was broken up on August 10, 2006, when British authorities arrested twenty-five suspects. Seven more were arrested in Pakistan shortly afterward. It is thought that the alleged terrorists planned to detonate liquid explosives hidden in their carry-on luggage when the planes were in flight.

Seven men were arrested during an FBI raid on a Miami warehouse on June 22, 2006, for plotting to blow up Chicago's Sears Tower and the Miami FBI building; a couple of weeks later in New York, a plot to blast the PATH railway tunnels running under the Hudson River was foiled by the FBI. The agency said the plan's mastermind was detained by Lebanese authorities in Beirut, and the ongoing investigation involves six countries on three continents.

On May 8, 2007, it was reported that six Islamic extremists from the Middle East and the former Yugoslavia had been arrested for planning to attack Fort Dix, an American military base in New Jersey, in order to "kill as many soldiers as possible," possibly using rocket-propelled grenades to maximize the carnage.

Less than a month later four more suspects were charged with a plot to blow up a jet fuel pipeline that supplies

---

New York's JFK International Airport. One suspect was once a member of Parliament in Guyana, while another appreciates the value of a symbolic and heavily populated target. According to the indictment he said, "It's like you can kill the man twice."

On June 29, 2007, two car bombs were left outside a busy nightclub in London at about one in the morning, but both failed to detonate. A day later, two men in a green Jeep Cherokee rigged with gas cylinders rammed into the main terminal of Glasgow International Airport in Scotland. The eight suspects arrested so far are mostly licensed physicians who were trained in India, Iraq, Lebanon, Jordan, and elsewhere in the Middle East. Two months earlier, a British priest working in Iraq was told by an Al Qaeda member, "The people who cure you will kill you."

AL QAEDA AND KIDNAPPED CANADIANS

Several Canadians have been kidnapped by Islamic terrorists since 9/11, and certainly not all incidents have involved Al Qaeda and its associated groups; some may have been executed by common criminals. Nevertheless, the following have been reported from Afghanistan and Iraq.

Ken Hechtman, a freelance journalist working for the alternative *Montreal Mirror*, was believed to have been kidnapped on November 27, 2001, in the town of Spin Buldak, Afghanistan, but it was not clear by whom, reported the London-based *Guardian* newspaper. Witness Mohammed Zai said Hechtman was being guarded by about eleven armed men who wanted money and threatened to kill him. Francois Bugingo of the group Journalists Without Borders told Radio-Canada that he was "tied down to the ground and apparently he's been brutalized at least a couple of times." Hechtman had approached the *Mirror*'s staff in Montreal and offered to file stories from the wartorn region. His disappearance came just several hours after Foreign Affairs Canada frantically called news organizations here warning of a Taliban plot to invite western journalists to Kandahar in order to trap them and use them as bargaining chips.

Zaid Meerwali, a wealthy Kurdish Iraqi-Canadian who returned to Iraq to do business, was kidnapped and murdered in August 2005. Wearing Iraqi police uniforms, the kidnappers overpowered his bodyguard. Meerwali was later beaten, his throat was cut, and he was shot in the back of the head execution style. The ten abductors arrived in police cars, and they drove away with him in the trunk of one of their cars. The kidnappers had demanded US$250,000 in ransom. A brother of Meerwali's living in Iraq had already killed two terrorists trying to abduct him in a separate, previous incident.

Fadi Ihsan Fadel was kidnapped and held for ten days for political purposes. Fadel is a Canadian of Syrian origin who worked in Iraq for the New York–based International Rescue Committee. In the middle of the night on April 7, 2004, several men broke into his residence in Najaf. He said that he was tied up and blindfolded for the first two days as his captors beat him, stubbed out burning cigarettes on his neck and back, and repeatedly put a machine gun to his head. His abductors tried to force him to say he was working for Israel, and videotape shown on Arab TV stated he was an Israeli spy. The group called itself the Saraya al-Mujahideen and is believed to belong to cleric Moqtada Sadr's Mahdi Army.

Mohammed Rifat was kidnapped in Iraq on April 8, 2004. Rifat is an ethnic Kurd and was working in Abu Ghraib prison under contract for a Saudi firm. He left the prison after work and has not been heard from since. Rifat had immigrated to Canada from Iraq after his father was killed by the Hussein regime in 1980. The motives for this kidnapping still remain unclear, and Arab media are now printing and broadcasting Rifat's picture and story hoping that increased exposure will lead to his safe return. Foreign Affairs Canada has stated that there have been reports that Rifat is alive and healthy, but that there has been no contact with his kidnappers to date. The only thing found of Rifat's was his green Jeep Cherokee, later put up for sale. No demands were placed and no videos have been distributed so far.

Naji al-Kuwaiti was kidnapped in Baghdad, Iraq, on April 28, 2004. Three cars surrounded his vehicle and several gunmen blindfolded the businessman and hustled him into a van en route to a safe house. He was threatened with decapitation if a ransom of $50,000 was not met. Latter he learned that the kidnappers had been following him for months. The criminals did not seem to be motivated by politics, and with the help of Foreign Affairs Canada officials and intermediaries al-Kuwaiti was released unharmed and was escorted out of Baghdad to the Canadian Embassy in Amman, Jordan. It is rumoured that the ransom was paid.

Scott Taylor, publisher of the Canadian magazine *Esprit de Corps*, was kidnapped in September 2004 about sixty kilometres from the Turkish border in Iraq. He was held for five days and beaten while being accused of working for Mossad. His captors always wore black hoods to avoid identification, and he was moved to a second safe house after an American Apache helicopter assaulting Talafar destroyed the first. At three different times he was told that he would be beheaded. Eventually, his initial captors turned him over to another non-Arab who put him in a cab and drove him to the main highway between Mosul and Turkey in Kurdish territory without explanation.

Fairuz Yamulky, a Baghdad-born Kurd from Calgary, was kidnapped in Iraq on September 7, 2004, but she escaped after sixteen days in captivity. Yamulky was taken at gunpoint by a group of heavily armed men from a pickup truck alomg with two employees of the GSS Cement and Sand Co., who were later released. A short video clip of Yamulky was included with a statement demanding that GSS Cement build 150 homes in Iraq to replace those destroyed by American bombs during the initial start of the war, arrange the release of 50 female Iraqi prisoners, leave Iraq, and pay US$2.5 million in ransom. The group called itself the Brigades of the Victorious Lion of God. Yamulky engineered her own escape by convincing one of the guards that she would assist him in coming to Canada as a new immigrant. American helicopters were diverted to an open area where she stood with the lights of a car shining on her. She boarded a Blackhawk, and the car disappeared into the night.

James Loney and Harmeet Singh Sooden were among four peace activists kidnapped on November 26, 2005, in Baghdad and held in captivity for 118 days. The two Canadians, along with Briton Norman Kember and American Tom Fox (who was separated from them and killed two weeks later), were pulled from their vehicle at gunpoint while driving to a mosque to visit the Muslim Clerics Association. Videos of both Canadians wearing orange jumpsuits were aired on Al Jazeera on January 28, 2006, accusing them of being spies. Ironically, Christian Peacemaker Teams work for the rights of Iraqi prisoners. Their guards said they belonged to a group called the Sword of the Righteous Brigades (not associated with Al Qaeda) and described Shiite Muslims as worse enemies than Americans. In fact, it is believed that the group belongs to the Islamic Army of Iraq, which has killed several kidnap victims before. In a bizarre twist, an Iraqi hostage negotiator went missing when working on the release of the victims and is believed to have been kidnapped himself. British soldiers rescued Loney, Sooden, and Kember on March 9, 2006. "You go as a peace activist and you are rescued by the SAS," Kember said.

INTELLIGENCE COMMENTS

Terrorism is the weapon of the weak. Al Qaeda is using it to politicize and militarize Islamic countries. Al Qaeda is not a small gaggle of bandits, but an umbrella network consisting of dozens of terrorist groups, affiliates, and alliances supported in principle by millions of people across the world. The terrorists are attempting to spread Islam via tactics of intimidation. Any war polarizes people politically, and casualties in war equate to the need for revenge on a personal level. Both these facts will continue to provide Osama bin Laden with new recruits willing to die for Allah.

Even if Al Qaeda is broken in the future, offshoot groups will form from its survivors that will be even more ruthless. Destruction can only be guaranteed by the elimination of all sponsor states, all the group's financial resources, and all public support for the cause. The Al Qaeda idea was created and spread during a period of more than a dozen years, not counting the five years that MAK operated. And with the tens of thousands of potential recruits that have passed through Al Qaeda training camps, there will be no trouble in finding capable bodies for the group's support network. So the job will be a long and tough one for the West's security forces.

There was a sharp rise in anti-American sentiment during Gulf War, especially when the Arab mujahideen were perceived as being threats within their own countries, and it was seen by many that the invasion of Kuwait should be handled as an internal Arab matter. The Second Intafada also damaged the Americans' image. The buildup of anti-American sentiment was gradual but steady over the decade leading up to 9/11. And although Sudan has officially turned its back on bin Laden and even arrested several dozen low-level Al Qaeda members, the country's leadership remains the same, with its original mindset intact. It is only due to international pressures that Sudan is currently behaving, shall we say, properly. In fact, covert assistance to Al Qaeda could probably still be organized from within the Sudanese government, which also has an active chemical and biological weapons program.

Finally, the authors would like to stress a point. Although it is not usually acceptable to kill women, children, and non-combatants according to the Koran, the Al Qaeda fatwa that was passed by bin Laden allowing Muslims to kill all sorts of Americans justifies the group's attacks to many Muslims. This may be the deepest root of the problem. With a fatwa, any action can be condoned by Al Qaeda.

7: Cat Fight

INTELLIGENCE FILE 005/2007 — LIBERATION TIGERS OF — TAMIL EELAM

INTRODUCTION

The Tamil Tigers are the only terrorists in the world to succeed in assassinating two heads of state by suicide bombings. Their cause is rooted in a civil war in Sri Lanka between the Tamils and the Sinhalese that is almost a quarter of a century old. More than seventy thousand people have been killed so far, a further 1.6 million have been displaced, and the Sri Lankan government is blamed for the disappearance of sixty thousand more. Tamil terrorists have been fighting for an independent state (*eelam*) in the northern part of the island since 1983. The country is only about forty kilometres from the Indian subcontinent, which includes the semi-autonomous Tamil Nadu state of India. While the Tamils are Hindus and the Sinhalese are Buddhists, the basis of this conflict is ethnic.

The Liberation Tigers of Tamil Eelam, which is the main Tamil terrorist group, has between eight and ten thousand armed insurgents and more than thirty thousand in direct support. The Tamil Tigers have their own military-style navy, along with SA-7 missiles from Cambodia and Stingers from Afghanistan. The Tamil Tigers are an extremely serious group to be reckoned with in Sri Lanka — and possibly in Canada, if their policies were to ever change. Believe it or not, the largest Sri Lankan diaspora is right here, so it should be of no surprise that the conflict, in one form or another, has spread into our country. Canada for many years has been used by groups like the Tigers as a place for locating funds, for rest and recuperation, and for uninterrupted planning by key members of their leadership that live here. Their ties are so strong that the volunteers who operate in Canada have been given their own name: the Snow Tigers. That gives you an idea of the influence that some Tamil Canadians must have in supporting the war in Sri Lanka.

The Tamils were originally brought to Ceylon (now Sri Lanka) from India by the British to work on tea plantations in the mid nineteenth century. Today, they make up about 15 percent of the population. Independence was granted to Ceylon in 1948, but Indian Tamils were refused the vote and citizenship by the new Sinhalese government. Tamil participation in the civil service was limited, and the group's unemployment rate has hovered at about 40 percent since independence. Tamils were denied language rights in 1956, and Sinhalese anti-Tamil riots broke out that year as well as in 1958.

In the first Tamil Tiger action on July 23, 1983, thirteen Sri Lankan soldiers were killed. This attack led to reprisals against the Tamils, and hundreds were murdered while police just stood by and watched. This, combined with many indiscriminate arrests of Tamils by security forces, greatly bolstered the terrorists' cause. By the mid 1980s, twenty terrorist organizations existed in Sri Lanka, and by 1986 the Tamil Tigers were one of the most powerful of them, numbering about three thousand operatives.

A basic rule of terrorism is that rival groups will often engage in open warfare despite sharing the same strong ideological beliefs. On April 29, 1986, the Tamil Tigers attacked the Tamil Eelam Liberation Organization, killing more than two hundred of their number. In another incident in 1994, the Tigers shot to death Sadaratnam Sabalingam, an anti-Tiger activist about to publish a book that would have put a negative spin on the group and some of its criminal activities, such as extortion, blackmail, and fraud. When Canadians and even the government talk about Tamil terrorists, they usually refer exclusively to the Tigers. But just as in the case of the IRA, which is not the only nationalist terrorist group in Ireland, the Tamil Tigers are certainly not the only Tamil terrorists. Below is a list of some of the original groups, most of which are now defunct thanks to the aggressive posture taken by the Tamil Tigers in ensuring their own dominance.

TELO: Tamil Eelam Liberation Organization
EROS: Eelam Revolutionary Organization of Students
PLOTE: Peoples Liberation Organization of Tamil Eelam
EPRLF: Eelam Peoples Revolutionary Liberation Front
TEA: Tamil Eelam Army
TELE: Tamil Eelam Liberation Extremists
TELF: Tamil Eelam Liberation Front

Eventually, often through assassination of rival terrorist leaders, the Tamil Tigers emerged as the major Tamil terrorist group controlling most of northern Sri Lanka. The group's founder, Vellupillai Prabhakaran, holds almost a mythical place in leading the Tigers' campaign. It was he and his military commander who decided to use suicide attacks to offset numerical and weapons inferiority. The Tigers control most of the northern and eastern coastal areas of Sri Lanka but have conducted operations throughout the entire island. They also have a significant overseas support structure for fundraising, weapons procurement, and propaganda activities.

Prabhakaran has established an extensive network of checkpoints and informants to keep track of any outsiders who enter the group's area of control. With time, Prabhakaran has silenced all the opposition to Tiger control over the Tamil insurgent movement by assassinating all his opponents. In a macabre twist, he is rumoured to have all terrorist acts photographed and chronicled for his own personal collection. The Tigers also demand that one child from every Tamil family in Sri Lanka serve with them. Although abduction is rare, and it is considered to be an honour for the Tamil family, they are nonetheless child soldiers.

There have been several ceasefires between the Tigers and the Sri Lankan government over the years, but none have held. The last was declared in February 2002; today the foes have returned to bitter fighting.

BLACK TIGERS

The Tamil Tigers actually pioneered terrorist usage of the lone suicide bomber in a vest. By 2000, they had carried out 168 attacks this way, killing fifty people and wounding thousands. Created in the early 1980s, the Black Tigers are the suicide battalions. Like the Palestinian *shaheed*, Black Tiger recruits tend to be young, unemployed, and unmarried. They are not trained to become mere human bombs, however; both male and female volunteers come from the organization's toughest combat battalions, and males, for the most part, must bring with them a superb fighting record. Operatives at first used a belt bomb filled with Semtex H, a Czech-produced plastic explosive, but in time there were improvements in design and a move toward vests (see illustration section).

The Tigers have fully integrated their suicide units with the organization's secular nationalist army, whose recruitment process employs neither religious rites nor religious oversight. Just like other Tamil Tiger fighters, members of suicide squads are socialized into a culture of supreme sacrifice that glorifies death in action and reveres a long list of dead heroes. The recruitment process involves a tough military program aimed at selecting the most able and devoted soldiers. Although designated to die in kamikaze-style attacks, many of these volunteers are often called upon to carry out sophisticated commando operations that do not require killing themselves.

The Black Tigers launched their first attack in July 1987, and since then suicide bombings have become an enduring feature of the Tamil Tigers' campaign. The assassinations of two heads of state, various political leaders, and high-ranking military officers have made it clear that no public figure is immune from their wrath. Amazingly, the Tamil suicide bombers are not the result of a religious belief or other ideology but of the aura of a single man. Prabhakaran, the charismatic leader who initiated the practice, created the suicide units largely by the strength of his personality and his unlimited control of the organization. He also appears to have been greatly influenced by the spectacular successes of Hezbollah in Lebanon. The Black Tigers constitute significant proof that suicide terrorism is not merely a religious phenomenon and that under certain extreme political and psychological circumstances, secular volunteers are fully capable of "martyrdom." Black Tigers don't believe paradise awaits them — only processions, flowers, and shrines.

The birth of the Black Tigers was greatly facilitated by an already existing practice of the organization's members. Since the early 1980s, both male and female fighters have been required to carry potassium cyanide capsules with them, and a standard order makes it clear that soldiers are to consume the capsule if capture is imminent. The suicide units are essentially an extension of the organization's general culture of martyrdom: members of Tamil Tiger units are not allowed to marry, as they are already considered to be married to the cause, and they are indoctrinated that it is a disgrace to be taken alive. In what is considered a great honour for their extended families, Black Tigers traditionally eat their last meal with Prabhakaran.

There are probably close to ten thousand Tigers today, of which only one-third are female, yet women provide 60 percent of their suicide bombers. Their logic is that men are stronger and are needed to fight in the regular army. The first female units were formed in 1984 and they have had their own training camps since 1987. An advantage of being a female suicide bomber is that women are often not checked by security because of cultural taboos in both India and Sri Lanka. It is also easier to conceal a bomb under a sari, especially if pretending to be pregnant. Using such a disguise, a female bomber can carry more explosives than a man in a specially designed belt (like the ones used in the early 1970s by the Baader-Meinhof Gang when planting bombs in washrooms of government buildings).

THE ASSASSINATIONS

On May 21, 1991, a Black Tiger known as Dhanu arrived by bus in Sriperumbadur wearing a garland of flowers around her neck. Indian Prime Minister Rajiv Gandhi was on the hustings with a local politician in India's Tamil Nadu and would make a public appearance later that day. Gandhi could always draw quite a crowd, and as the day's events began several of his bodyguards tried to restrain onlookers, although not always successfully. In this semi-chaotic scene, Dhanu managed to edge herself close to the prime minister before she bowed down and detonated a grenade-packed girdle hidden under her traditional Indian sari. Little was left of Gandhi's body afterward.

The Black Tiger who killed Gandhi was in her early thirties. Part of her motivation for conducting the suicide assassination probably included a need for revenge. Her home had been looted, she had been gang-raped, and the Indian Peacekeeping Force that had been sent to northern Sri Lanka by Gandhi's government in 1987 had killed four of her brothers. It's important to note that backup suicide terrorists were also present and later killed themselves with cyanide, a standard operating procedure for the Tigers.

On January 28, 1998, twenty-six people were found guilty of killing the prime minister, and all received death sentences. Sixteen of them were Sri Lankans while the rest were Indians. But Prabhakaran and his two key aides were not on the list. India had already declared the Tiger leader a "proclaimed offender"; they have sought his extradition from Sri Lanka since 1995. From the evidence, the prosecution established that conspiracy was planned by Pottu Amman, chief of the Tiger's intelligence wing, and a woman known as Akila, deputy chief of the female wing. But the group did not claim responsibility for Gandhi's killing and has since denied it. Twelve suspects, including the man believed to have led the hit squad, swallowed cyanide in 1992 to avoid being captured by police.

On May 1, 1993, Sri Lankan President Ranashinge Premadasa was assassinated by a Black Tiger who had infiltrated his inner circle and spent a year in his proximity before carrying out the hit. The suicide bomber had explosives wrapped around his chest. Twenty-two others were also killed.

On December 17, 1999, the current president of Sri Lanka, Chandrika Kumaratunga, survived a female Tiger suicide attack but was permanently injured in his left eye. Thirty-four other people were killed in this assassination attempt, however.

TIGER TARGETS

The Tigers target Sri Lankan and Indian decision makers and political figures at all levels, the countries' vital infrastructures, and their military installations and personnel. Only on occasion are their targets symbolic. Typical targets have included the headquarters of a Special Forces unit, the oil reserves in Kolonnawa, and the Temple of the Tooth, an important Buddhist shrine. Here are more significant suicide operations.

In July 1987, a Black Tiger in a truck full of explosives killed forty soldiers when he rammed the vehicle into an army barracks.

In February 1988, a female suicide bomber detonated her charge outside the Sri Lankan Air Force's headquarters in central Colombo, killing nine.

In May 1991, a suicide cyclist blew up the Sri Lankan defence minister.

In 1991, a Sri Lankan warship was sunk by a suicide attack by the Tamil Tigers at sea. Admiral Soosai is the Tigers' commander for its naval operations.

In 1994, a female suicide bomber killed Sri Lankan opposition leader and presidential candidate Gamini Dissanayauae and fifty others in Colombo.

The Black Tiger attack that has caused the most damage to date happened on January 30, 1996, in the financial district of Colombo, when a truck was driven through the main entrance of the Central Bank in the heart of the capital. More than one hundred were killed and fourteen hundred wounded. Seven buildings were destroyed in the attack, and many others were damaged. Panic set in amongst the survivors, and dozens of people were trapped on top of burning buildings waving for help. Helicopters hovered over rooftops and tried to pick up survivors, but flames and fears of additional blasts hampered rescuers. The truck had been packed with two hundred kilograms of explosives.

On July 17, 1996, two bombs rocked the Dehnvala commuter train on its evening run, killing seventy-eight people and wounding more than six hundred. This strike was initiated after government troops mounted a successful offensive on the east coast of the island.

On July 4, 1997, twenty-two people were killed when a female suicide bomber targeted the Sri Lankan housing minister. Even though the minister survived, an army major-general was killed in the blast.

In June 2000, a Sri Lankan cabinet minister, his wife, and twenty-three others were killed by a suicide bomber while meeting constituents in a southern Colombo suburb. Ten of the minister's bodyguards died in the incident.

On July 24, 2001, at Colombo International Airport, thirteen civilian and military planes were destroyed or damaged by a Tiger suicide attack. This hit paralyzed Sri Lanka's only major airport and destroyed half of its air force. There was also a huge effect on tourism, which dropped considerably for some time. This was devastating for the local economy, as tourism is often the only real means of financial support in some parts of the world.

Conventional tactics have not been ignored by the Tamil Tigers; use of landmines on and off the roads is common, as is use of car bombs. Bombings of bus stations, bridges, railways, hydro plants, airports, and town halls are frequent as well. The Tigers are also one of the few terrorist groups to use multiple bombs striking at targets simultaneously.

INTERNATIONAL SUPPORT

Overt organizations linked to the Tamil Tigers support Tamil separatism by lobbying foreign governments as well as the United Nations. The Tigers also use their international contacts to procure weapons, communications materials, and any other equipment and supplies they need. Large Tamil communities in North America, Europe, and Asia are also exploited to obtain financial support for Tiger operations.

Liaison with different terrorist groups has been maintained for years. Contact with the PLO was established many years ago, and the PFLP at times has had as many as two hundred advisers training and

Cat Fight | 117

attached to Tiger units. The Tigers have also had a limited relationship with both the Lebanese Resistance (Amal) and Hezbollah. It is rumoured that the Tigers sold their suicide technology (a four-pocket vest made from canvas containing plastic explosives and a detonator) to Hezbollah as part of a quid pro quo. This is one of the reasons why Israel has supported the counterterrorist campaign of the Sri Lankan government by providing advisers and other specialist material.

For many years the Indian government and their intelligence services (such as RAW, the Research and Analysis Wing, their foreign intelligence agency) provided direct and indirect support to the Tamil insurgency. Training bases were allowed in Tamil Nadu and other Indian states, and its military provided support for training of the Tigers' navy and combat swimmers. The Tigers' infiltration route from India was mostly by sea, as the Palk Strait is only forty-three kilometres wide. Overt Indian government support ended, though, when its troops were used as peacekeepers in the conflict, which in turn led to the assassination of Rajiv Gandhi. It has also been rumoured that the Tigers have been in touch with MAK and later Al Qaeda on an on-and-off basis since 1986.

PROPAGANDA MACHINE

One of the great strengths of the Tamil Tigers has always been their ability in the field of propaganda — or, if you wish to use the modern term, perception management. The amount, quality, and varied forms of this force multiplier make the Tigers a powerful foe. Materials include mystical stories and songs, videotaped combat scenes, pamphlets, books, stickers, and flags, which have been prominent in many of the demonstrations in the streets of Toronto, in front of Queen's Park, and at Canadian universities.

FINANCING

"Revolutionary taxes" are often levelled on people and businesses living and operating in terrorist/guerrilla–controlled territory. But the Tamil

Tigers also receive about $1 million per month from the Sri Lankan diaspora. This money comes from the sale of narcotics, extortion, and fraud, as well as contributions to front groups. Canada is key to financing operations in that it has the largest portion of Tamils outside of Sri Lanka. It's obvious that to halt or impede Tiger operations overseas, this money trail must be interdicted.

For many years the RCMP has had its hands tied by the fact that Canada did not classify the Tigers as a terrorist group. Thankfully, this situation has now changed, and with this new status, combined with improved counterterrorism laws (due to the misfortune of 9/11), the Mounties might have some luck. Unfortunately, it will probably be several years before they can make a substantial dent in financing operations in Canada.

SNOW TIGERS

Many Canadians do not realize that violence and intimidation have been used by the Tigers against the families of local Tamil and even Sinhalese businessmen. These people are often Canadian citizens that deserve all the protection that Canadian law can provide. The real tragedy is that many of these victims are not used to trusting any police force whatsoever, as security forces in their homeland are often used as tools of repression instead of defenders of their rights. It takes many new immigrants to Canada some time to realize that those in uniform are not always their enemies.

Nearly two hundred thousand Tamils live in the Greater Toronto Area, and many are still involved in their old national politics. On September 26, 2004, a rally at Queen's Park organized by the Canadian Tamil Students Association drew a crowd of ten thousand urging Ottawa to play a prominent intermediary role in peace talks with the Tigers. Talks had stalled in 2003 after Norwegian mediators failed in the latest bid to bring peace to the region.

Even though Tamil terrorists have rarely targeted Canadians of non-Tamil origin, they did in 1986 when the Eelam Revolutionary Organization of Students threatened to poison Ceylon tea sold here with cyanide. Another problem for Canada is the ease with which a Tiger can disappear into the large diaspora and become very difficult to track down. Once they are are here, illegal travel into the United States is sometimes their goal. On August 20, 1986, out of 155 Sri Lankan refugees in Toronto, 31 were found to be under investigation by German authorities for having terrorist ties. But most importantly for Canada, at least five Tiger front groups are currently active in this country. Due to legal considerations, their identities are not listed here.

While a Sri Lankan citizen has been under the watch of a National Security Certificate since 1995 over suspicions of raising Tiger funds here, it wasn't until April 2006 that the government banned the organization from Canadian soil. Within days, police raided the offices of a suspected Tiger front group in Toronto and Montreal, and within a couple of months several alleged Canadian connections began to appear. On August 21, 2006, three Canadians were arrested in New York City and accused of attempting to buy nearly a million dollars' worth of Soviet-made SA-18 surface-to-air missiles and AK-47 assault rifles for the group. A fourth Canadian who was tied to those suspects and was referred to as a "wireless specialist" was later arrested here and is awaiting extradition to the U.S.

The weapons were intended to be smuggled into Sri Lanka via a ship-to-ship transfer in the Indian Ocean; payment was to be arranged by a Canadian resident known only as "Big Guy."

A fifth suspect arrested in Canada shortly afterward is believed by authorities to have facilitated the purchase of submarine and surface warship design software as well as aviation and communications equipment for the Tamil Tigers in the past. In addition, it is alleged that he had instructed student couriers from the University of Waterloo to smuggle compasses, GPS locating devices, and computers into Sri Lanka in their suitcases, under such items as teddies and chocolates. The sixth suspect to be arrested is also believed to have facilitated smuggling material for the Tigers as well as to have been involved in a bribery scheme to have the Tigers removed from the Americans' list of designated terrorist groups. He faces extradition to the U.S. as well. A seventh Canadian suspect was arrested on August 24, 2006, in San Francisco where he was working for Microsoft; he is believed by authorities to be involved in a conspiracy to buy weapons for the Tigers.

With the cooperation of the RCMP, the University of Waterloo is now investigating whether or not it was involved with any humanitarian projects tied to the Tigers via its esteemed engineering co-op program, which many of the suspects were members of, and whether or not its

Tamil student club was linked in any way to the alleged activities. Authorities believe some of the suspects used their cover as students to procure high technology from companies for "school projects."

At about the same time, it was revealed that two brothers formerly from Montreal were arrested in Buffalo and accused of being involved with plans to smuggle Tamils into the United States for a fee of $6,000 per person. In the latest development, yet another suspect was arrested in Indonesia on January 12, 2007, linked with the initial group in the New York weapons deal. Authorities believe he is the principal liaison between the Tiger leadership and its North American operations. As of June 2007, the results of RCMP projects CRIBLE and OSALUKI had identified sixty-three suspects, and the investigations are still ongoing.

Despite this flurry of enforcement activity, the U.S.-based group Human Rights Watch claims street-level fundraising for the Tigers continues in Canada despite the group's outlawed status. According to a disclosed FBI wiretap, one of those accused of attempting to buy the missiles in New York said that the vast majority of money to fuel the civil war comes from Canada. When contacted by the Reuters news agency in Sri Lanka after the slew of arrests, a Tiger military spokesman said, "We have no connection with these people. It is not our way of operating."

INTELLIGENCE COMMENTS

Many countries long ago banned Tamil terrorist groups from their soil. Canada did not do so until last year. This was a very important step forward in establishing credibility with fighting international terrorism in the eyes of the world. It does not bode well when a country talks tough about terror in the global political arena, yet everyone knows it harbours known terrorists and allows them to finance a good part of their operations through illegal means there.

So far, the Tamil Tigers have refrained from targeting foreign diplomatic and commercial establishments in order to avoid complications with the support that they receive from the Tamil diaspora. But despite the fact that the group has a worldwide network it does not want jeopardized, Prabhakaran has threatened any nation who gives support to Sri Lanka. As well, the Tigers are very media-savvy and politically astute. On more than one occasion, Tiger representatives in

Canada have wined and dined both federal and provincial politicians to glean favours and good will. In Sri Lanka, on the other hand, such individuals would have been executed.

Finally, the Tamil Tigers are very significant terrorist organization, as they have proven extremely adept in committing assassinations of national leaders with suicide bombers. Other terrorist groups already employing suicide bombers will in time pick up this tactic. Al Qaeda used such a suicide strike against one of the most influential leaders of the Northern Alliance the day before 9/11, and assassination has been practised by the group on all levels of government officials in both Afghanistan and Iraq. Al Qaeda has not yet targeted Western leaders. A few angry young men inspired by them allegedly have, though.

8: Bodies

INTELLIGENCE FILE 006/2007 — RECRUITMENT AND — DEVELOPMENT

INTRODUCTION

In the past here in Canada, the recruitment of domestic terrorists and their direct support networks has been accomplished not only in university settings but also in certain progressive boutique bookstores that distributed terrorist propaganda (some of which is shown in the illustration section) in addition to the typical tomes promoting national liberation in Third World countries, the peace movement, environmentalism, animal rights, women's rights, and various left-wing ideologies. New customers were always approached by a very friendly clerk who would attempt to determine their areas of interest — in itself not unusual — but depending on the answers given and the books bought, an invitation to have a cup of coffee might follow. This in turn could lead to further invitations to attend after-hours gatherings to watch films or attend special presentations on different subjects. Avid readers could eventually find themselves in demonstrations or in direct action operations.

Terrorist organizations have different methods of recruitment and development, and these are always tailored to the operational environment. The style can be divided along geographic lines as well as by group.

In Western Europe, Australia, and North America, the profile and development of a recruit for a traditional terrorist group was generally similar. The average age was twenty-two, one-third were female, and 80 percent were single (although this was not necessarily true at recruitment time, as many divorced soon after getting involved in the process). Most were from the middle or upper classes and had above-average IQs. Many had at least partially completed university or college. Key parts of the personality profile were a need to feel important and a desire for publicity. Recruits often lacked friends and therefore needed companionship and a sense of belonging. They were rarely stupid people and definitely not crazy, and all possessed a desire for self-sacrifice. Some would flip-flop from an extreme right-wing ideology to the extreme left, and all believed that violence is morally justified to support the cause. Individuals who have a need for revenge or strong hatred are ideal. This was the personality profile of those that often became terrorist cell or group leaders. Another key profile was an individual whom we can call a clean slate, someone with few friends and no strong beliefs about anything. Such individuals are easy to mould and often make good foot soldiers.

RECRUITMENT TARGET GROUPS

Although there was generally little difference in the steps of development taken by terrorist groups in advanced countries, there were sometimes differences in where recruits were found. Mostly they came from universities and colleges, but the Italian Prima Linea and the U.S.–based Weather Underground recruited actively in high schools. Recruits from high school may not be well educated or smart, but they will be more violent if properly prepared psychologically — the younger they are, the more easily moulded. The Symbionese Liberation Army of Patty Hearst kidnapping fame recruited predominately in prison, as did the Black Liberation Army.

THE MAKING OF A TERRORIST
IN EUROPE & THE AMERICAS

Terrorists and their supporters are always looking for talent. Once a potential recruit is identified, he is invited to participate in some social activity: a book reading, a documentary viewing, a discussion group, or even a party. What follows is the standard recruiting process that is used by many terrorist groups that have existed (and still exist) in developed countries.

1. The potential recruit is slowly integrated into a group that can provide personal psychological comfort, friendship, and sometimes even sex. The recruit is introduced to the cause. The group consists of supporters of the cause, but it is not necessarily part of the direct support network or the military action arm.

2. The individual gets involved in attempts to change the system through legitimate means, such as a letter-writing or phone-call campaign in support of a cause. If the recruit has not been introduced to his controller, he is at this point. The function of the controller is to mould and psychologically prepare the recruit for terrorist activity.

3. The recruit is now invited to non-violent protests and demonstrations in support of the cause. When he feels strongly enough about it and sees that legitimate means of protest to change the system do not work, the next step is taken.

4. The recruit is encouraged to commit acts of civil disobedience, such as participating in a sit-in, painting graffiti, destroying property, and trespassing. In time, such activity can lead to the arrest of the recruit — or an arrest can be arranged, as it builds hatred for the targeted establishment. During this propaganda and agitation phase, the recruit feels a growing sense of power, and the controller starts requesting small actions. Now he is breaking the law. The controller further legitimizes

the cause in the eyes of the recruit and appeals to others to demonstrate and protest (forms of propaganda) in order to drive the movement forward. The controller creates and then exploits prejudice in the recruit: emotional appeals are made constantly, as this is one of the most powerful tools of manipulation. A strong sense of belonging is also created by the controller at this time.

5. The recruit is invited to what should be a peaceful, legal demonstration led by a legitimate group or coalition, but it is often turned into a riot by infiltrators. The recruit is encouraged to enter physically into the fray against the police. Blows or beatings may be the result, and participation can also lead to another arrest and more hatred for the system.

6. Once out of jail (if an arrest was made), the recruit is encouraged to make threats of violence by letter, phone, or even in person. During all the time the recruit spends with the group, he is also encouraged to keep going to demonstrations and continuing in other support efforts.

7. When the controller decides the time is right and the recruit is psychologically ready, he persuades the recruit to commit his first real terrorist act. Often it is a simple task, with the target chosen to allow a good getaway. An act of arson on a police car, government offices, or a recruiting centre is a good beginning, as arson is easier to commit than bombing. Once a recruit is at this point in his psychological preparation, he is no longer a petty criminal but a felon. At this time he can be introduced to weapons training, terrorist tactics, and bomb making, among other things. After some training in select specializations, the recruit may be asked to join a direct support cell of the group, but he is still short of being psychologically prepared to be a real terrorist. He continues training and participates in covert support operations but now associates with only the direct support cell, having been ordered to forgo his old friends in the

political arm of the organization. The recruit is at last involved in the military arm, the people who directly support the individuals who commit the dirty deeds. He is to an even greater extent cut off from the real world. Groupthink from the covert direct support cell starts to creep in, and clandestine operations lead to a need for security, which can become a form of paranoia; police and intelligence now seem to be lurking behind every corner. The recruit feels that he is different from everyone else and his only friends are within the direct support cell; rhetoric about the cause and the ideology becomes more real, and hatred for the system grows. The cell has its own terminology, which, according to the science of neuro-linguistics, will change how a person thinks. Common words are replaced with new revolutionary terms, such as "expropriation" instead of "robbery" and "direct action" for other terrorist acts. The word "execution" veils the harshness of the terms "assassination" or "murder."

8. As a new generation is required, the recruit may move up to a direct action cell and start committing full-fledged terrorism in the name of the cause. This often requires him to commit bombings. These may be conducted with improvised explosive devices (IEDs, or homemade bombs), stolen dynamite, or even plastic explosives depending on availability, the level of training the recruit has received, and tactical considerations.

9. The recruit may be asked to commit a kidnapping.

10. The recruit is asked to beat someone physically, if this was not achieved during the riots that he has participated in. Somewhere during the preceding few stages someone will die, at which point you have a terrorist on your hands. The recruit continues to harden with involvement in more operations.

The recruitment and development process is one of natural selection and progression. Recruits are given assignments based on their psychological and technical preparation. If they refuse or are seen as not being fit, they remain at the levels achieved or are shifted to terrorist support work like intelligence gathering, theft of needed equipment, or safe house support. The Red Brigades began by burning cars, then graduated to Molotov cocktails, beatings, knee-cappings, bombings, kidnappings, and then murders. Using these steps and a few other tricks not mentioned here, anyone can create a terrorist cell in a matter of five or six years with the proper selection of a cause.

URBAN GUERRILLA THEORY

This is also known as the Revolutionary School or FOCO Theory. Most communist theories state that a revolutionary (terrorist) must wait until the economic and social conditions are ripe for armed resistance, but Urban Guerrilla Theory states that you do not have to wait; rather, as a terrorist, you can create such conditions by direct action. Left-wing icon Che Guevera, who was killed in Bolivia in 1967, was a true believer in this theory, but there have been no successful terrorist overthrows of governments using it. If there are not sufficiently strong causes for terrorism, a regime change is not possible. Only if there are enough legitimate or perceived causes can you recruit enough terrorists to attempt something substantial.

AFRICAN TRIBAL BASE

Whether you analyze current terrorist groups in Uganda or older terrorist groups in other parts of Africa like Zaire and Zimbabwe, recruitment is always based on tribes. The Zimbabwe African Peoples Union, the military arm of the Zimbabwe People's Revolutionary Army, had their recruiting base in the Matabele tribe, with a population of 1.6 million. Their opposition in the Rhodesian terrorist game was the Zimbabwe African National Union, the military arm of the Zimbabwe National Liberation Army. Their leader, Robert Mugabe, who has been the country's president and dictator since 1979, had his recruitment base in the Shona tribe, consisting of 5.3 million people. Recruits for the African National Congress were selected from all tribes except the Zulus, who had special status in South Africa during the Apartheid era and usually took the side of the white regime in political matters. In the old Portuguese colony of Angola, the National Union for the Independence of Angola drew from the Ovambundu tribal base, the Front for the National Liberation of Angola used the Bakongo tribe, the Popular Movement for the Liberation of Angola used the Umbundu tribe, and the South West African Peoples Organization recruited from the Kwanyaba tribe of the Ovambos.

The Polisario terrorists operating against Moroccan security forces can also be considered tribal. But there are exceptions to the African rule. In Somalia, recruitment is based on clan or family, so it is no surprise that the Canadian citizen who was detained in Ethiopia this year, as that country's army battled various Somali Islamic factions, is the grandson of an Ogaden Liberation Front founding member. Meanwhile, in North Africa, the Egyptian Islamic Jihad and the Algerian GIA are both linked to Al Qaeda and operate in a Middle Eastern fashion.

In Africa, there is another basic rule to terrorist recruitment. The kidnapping and indoctrination of young children is common from Uganda to Angola, from Nigeria to Zimbabwe. A colleague of one of the authors recently returned from Uganda and says it's believed that an obscure Christian terrorist organization known as the Lord's Resistance Army still uses cannibalism to coerce young boys into their ranks.

THE SYSTEM IN THE MIDDLE EAST & FAR EAST

Here again there are differences between groups, but there are key similarities as well.

Pay, religion, nationalism, tribalism, and the fight against outside military forces are all key motivators in the Middle East. Revenge is also a common motivator in insurgent warfare. Money is important in areas of the world where there are high levels of unemployment, as is the case in Gaza, the West Bank, southern Lebanon, Iraq, and Afghanistan. Each terrorist group has its own recruitment procedures; here we will look at Al Qaeda as an example.

Al Qaeda bases its support on Muslim ex-fighters who were active during the Soviet occupation of Afghanistan from 1982 to 1992. It is said to have connections with seventy thousand people, thirty-five thousand of whom were volunteers from forty countries around the world. The group recruits from all Muslim sects, Sunni and Shite alike, the same as it was in the days of MAK. Recruitment is also done according to broad-based family clans, close family members, and close friends. Al Qaeda recruits at local mosques and madrassas. Among the most sought after recruits are Muslims living in Western Europe and overseas. There are between 5 and 6 million Muslims in France — an important internal political fact that probably plays havoc with any French position on the situation in Afghanistan or Iraq.

The process for Al Qaeda is informal but detailed. Recruitment most often starts with a recommendation by a close friend or relative, and then the group evaluates the personality profile of the individual and carries out a security check. There are fourteen traits required to join the military arm of Al Qaeda: knowledge of Islam, ideological commitment, maturity, a spirit of self-sacrifice, discipline, the ability to maintain secrecy, good health, patience, determination, intelligence and insight, caution and prudence, truthfulness and wisdom, the ability to observe and analyze, and the ability to act. If possible, the recruit should have language and technical skills of some kind.

Once selected, possible male recruits undergo basic military training. (In a strict Islamic culture women cannot participate in a military jihad, their function being to breed more soldiers.) All wear the *shalwar kameez*, a loose tunic over their pants, and Afghani *pakul* hats. All are treated as one. Recruits who show merit the recruit serve in Afghanistan, Iraq, Chechnya, or another Islamic front.

If he is found worthy, somewhere during the process the recruit swears a *bayatt*, or blood oath, when he becomes a full-fledged member of Al Qaeda, swearing allegiance directly to Osama bin Laden. What the recruit does not know is that he must pass commitment and dedication tests before and after being accepted.

In Al Qaeda, a recruit is asked what he would like to do. A terrorist could choose to be assigned to the fight in Iraq or to go for specialized training, but he could just as easily say that he is ready to be a *shaheed*, or "martyr." We know them as suicide bombers. Groups like Hamas, Hezbollah, the Al-Aqsa Martyrs' Brigade, and others simply wait for volunteers; such is the power of the cult of martyrdom under the influence of propaganda. Suicide recruitment and development is covered in greater detail in Chapter 12.

CAUCASIAN RECRUITMENT

The recruitment of white converts to Islam is a priority for the Al Qaeda umbrella organization, as there are numerous advantages to such a man, including, usually, a passport from a non-Muslim country. Caucasian features tend to blend in during operations in Western countries, and the understanding of Western languages and cultures can be indispensable. One example is George Holland (aka Jack Roche) who was arrested in November 2002 and later convicted of plotting to blow up the Israeli Embassy in Canberra, Australia. He was part of the network of Jemaah Islamiyyah operatives. Holland received training overseas from Jemaah Islamiyyah and managed to conduct surveillance of certain targets.

INTELLIGENCE COMMENTS

As long as an appropriate cause can be found, impressionable youths can always be manipulated to join a terrorist organization, and, through progressive indoctrination, coercion, and steps of increasing violence, they will be prepared to kill and even commit suicide to accomplish a set terrorist goal. If recruits do not readily volunteer, properly selected individuals can be indoctrinated to achieve the same objective.

There is no shortage of suicide bombers based on current military, political, social, and economic conditions. Keep in mind that terrorists are not mentally unbalanced. Different cultures have different patterns of thought and see the world using a different template based on their life experiences, not ours.

Zimbabwe was suspended from the British Commonwealth in 2002. The Zimbabwe African National Union and its military arm, the Zimbabwe National Liberation Army, control the country. Under President Mugabe, a dictator for nearly thirty years, they wantonly killed defenceless white farmers and used kidnapped child recruits to win control. This is a very good example of a terrorist group that is now a legitimate power. Terrorism can work. Along the same lines, the African National Congress is currently in power in South Africa. Here, some will say the ANC was composed not of terrorists but of freedom fighters who rose against racist regimes. But both the African National

Congress and the Zimbabwe African National Union were the political arms of their respective terrorist organizations, and they used terrorist tactics as part of their military campaigns. Therefore, they must be classified as terrorist groups, regardless of the legitimacy of the reasons for their actions.

It must be remembered that throughout the world, revenge is one of the key means for recruitment; the Chechens are a prime example of a blood feud culture. If you were to lose a family member to the actions of an occupying army or repressive state, revenge would probably be on your mind as well. This emotion is also one of the biggest reasons why it is difficult to stop a terrorist campaign once it starts. The latest IRA campaign was over thirty-five years old when peace was finally reached. The Basque ETA is still going strong after the same length of time, and the Red Brigades and the RAF lasted for twenty-five years. The campaign against Al Qaeda will be considerably longer.

9: Train Hard, Fight Easy

INTELLIGENCE FILE 007/2007
— AL QAEDA TRAINING —
AND TACTICS

INTRODUCTION

In the wet and freezing week after Christmas 2005, several young men in white camouflage coats and guns allegedly trained to be terrorists near Washago, Ontario, one and a quarter hours north of Toronto. According to a report, the group's leader told one nosy neighbour, "I've got to show these kids everything. They don't know anything. They can't even keep their feet dry." Sounds like basic training at Camp Borden, but we didn't call it "extreme camping" in those days. We weren't inspired by Al Qaeda, either.

Actually, Al Qaeda training emphasizes psychological preparation for war, which is considered more important than military training. In many cases, training of a specialized nature is conducted only for specific small groups within the organization; counter-surveillance training was conducted only for Shura members, for example. This is not to say that less detailed military training is not provided to other Al Qaeda operatives under certain circumstances. Note that the term "suicide bombing" is never used by Al Qaeda, as it is with Hamas, the Palestinian Islamic Jihad, and Hezbollah; instead, they prefer to say "martyrdom attack." Al Qaeda's presence has been detected in seventy-six countries, and many of those have training facilities. In some cases volunteers that come to the organization already have military or police experience from their countries of origin. This is often because they faced a policy of conscription, but now we find that volunteers will intentionally join local military or police forces to gain experience before trying to join Al Qaeda. It's also the group's policy to encourage this.

SECTION 1: TRAINING

BASIC COURSES

Tens of thousands have graduated from the basic Al Qaeda military course, but only several thousand have been asked to join the group and continue training. In this way, Al Qaeda retains and utilizes only the best of the best. Basic training consists of the tactics of guerrilla warfare, the fundamentals of Islamic law, an introduction to small arms, and other fundamentals such as using cover and concealment, setting up ambushes, and conducting infiltration.

Safe house training is restricted to cell members operating in foreign lands, covert operatives working on infiltration or "martyrdom" operations, or recruits who have limited time and capability to be shipped to proper training camps. These sessions are conducted in homes or apartments and often cover all aspects found in basic camp training, except that firing weapons and detonating explosives have to be done at a different location or skipped altogether. So it's no surprise that some of the alleged terror suspects in the Toronto 17 group went well north of the city for their target practice.

The third step in training is usually (but not always) military action in the field. After the first levels of training are conducted, the recruit can be sent to fight in Chechnya, Uzbekistan, China, or other locations where there is combat. This not only teaches him but also tests his resolve.

ADVANCED PROGRAMS

Among the advanced courses a recruit can take are training in more complex explosives, assassination, kidnapping, and torture (which covers both the methods to be employed by Al Qaeda operatives and resistance to interrogation). Others cover special killing techniques, heavy weapons, and the use of surface-to-air missiles, among other things. These are generally offered to recruits who have been selected to conduct guerrilla warfare and terrorist operations. Specialized training like surveillance, the forging and identification of documents, or using improvised NBC weapons is reserved predominately for those operating overseas in an urban capacity.

MISSION-SPECIFIC TRAINING

This is training provided for Al Qaeda members who have usually been selected for "martyrdom" operations. These courses may include maritime suicide operations, such as the skills used in the attack on the USS *Cole* and the French oil supertanker *Limburg*. Another may teach the skills required for vehicle-based suicide operations, such as those used in the embassy attacks in Kenya and Tanzania in 1998, or cover air-based tactics used in operations like 9/11.

Al Qaeda uses a standard operating procedure that is employed by intelligence organizations everywhere: never teach more than is required to do the job. If a terrorist is captured, he cannot reveal more than he knows, and the less he knows in this case, the better. Suicide terrorists are on occasion captured; Israel has a whole slew of Hamas, Palestinian Islamic Jihad, and the Al-Aqsa Martyrs' Brigade operatives in jail today. In addition, if terrorists are going on a one-way mission, there is no point on wasting additional time, energy, and money on them. But there is an exception to this rule: Al Qaeda does send out group liaison officers to work with foreign cells that require extensive knowledge. They act as trainers, in addition to being the planners, financiers, and initiators of the operations.

TRAINING CAMPS

Camps can be located in any country that Al Qaeda operates in. The ones in Afghanistan are well known, but there have been others in places like the Sudan (while Osama bin Laden was living there), the Philippines, and even distant places like the Pankisi Gorge region of the newly independent Georgia. It has also been reported that counterterrorism investigators worldwide have been finding many connections between suspected homegrown terror cells (including the Toronto 17) and the Pakistan-based Lashkar-e-Tayyiba network, which runs camps in that country. Training camps are common for terrorist groups: even the FLQ had them north of Montreal in the Canadian Shield and in the Eastern Townships near Sherbrooke, Quebec.

The site selected for the camp is always secluded. Movement to and from the location is controlled by only a few, and careful selection of visitors is followed by a security check before arrival. Potential recruits travel in trucks at night so the location is kept even from them. Trainers do not reveal their identities to recruits; recruits do not reveal their identities to each other. Commanded by an emir, camps are guarded at all times and are self-contained, with their own medical facilities, fitness training areas, firing and explosives ranges, tactical rehearsal areas, eating facilities, showers, and washrooms. As an added security measure there are numerous escape routes from the compounds.

Al Qaeda also expanded to caves during the Soviet occupation of Afghanistan by blasting tunnels and eventually using machinery that bin Laden had brought there. The caves are huge — some several kilometres long — and capable of holding field hospitals, army depots, and accommodations for hundreds of mujahideen. Parts of these complexes were used for training at different higher levels. Bin Laden kept building after the Soviets were defeated, and this is why some intelligence analysts believe that he is somewhere in the mountains today.

TRAINING MANUALS

Different textbooks have been discovered in raids on Al Qaeda positions, safe houses, and training camps. There are various editions, some with more and newer material, and often they have been photocopied or are found on computer discs or hard drives. *Declaration of Jihad against the Country's Tyrants: Military Series* (*I'alan al-Jihad 'ala al-Tawaghit al-Bilad*) was written from 1993 to 1994 by a senior member of the Egyptian Islamic Jihad and is divided into eighteen lessons, including one called "Cold Steel Torture Methods." Instructions about how to produce ricin have also appeared in a chapter on assassinations from this book, a copy of which was seized in 2002 by the Manchester police.

Another example is the *Encyclopedia of the Afghan Jihad*, also known as the *Encyclopedia of the Afghanistan Resistance*. This easy-to-understand set is about seven thousand pages in length and was started soon after the Soviet withdrawal in 1989. It took five years to complete, so different editions were published even before completion. Jordanian Intelligence managed to provide the first complete set of volumes to the CIA in 1997. American and British military texts were used as part of the research. It was planned as a ten-volume set, but an eleventh was found on CD, discussing improvised NBC warfare with precise formulas for manufacturing botulinum and ricin. Also found with it were videotaped experiments on dogs using toxic vapours from a white liquid.

It must have been extremely time-consuming to translate this type of text due to the linguistic difficulties of technical terms used in military manuals. But in spite of this, and with limited translator availability, Al Qaeda managed to produce a comprehensive product that includes technical direction on how to blow up bridges and buildings and how to shoot down an aircraft using a Stinger surface-to-air missile. Not surprisingly, the encyclopedia is dedicated to Allah.

Yet another example is *War Cry of the Mujahideen* (*Mujahidin ki Lalkabr*), which spans more than a thousand pages and was a joint project of Al Qaeda and the Harkat-ul-Mujahideen. Videos with indoctrination lectures and instructions on weapons have also been confiscated at safe houses and camps. These have included instruction on SA-7, SA-14, and Stinger missiles in addition to rocket-propelled grenades and even the Milan anti-tank missile system.

SECTION 2: AL QAEDA CONVENTIONAL TACTICS

CODE NAMES AND ALIASES

Al Qaeda is also known as the Islamic Army for the Liberation of the Holy Places and the World Islamic Front for Jihad against Jews and Crusaders, which is the official name of the umbrella organization of the different terrorist groups under its control. Two other names for the group are the Islamic Salvation Foundation and the Islamic Army.

Individual members have different aliases for different purposes. Some operatives have more than twenty-five, with documentation to match, and up to fifty can be used for the higher leadership. This is one reason why security forces have great difficulty locating and apprehending key operatives and leaders. They are someone different to everyone they meet. This enhances security in that connections are difficult to make, especially if disguises are used for each identity. This practice also emphasizes the importance of forgery and documentation theft, which is a specialty of Al Qaeda: the organization produces a high-quality product and can charge top dollar.

PLANNING AND PREPARATION

Planning is an essential element of any terrorist act, and Al Qaeda plans more than other groups. It also does so more carefully. The collection of basic information is often done via the Internet, and surveillance and investigation, which includes video and/or still photography, follows. Surveillance video footage was discovered in Afghanistan of targets in Toronto, and all this information has been passed on, with copies probably made and stored in different locations to be used when the time is appropriate.

In the Philippines in 1995, Ramzi Yousef was plotting to kill four thousand people with the mid-air bombings of a dozen American Trans-Pacific flights. Yousef even conducted a dry run in which he actually planted an explosive charge on a Philippine airliner that was seriously damaged. He undoubtedly informed his superiors that either the explosive would have to be placed in a different location or a larger, more powerful charge would have to be used. Even though Yousef was captured in Pakistan, the information he provided in terms of explosive type and charge placement still remains at the fingertips of Al Qaeda for future possible operations. Millennium bomber Ahmed Ressam, who was arrested on the Canada/U.S. border, was planning to set off a bomb at Los Angeles International Airport on December 31, 1999. But even though he was not successful, all the preparation that went into planning his operation is still mostly valid and probably requires nothing more than verification.

Regarding reconnaissance, what conclusions should we draw from the file of Samir Ait Mohammed, a failed Canadian refugee claimant who spent over four years in a Vancouver remand centre before being deported to Algeria in January 2006? Security services allege he was linked to the GIA, helped supply false passports, tried to establish a training camp, and was hatching a plot to bomb a Jewish district of Montreal. A plan gone wrong — but the effort was not totally wasted. This is the Al Qaeda mentality: two steps forward, one step back, but eventually they will get where they want to go.

There have also been other spectacular plans that thankfully never made it off Al Qaeda's drawing board. One was to slam a commercial airliner into an aircraft carrier while the ship was in port, specifically in Norfolk, Virginia. Mohamed Atta of 9/11 fame visited Norfolk and certainly passed on the information he collected there. An American Nimitz-class carrier is worth $18 billion and has a compliment of approximately six thousand sailors and eighty-five combat aircraft on board. They are powered by two nuclear reactors, store 13.2 million litres of aviation fuel, and have flight decks covering 1.8 hectares. In addition, an American aircraft carrier usually has a very patriotic name (such as the USS *Dwight D. Eisenhower*) and is a symbol of the most powerful warship afloat.

In addition to the alleged plots of the Toronto 17 group (who will go on trial in Canada) and the London–New York aircraft bombings that were prevented in August 2006, here are some other schemes that Al Qaeda has had in mind.

Computer files seized in Pakistan provided detailed plans of buildings and diagrams for a stretch limousine packed with explosives. It was determined that a helicopter tour of New York was used for this reconnaissance. These files belonged to Mohammed Neem Noor Khan, an Al Qaeda communications specialist based in Lahore. Other related files in Gujarat belonged to Ahmed Khalfan Ghailani, one of those responsible for the 1998 U.S. Embassy bombings in Africa.

The Singapore Internal Security Department arrested thirteen members of an Al Qaeda cell planning simultaneous bombings of the British and Australian High Commissions and the American and Israeli Embassies there. Hashim Bin Abbas, an engineer, pointed out where bombs could be hidden in bikes and motorcycles on a video recovered from raids of safe houses. Other plans included attacks on a railway station and on American corporations in Singapore and Hong Kong. Six of the arrested cell members were members of the Singapore Armed Forces.

Great Britain's Special Branch believes that an Algerian group loosely connected to Al Qaeda planned to detonate a bomb on an M 4 motorway overpass during rush hour in London's west end. This plot was uncovered when two men were arrested rappelling after writing graffiti. Six other terrorists fled with the bomb when they saw police arrest the other two, and the pieces to the puzzle were put together only after the release of the graffiti artists.

The U.S. Office of Homeland Security has issued warnings of attacks in regards to the New York Stock Exchange, the headquarters of the International Monetary Fund, and the World Bank in Washington.

Note that Al Qaeda likes to modify plans. While planning the 1993 World Trade Center bombing, a plot to skyjack an airliner and crash it into CIA headquarters was also considered. Jose Padilla, who planned to construct and detonate an RDD, also had a plan to seal off twenty apartments in the U.S., let out the gas, and ignite it, causing a massive explosion that would have levelled the apartment complex. This was a different take on the supposed Chechen apartment explosions in Moscow. One can readily see how this plan may be tweaked to cause a gas explosion in downtown Toronto, causing the destruction of the financial district.

TARGETING
Al Qaeda targets political, military, and economic installations, including businesses. The 9/11 targets all fit the above criteria, and the direct cost of the attacks to the American people was estimated at between $40 and $45 billion.

MOVEMENT
Stated tactics for infiltration into foreign countries are to use illegal immigration groups or to apply for refugee status. When travelling, Al Qaeda terrorists may be with their families or pose as a member of another's family. Millennium bomber Ahmed Ressam was disguised as a woman to cross the border from Pakistan to Afghanistan before receiving training. As of 2000, it was estimated that Al Qaeda had effectively infiltrated 20 percent of all Islamic NGOs in the world, and these organizations often provide excellent cover for travel. Terrorists dress just like you and me, and they can tint or dye their hair and shave or closely crop their beards.

INFILTRATION
Infiltration of police and intelligence services, the military, political parties, and even key government positions can be expected from Al Qaeda in any country where they can manage it. Infiltration was the method used to take control of many mosques and madrassas to provide recruiting and indoctrination bases.

AL QAEDA CELLS AND CONTROL OFFICERS
Al Qaeda in an urban context operates in circular or cluster cells. The chain of command for international cells consists of a senior agent handler (who is usually a Military Committee member), an agent handler, a cell leader, and the cell members. For operations such as 9/11, the cells are self-contained and self-sufficient. They can even be tasked

to operate independently of central command once a target and method of attack are sanctioned. It is important to note that the agent handler will use different communications tactics for each cell that he controls. Human couriers are often used.

LOCAL ETHNIC POPULATION

Like many terrorist groups, Al Qaeda makes use of migrant populations and gains great benefits from these community members for handling their requirements in foreign countries. This includes financing, provision of safe houses, transport, and, most importantly, assistance with propaganda and recruitment. The 9/11 operation was very secretive and self-contained, but this has not been the case for other operations. One thing that may explain this is that some Al Qaeda cells are formed by citizens of first-generation immigrants who are drawn into the idealism of jihad, as was the case for the London Bombers of 7/7 and the cells arrested last year in Toronto. Such people would usually be known within their own ethnic community.

A British support cell was found to have shipped scuba gear, range finders, and satellite phones from Germany and night vision goggles and sniper scopes from the U.S. to their counterparts in Afghanistan. Other items that have been shipped to Al Qaeda include video equipment for surveillance and target planning, .50-calibre sniper rifles, and even a T389 jet trainer. (The trainer was lost in Sudan in the mid 1990s; it was meant for basic pilot training for suicide attacks.)

SLEEPER CELLS

As with all terrorist groups, the most dangerous type of Al Qaeda unit is a sleeper cell, activated only when required. These dormant cells are extremely difficult for intelligence services to uncover until they are activated. Sleeper agents were used in the 1998 Nairobi and Dar es Salaam bombings, which were planned for several years in advance. Sleeper cells can operate anywhere in the world, even in Canada.

SAFE HOUSES

Al Qaeda avoids isolated locations and prefers the protection that is provided by an inner city if operating in an urban context. A ground floor is preferred. It is important that the room and its occupants cannot be viewed easily from an adjacent building. The preparation of an evacuation plan is one of the priorities upon arrival, but much of the groundwork has already been done by a safe house selection team. Safe houses are separated by function. There are separate houses for meetings, storage, housing fugitives, and planning. Safe houses are rented by using false ID, with supporting documentation and a cover story by someone who has a non-Muslim appearance. Hidden areas for documents or weapons are found or constructed. All visitors need proper cover before visiting, and they are not to come and go at suspicious times. There are also prearranged warning signals and all-clear signs. All locks are replaced upon moving in, and around the safe house three circles of security are developed: outlying posts for early warning, sentries inside or outside (depending on the house's location), and a final internal layer of bodyguards. Sleeping mats are often used in Al Qaeda safe houses, but if living in the West, proper Western furniture should be used. Some of the 9/11 terrorists did not follow this rule, but unfortunately those who noticed this odd behaviour did not know its significance and never reported it to the authorities.

COVER

Supporting documents may include a diploma, a driver's licence, a union card, a permit of some sort, and even photographs of a fake family. The terrorist must have knowledge of his cover occupation, whether it might be medicine, engineering, or architecture. Most importantly, the terrorist must be able to blend with local population where he resides and operates. His means of transport must match the cover, and the terrorist must act according to his cover's financial capability.

COMMUNICATIONS

Communications in the past have often been by satellite cellphone, often registered to a front company. This is probably in the process of changing since several cells in Europe and other parts of the world have been identified and apprehended because of such communication, thanks in part to Echelon, a satellite technical monitoring system that is employed around the world. Satellite phones are starting to be restricted to the group's leadership only. Al Qaeda often positions satellite phones near high-frequency sources like TV stations or embassies. They talk for less than three minutes and always disguise their voices. Remote systems and main street phones are often used, and a pre-recorded tape is sometimes played to deceive listeners about where the individual is located. All conversations must be quick, explicit, and pertinent.

Human couriers, encrypted e-mails, and ordinary commercial courier companies continue to be used with success in addition to other methods. Intermediaries used to send and receive messages may be non-Islamic, possibly not even Al Qaeda members. If sending messages via a courier service, the sender's name and address must be fictitious. If a message is sent by mail, the correct amount of postage must be paid attention to. The envelope has to be typed, as written script may be identified as Middle Eastern, and its coded contents should be only a few pages so as not to attract undue attention.

COVERT MEETINGS

Al Qaeda uses three types of secret communications: "common," when not under surveillance; "standby," when surveillance is suspected; and "alarm," when security forces have penetrated the cell. Little time is given after the message for meeting is sent, and disguises are always used. Operatives are instructed that if they travel by taxi, they don't speak to the driver, as in many countries drivers are informants for the intelligence services or for whoever pays best. Meetings always take place at a predetermined place, with set arrival and departure times and signals for verification that can be as trivial as carrying an object. There will also always be an alternate time, date, and place for the meeting. Often, higher Al Qaeda leadership organizes some or all of these details.

Counter-surveillance is conducted before, during, and after the meeting by all parties involved. A separate counter-surveillance team may be present in support if the assembly involves a high-ranking Al Qaeda leader. Guidelines for meeting an unknown terrorist may be different from those for meeting a known one, but there are key behaviours to follow at all time. The terrorist must act normally and speak quietly (but not in a whisper), and nothing is committed to writing. A standard rule is to wear gloves to avoid leaving fingerprints. As well, there is a plan if the meeting should be compromised, including a plausible cover story, an escape route, and even a blocking group if required. All the terrorists must know the location intimately, and it must be a public place. They must all travel by secondary roads or by bus, subway, or commuter train. There are many risks in a meeting: being captured, killed, or photographed or identified. There is also the chance that security services are recording the clandestine conversation.

TRANSPORTATION

Proper registration documents should be carried according to the vehicle used. The vehicle selected must match the cover used. A transport vehicle is not to be used in attacks, but rather for meetings or other non-attack reasons. Traffic rules must be obeyed. Counter-surveillance must be conducted at all times, on foot or in a vehicle. The vehicle must be purchased using forged or adapted documents. It must always be parked securely with exit routes available and known. Colour can be changed for operations, then changed back if need be. Licence plates on the vehicle are to be changed before and after it has been used for meetings. Gas stations should be avoided before and after meetings because of closed-circuit televisions. By 2000, Al Qaeda started using sea routes more frequently for international travel because of lax security at ports as compared to airports. The Al Qaeda shipping network ceased to function in 1996 after leaving Sudan. Currently, Al Qaeda charters vessels as required or uses one owned by affiliated terrorist groups.

PURCHASES, TRANSPORTATION, AND STORAGE OF EQUIPMENT

The pre-purchase of equipment for operations is preferred, which means members like to use a broker. The location of the buy must allow for 360-degree observation, as counter-surveillance must be conducted during the purchase. A cover story is at the ready, if not already given to the broker. Operatives are told to inspect, test, and pay with a limited amount of time spent at the purchase location, always watching the body language of the broker or seller. Transportation to and from the buy must be at a suitable time and by an obscure route known in advance, and counter-surveillance is again conducted. Equipment is never stored at an operative's residence, but near the target location and definitely not in a park or close to public buildings. Members are encouraged to rent an apartment with a long-term lease and to not visit the storage area frequently. They should also make sure that the equipment storage safe house is known to only a few.

SURVEILLANCE OPERATIONS

Al Qaeda operatives have been reported to use disguises while collecting information on potential targets, including dressing up as panhandlers, street sweepers (which are common in the developing world), city workers, and street people.

Previous page, above, and opposite page: Continued overt military intervention abroad in the war on terror will prove the salient straining point for Western democracies in the future. Governments are at the beginning of a steep learning curve; in this new era, wars will likely be protracted and cannot be won in the conventional sense.

Note: The illustrations contained herein are a selection of my work as a photojournalist from 1983 to 2007. Some are my subjective interpretations of the many events described in this book.
— Dwight Hamilton

Top: Peter Worthington, founding editor of the *Toronto Sun*, has said that the June 2006 arrests of the terror suspects in Ontario "served clear warning that Canada is also a target viewed as an enemy too. So get used to it — until the threat is diminished, which is unlikely in the foreseeable future." Above: Scion of the intelligentsia William F. Buckley Jr. on the war on terror: "To what extent does this society elect to fight it? Because if it doesn't care that much about it then to hell with it." Opposite page: Inspection officials' training aid in the wake of Heathrow's August 2006 thwarted transatlantic airline plot allegedly involving liquid explosives.

Above, clockwise from top: A plastic knife concealed inside a comb; a plastic copy of an Office of Strategic Services (OSS) thumb knife ideal for sewing underneath a coat collar or lapel; an older design of a concealed edged weapon, a plastic Russell knife; two different types of ballpoint pens, one concealing an edged weapon and the other a pick. All items can be used in an attempt to evade airport security. While inspectors are on the lookout for these, the goods may be easily missed during peak hours. Opposite page, clockwise from top: An adhesive sticker version of the Front de Libération du Québec's flag; a Makarov (PM) automatic (9mm short); a Baby Browning automatic (.25 cal); an English-language communiqué from Germany's Red Army Faction featuring the organization's history, illustrations, and motivational prose; a handy and illuminating pocketbook for political "agitators" in Quebec that includes on its first three pages the telephone numbers of labour unions, various Marxist-Leninist organizations, many of the province's radio stations, Montreal's daily newspapers, and the burn units of some local hospitals, while the remaining pages are apparently for "notes"; a rare English-language copy of the classic textbook *Minimanual of the Urban Guerrilla* by Carlos Marighella, printed in Vancouver in 1970; a Tokarev (TT) automatic (7.65mm).

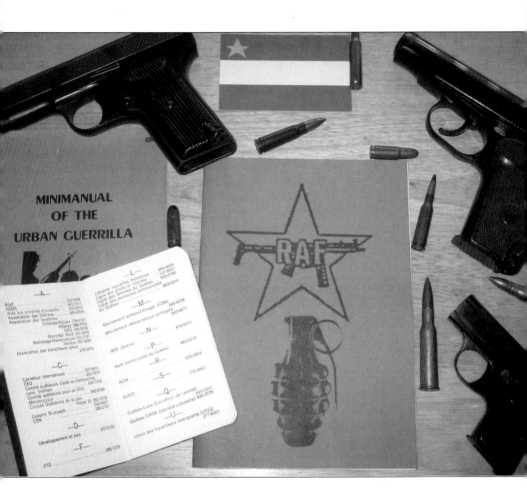

Two cabinet members during the FLQ era were Lester Pearson's minister of national defence, Paul Hellyer (top), and Pierre Trudeau's justice minister during the October Crisis, John Turner (above). "Some of my most embarrassing moments were caused by FLQ break-ins to steal arms and ammunition from defence establishments," Hellyer said about the first generation's reign of terror, which had begun in 1963. Opposite page: An electrical substation constructed circa 1970 in Montreal; note the thirty-foot-high concrete walls and the corners' curvature. The FLQ specialized in bombs and was one of the first terrorist organizations in the world to strike at multiple targets simultaneously.

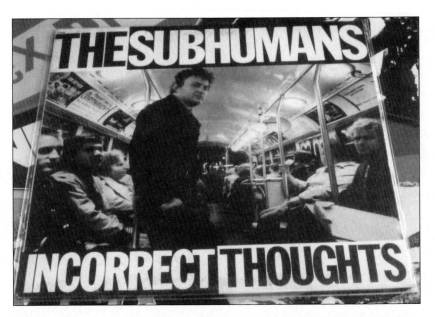

Above: Anarchy in the 1980s. Subhumans bass player Gerry Useless (far right) before joining Direct Action. One of the heaviest Canadian punk bands, their album contains a life-imitating-art number entitled "Urban Guerilla." Opposite page: One of the more prominent anti-war protests in the nation's history occurred in October 1983 at Toronto's Queen's Park and concerned the testing of American cruise missiles on Canadian soil. (A year earlier the local plant of Litton Industries, which manufactured the missiles' guidance systems, had been bombed by Direct Action.) Rounding out the usual suspects that day were Marxist-Leninists, Trotskyists, FOCO theorists, Maoists, Feminists, Hippies, Yippies, Dadaists, Nihilists, Punks, Pacifists, Beats, Diggers, Taborites, Bakuninists, International Situationists, opponents of the Military Industrial Complex, many miscellaneous malcontents, and me. Earlier that month, one of my fellow students had been convicted of public mischief for perhaps the most classic anarchist statement one can make when he defaced the law's original parchment during a visit to the National Archives in Ottawa. During his trial he stated, "The most important part of the Constitution is the Charter of Rights. One of the most basic rights is to be alive. The Trudeau government has violated that right." Even the judge admitted he was "an excellent student, with a possibly brilliant artistic future."

Top: The CN Tower was allegedly on an infrastructure target list produced by the U.S. government in 2002; Secretary of State Colin Powell would neither confirm nor deny its existence, but if it did exist he said he didn't have it. Above: One of the alleged targets in Operation Badr was the CBC building in Toronto. Opposite: Union Station in North America's fifth-largest city has been on Al Qaeda's hit list for some time, according to a videotape discovered by an American journalist in Afghanistan and passed over to coalition security forces.

Above and opposite: An exact replica of a suicide vest manufactured by Securesearch Inc. and used as a counterterrorism training aid. Utilized by many terrorist organizations today, the vest idea was originally conceived by the Tamil Tigers, and the technical expertise to manufacture it was passed on to Lebanon-based Hezbollah in the mid 1980s as part of a quid pro quo between the two groups. The Czechoslovakian-manufactured plastic explosive Semtex H was initially used, as it was untraceable by airport detection methods and Libya had dumped about one hundred tons onto the international black market in the 1980s. But since the Montreal Protocol made it mandatory to include chemical "taggants" when making plastic explosives, the formula would seemingly have no advantage over American C4, British PE-808, or other "cap-sensitive" high explosives when employed in these lethal and psychologically devastating weapons. Vests are composed of about six kilograms of plastic, separate arming and firing switches, and a series of detonators; shrapnel can include anything from nails to ball bearings and is often mixed with feces or other toxins to infect the victims' wounds. Coming soon to a Canadian shopping mall near you if present trends in unconventional warfare continue. Overleaf: The authors.

REGIONAL FUNCTIONS
Divisions in labour are often due to the linguistic difficulties in communication. Ethnic Al Qaeda terrorists are tasked to perform specialized functions. Libyans in the past have specialized in forged documents, the Algerians in conducting credit card fraud, the Philippine More Islamic Liberation Front in training in Southeast Asia, and the Egyptians in training terrorist groups in North Africa, for example. The weakness with this approach is that all members working in that specialty are of one nationality. Find one operative and it is easier to locate the rest.

INTELLIGENCE COMMENTS

There is much to know in order to be a truly professional terrorist — many never live that long. Unfortunately, it takes only a few pros with leadership skills to set the world on fire. The Al Qaeda doctrine can be stated as follows:

- As long as we learn from our mistakes, it is not a loss. We may revisit past or planned operations.
- We are goal-orientated and flexible. We are capable of switching the types of targets and how they will be struck or a combination of both.
- We strike at the centre of the enemy. Whether in the U.S., Great Britain, or Spain, we have always targeted key cities. This is not to say that we do not strike the periphery, but we do it by using local or regional allies.

Many volunteers have been trained by this terrorist organization, but only the best were recruited into the Al Qaeda fold. From these, only a small portion become the true terrorists you hear about in the media. They are the best that Al Qaeda can recruit.

Meticulous planning is a hallmark of Al Qaeda operations, and they can spend years plotting against a specific target. This is not indecision on their part, but rather a demonstration of care that few terrorist groups in the past have matched.

The group's operations are relatively cheap compared to the damage done. The 9/11 strikes cost less than $500,000 and killed more than three thousand people, and the Bali bombings cost just $35,000 and killed more than two hundred.

10: Order of Battle

INTELLIGENCE FILE 008/2007 — TERRORIST GROUP — ORGANIZATION

LEADERSHIP

Terrorist leadership, as in any organization, attracts above-average individuals; it is a fallacy that terrorists are mentally disturbed. Some terrorist groups are almost exclusively middle and upper class, and many are professionals. A good example was the Bolivian ELN, which was commanded by a university professor, a university student, and a Marxist theorist. The Weather Underground had three key leaders: Bernadine Dohrn was a lawyer trained in Cuba and Yugoslavia, Mark Rudd was from the upper middle class, and Bill Ayers was from the moneyed society of Halifax and Saint John. Professor Robert Comeau of the University of Quebec at Montreal founded the Viger cell of the FLQ. Ann Hansen of Direct Action was a University of Waterloo student who studied in Europe. Her colleague-in-terror Brent Taylor's parents were both university professors from Victoria. An exception to such backgrounds was David Defreeze, the leader of the Symbionese Liberation Army of Patty Hearst kidnapping fame. He was a career criminal who escaped from an American prison in 1972.

Yasser Arafat of Fatah came from high lineage. His mother was related to the mufti of Palestine and his father was a member of the Muslim Brotherhood. Arafat received a civil engineering degree in Cairo when he was president of the Palestinian Students' Union, and he underwent military training as an officer in the Egyptian Army before he and five others organized Fatah (a major Palestinian political party that eventually became the largest group in the Palestine Liberation Organization) in 1963. The first attack launched by Al Asifa, the military arm of Fatah, occurred on New Year's Eve in 1964 against Israel. Arafat became the chief spokesman for the PLO in 1968, but it was not until the next year that Fatah joined that umbrella organization, which they have subsequently dominated. A covert Fatah group known as Black September was formed in 1970 to attract attention on an international scale when using terrorism. It worked. Eleven Israeli athletes were murdered by the group at the 1972 Olympics held in Munich, Germany, and the entire event was broadcast on television around the world. A routine tactic today, but not in that era. It was not until 1974 that Fatah rejected terrorism officially.

Giangiacomo Feltrinelli was a multi-millionaire who led GAP until his death in 1972. GAP then united with the Red Brigades. Their first leader, Renato Curcio, was a university professor who was captured in 1976 and replaced automatically, as is always the case in well-organized terrorist groups. The Red Brigades' security was so tight, only one other member from its inner leadership circle, known as Strategic Direction, was ever brought to justice.

Carlos Marighella was the Brazilian Communist Party leader and author of the classic *Minimanual of the Urban Guerrilla*. At about 8:00 p.m. on November 4, 1969, he was shot dead with several others in a police ambush staged at 800 Alameda Casa Branca in San Paulo.

Raul Sendic, one of the heads of the Tupamaros (also known as the National Liberation Movement) in Uruguay, was a union organizer, and another of the group's key leaders was a former art history professor.

Comrade Gonzales was a philosophy professor who led the Peruvian Shining Path for about twenty years. A major problem for this rural-based group was that its leaders often came from urban areas.

The leader of the El Salvadoran Popular Forces of Liberation was Soviet-trained Salvador Cayetano (Marcial) Carpio, a member of the Cuban Communist Party. Revenge was his true motivation for becoming a terrorist, as his daughter had been killed in a demonstration in 1980.

Former Chilean President Allende's nephew and his wife were killed in a shootout with police on October 5, 1974. They were members of the MIR's central committee. Allende's sister and her husband were also arrested on November 4, 1974, for aiding that terrorist group.

LIBERATION THEOLOGY

Religion is not the exclusive domain of Al Qaeda. Many extremists in the United States and Latin America that have planned or practised terrorism have used religion as the basis of their philosophy. "The kingdom of heaven can come about in our day only by Marxism," Mexican Bishop Mendez Arced once said. Slogans such as "Jesus was a revolutionary" and "You must live your Christianity through Marxism" were delivered from Latin American pulpits from the mid 1960s to the late 1980s. In fact, some clergy not only preached "liberation theology", they took up arms themselves to lead different terrorist units.

On May 25, 1974, five priests were deported from Chile for having strong ties with the MIR and belonging to a group called Christians for Socialism.

On August 3, 1971, various priests were arrested in Argentina for terrorist involvement.

On February 15, 1970, the public was informed that numerous priests had joined the ELN in Colombia. Led by a priest, the ELN also seized the town of San Pablo, Colombia, in a famous raid on January 7, 1972, and held it for several hours. The group killed two police officers, wounded four others, and stole $400,000 from public offices, city hall, and the telephone company. Also in that country, an ALPHA 74 cell led by a former Roman Catholic priest stole explosives on October 6, 1974.

In North America and Europe, informal terrorist support infrastructures exist to this day based on the concept of liberation theology. Religion and extremists have mixed for decades on all continents; that Al Qaeda is using religious schools and mosques as the bases for indoctrination and recruitment is nothing new.

THE OCTOPUS OF TERROR

Every terrorist group is subdivided into different categories of operations that are reflected in their structures. A group's organization can be viewed like an octopus, with the political division serving as the head and different departments as the tentacles. Unless the creature is beheaded, its tentacles will continue growing.

The political division is the head and central nervous system and can include a strategic direction unit, which provides the group's leadership and long-term planning. It can also be used to forward messages and deliver strategic propaganda. It is believed by some that Direct Action may have had a strategic direction unit behind their efforts in Canada.

A good example of how the political division of a terrorist organization works can be found by looking at the Palestine Liberation Organization's structure before it split between those for and against the Rejection Front in 1974. Formed at the Arab Summit Conference in 1964, the PLO was an umbrella organization for over a dozen different groups that used terrorism. The PLO had united most groups under its wing by 1969 and had formed the Palistinian Liberation Army, which consisted of several brigades with its headquarters in Jerusalem. Under its banner the PLO also formed a youth organization known as Flowers and Lions, as well as the Palestinian Red Crescent, which included departments such as health, information, and finance. In addition, different unions were formed for doctors, lawyers, engineers, teachers, women, workers, and journalists. In short, it was a working government. The process is very similar to what Hamas and Hezbollah have done in the last decade to get elected.

Prior to 1974, the PLO was ruled by the Executive Committee (or cabinet), with fifteen members; the Central Council, with sixty members; and the Palestinian National Council (or parliament), with 350 members. Arafat, the chairman of the Executive Committee, directly controlled the Department of Military Affairs, the Palestinian Liberation Army, the United Forces of Resistance organizations (terrorists), and the militias. This was the basis for self-government that was set up in the occupied territories, negotiated at Camp David in the early 1980s. This is why Arafat was held responsible for any terrorism committed even before more autonomy was given on the West Bank. For some years now, all positions in the PLO have been open to democratic elections. Hamas came to power by copying these same tactics of organization.

The political division of a terrorist group also includes separate units for propaganda and civil disobedience. The Weather Underground participated in many riots in the United States in 1968, known as the Days of Rage. Direct confrontation with the police was the norm, and the group was known for its helmeted women who knew karate. In the spirit of Bob Dylan's famous line from "Subterranean Homesick Blues" that "you don't need a weatherman to know which way the wind blows," the group ran into a cyclone, and about three hundred of its members were arrested, which was almost everyone they had. The Weather Underground also had an associated organization (these are generally known as affinity groups) that was heavily involved in street violence. Demonstrations, strikes, political support, and the direct influence of politicians by wining and dining are some of the tasks that can be performed by affinity groups. As well, different organizations are created to collect donations that finance operations or provide legal defence fees. Then there is a network of talent scouts that search for and provide new recruits.

Often (but not always) a group's political division is officially linked to its military arm. For example, the African National Congress had a military arm formed by Nelson Mandela known as the Spear of the Nation, which was banned in 1963. It conducted all the bombing and assassinations, while the ANC provided the political assistance to the cause.

The military arm is the one that gets the public's attention, due to the fact it delivers a good deal of the group's propaganda by its actions. Most people do not even think about the fact that the political division is much stronger. If a generation of the military arm is killed, wounded, or captured, a new generation springs up because of the political division, which keeps the ideology alive in the minds of the target audience. The military arm is usually subdivided into cells by function performed.

The direct support branch tentacle involves criminal activity; members directly aid the terrorists in their cause. Thefts of weapons, vehicles, explosives, passports, and documents are common tasks of this arm. Forgery, safe house procurement and maintenance, and cache security and communications support through dead-drop pickups and courier services are also required. A key role would be to collect intelligence before a terrorist attack.

Support infrastructures are pseudo-branches of direct and indirect support. They are groups that do not officially belong to the political division but, due to ideological beliefs, support the terrorists' cause, both legally and illegally. The Socialist Lawyers Collective supported all three key German terrorist organizations by providing lawyers for apprehended terrorists. As well, the Autonomous Collectives provided other forms of support for those terrorists as well as some other international groups. The Italian Autonomous Collectives did the same for their terrorist groups. They were not small, either: their propaganda gave them the strength of 150,000 members.

From the 1960s to the 1980s there existed networks in the United States for predominately domestic groups like the Weathermen and the Black Panthers, and this is a phenomenon to watch for if terrorism becomes more prevalent. Individuals who did not want to participate in armed action but who had political leanings toward different terrorist groups formed them. Red Help were anarchists, remembered best for their threats against the Pope on his visit to Holland in the 1980s. They gave assistance to all sorts of terrorists, as did Direct Support Network, which provided the Belgian Combating Communist Cells with safe houses in Germany and Belgium. Also in the same category are strictly mercenary organizations like Henrie Curiel's Paris-based group. Although these networks may have ties to foreign intelligence agencies, they always claim independence.

Regional unaligned support is an unofficial ad hoc branch of a terrorist group. Non-aligned networks exist that can be used by terrorists if necessary, although often these networks are unaware of the fact. Most of these networks are set up to support Third World charitable organizations that are meant to house and feed locals. Who would think that an illegal immigrant given succor by a church group was a terrorist?

The state sponsor liaison arm is a covert group undertaking. It may involve finance operations, exchanges of intelligence, or weapons and explosives delivery arrangements. Another function would be to arrange for foreign training by the sponsor state or from another terrorist group. This unit would carry out planning and cooperation and would provide political support at both the national and international levels for both operations and the cause.

Group liaison is another function of members from the military division. This includes maintaining contact and arranging for assistance from other (usually) like-minded or allied terrorist groups. Al Qaeda does this extremely well. Older networks included the Palestinian terrorist groups, especially the PFLP. The Basque ETA and ETA-M were both key players, often providing instructors to other terrorist groups, as was the Japanese Red Army. This type of liaison does eventually lead to joint terrorist group operations, such as those by the PFLP with the Red Army Faction and the Japanese Red Army. Here are some more classic team-ups:

- Joint RAF and Action Directe communiqués on January 15, 1985, announced that French Brigadier Rene Audran, director of arms sales for that country, had been assassinated.

- U.S. Ambassador to Brazil Burke Elbrick was kidnapped on September 4, 1969, and released three days later after the release of fifteen political prisoners. A twelve-man team of National Liberation Action and Revolutionary Movement of October 8 operatives were involved. The incident was the subject of the 1997 movie *Four Days in September*.

- On April 10, 1972, an Argentine general was killed in a joint assassination by the People's Revolutionary Army and the Revolutionary Armed Forces.

- A West German Lufthansa aircraft was bombed in Bogotá on February 17, 1978. Twelve RAF terrorists were operating in Colombia at that time in cooperation with homegrown groups.

- The PFLP cooperated with the German RAF in the famous Entebbe skyjacking in July 1976.

- The RAF hooked up with the Red Brigades for the kidnapping of Aldo Moro in Rome on March 16, 1978. His bullet-ridden body was found on May 9 exactly equidistant from the Italian Communist Party and Christian Democratic Party's headquarters.

- On behalf of the PFLP, the 2 June Movement participated in the famous 1976 OPEC raid that was led by perhaps the most famous terrorist in history before Osama bin Laden came along, Ilich Ramírez Sánchez, a.k.a. Carlos the Jackal, a self-proclaimed leftist mercenary and the son of a Venezuelan champagne Marxist. He was trained in guerrilla warfare by the Cuban DGI at Camp Matanzas near Havana in 1967, and after he gunned down two French undercover agents in extremely close quarters he became legendary and the most wanted man in the world. He is now serving life imprisonment in France after DST agents "rendered" him from Sudan on August 14, 1994.

• On February 26, 1965, in New York City an attempt to dynamite the Statue of Liberty and two other symbols of the U.S. government by the Black Liberation Army was thwarted. The explosives were provided by the FLQ.

Today, we see the mixed operations of Al Qaeda and Jemaah Islamiyyah, the Egyptian Islamic Jihad and various Chechens. Nothing has changed.

The finance branch, just like propaganda, is divided between the political and military divisions. For many well-established groups, a separate finance branch is established for each. Palestinian groups have multi-billion-dollar investments with highly educated financial officers. Since much of the business of terrorism involves international investments, this is now a key area for the West's security efforts. The problem until 9/11 was the lack of agreement by many countries to apply such pressure to terrorist groups. Areas of dispute included the possibility of retaliatory terrorist attacks and the loss of big offshore banking business as well as political differences.

Terrorist financial operations can be legal or not. Narcotics have been a big money-maker for different Palestinian, Tamil, Colombian, and Peruvian groups. Credit card and other types of fraud are practised by the Al Qaeda network, the Tamil Tigers, and may others. Tamil Tiger extortion among the community in Toronto is notorious. Contributions at one time could be made to the IRA in Irish bars, especially in Canada and the United States. In addition, the Irish National Liberation Army used to travel with prostitutes who would earn money then give it to a courier who travelled with them. But when donations from countries and sponsors reach in the millions, money-making turns to legitimate investments and businesses, as it did for both Palestinian groups and Al Qaeda.

Organized crime liaison is another type of unit that can be found in the different tentacles of the terrorist octopus. According to Merighella's *Minimanual of the Urban Guerrilla*, a terrorist group must have contacts with the mob. They are useful for the distribution of narcotics and make good partners in crime. The Red Brigades learned how to rob banks by sharing half of their take from their first bank robberies in exchange for planning and training from the Mafia. Often, organized crime also has lawyers and judges in its pockets.

Front groups can be found in all arms of a terrorist organization. These include charitable organizations that provide defence funds for captured terrorists or money for widows and orphans, and businesses fronts for legal or illegal activity. Whether they are newspapers or bookstores, fronts always appear legitimate. Where the money goes to is another question.

SOME FACTS AND FIGURES

The strength of the Red Army Faction in its fourth generation consisted of about one hundred hardcore terrorists, with only about thirty to forty operating at any given time throughout Europe. It was estimated the group had thirteen hundred people in support. The cost to the German taxpayer to eliminate this threat was in the billions of marks.

The 2 June Movement in Germany operated in three- to five-person cells. There were no more than fifty to one hundred serious terrorists in any given generation. They were organized into street action and terrorist cells known as "Night and Fog," which is an old Abwer (German military intelligence) term.

The Tupamaros of Uruguay were organized into numbered "columns" of forty terrorists divided into five-person cells that reported to a central committee. In addition, there were direct support committees, called CATs, for each column.

In Africa and even in Central America, organization has often been along tribal lines. The MISURA and Sata group was formed from the Miskitos, Sumos, Ramas and Sata Tribes and was three thousand strong. Based in Nicaragua and Honduras, they fought the Nicaraguan government as Contras because of the government's communal claim on their land. In addition to armed insurgence into Sandinista territory, they developed an eighty-kilometre no man's land around the area they held, burning all the villages in the strip.

The IRA's Provisional Army Council headquarters was in Dublin, with a tactical headquarters in Belfast. The IRA was organized into three brigades, with three battalions in Belfast, one in Derry, and one in Armagh. A battalion consisted of six to fifteen officers and one hundred men. Battalions were organized into active service units and youth companies, organized for warning and protection against British security forces. The active service units have been organized into four-person cells since 1978.

The Venezuelan MIR had only 500 terrorists operating in six brigades on four fronts, but the Fuerzas Armadas de Liberación Nacional divided that country into military districts with 60 to 120 terrorists to each one. They were organized into thirty-person groups called tactical combat units, and about twenty of them were operating in a classic rural terror campaign.

By one estimate, in 1970 the FLQ had about one hundred potential trigger-pullers, one hundred propagandists, and anywhere from two to three hundred operatives in direct support infrastructure roles like financing and providing safe houses. Another three thousand were assumed to be passive sympathizers in the Quebec media, labour, and transport sectors.

CELL STRUCTURE

Cells can come in different forms and sizes and can be found in the military or the political arm. Cells can be of different orientations and specialization, and be part of associated or affiliated organizations. The cell structure is intended to ensure mobility, flexibility, and, above all, security.

Circular or cluster cells are those that have one key person knowing everyone in a given cell, and are used in the initial stages of formation of a terrorist organization. Circular cells can grow as large as forty members before a linear cell structure is eventually adopted.

Linear structures, with terrorists working in three- to fifteen-person cells, are more common. Only one person in the cell, usually the leader, is in communication with higher leadership. The cell leader may or may not know the leaders of other cells. The cell leader may also only communicate through live or dead drops, telephone, computer, fax, or messenger, and he or she may not even have met in person his or her immediate superior within the structure. Cells are often detailed a specialty in operations such as expropriation, assassination, sniping, bombings, intelligence collection, and hijacking, to name a few.

The size of the cell may be decided based on its specialty work, if any. A cell that specializes in kidnapping may be up to fifteen strong; otherwise cells need to be combined for those types of operations. This can be problematic in that the leadership is new and the separate cell members do not know one another, so there is less trust among combatants. Cells can be found in the military arm, the direct support branch, and even the finance and propaganda branches; larger organizations even have training cells. Cells are sometimes grouped into units, which are given military designations such as companies and battalions to add to their legitimacy and for propaganda purposes.

Usually several cells are known to a designated leader, and several of those report to a higher commander, and so on. In addition to the military commanders, there are leaders in the political arm that plan at a high level; the Provisional IRA had a council, and some of its members were even known to the British government. Strategic leaders ruled the Red Brigades, and only one was a military commander at the highest level. Recruits for their armed action units were often kept in reserve as direct support personnel. They would already know how to operate in a cell structure.

The Canadian group Direct Action had only one five-person military cell with forty people in direct support cells operating out of Vancouver, Winnipeg, Toronto, and Montreal. Despite this size, it took about two years to destroy the military cell.

The 2 June Movement in Germany was split into three- to five-person cells. There were approximately fifty to one hundred terrorists operating from the military arm, and its direct support branch had a strength of about two thousand and was also divided into cells.

In Namibia, the South West African Peoples Organization and its military arm, the People's Liberation Army, avoided direct contact when possible between its A teams and B teams, with the former carrying out terrorist acts and the latter guarding the group's tactical base camps. This method, although not the best for security purposes, was efficient in gradually weaning a potential terrorist from a role in direct support to a B team member to, eventually, a full-fledged operative in an A team. An A and a B team made up what was called an operational group of about fifty to sixty terrorists. There were only eight of them operating in Namibia at any given time, for a total of about four to five hundred terrorists in the front lines. That's very different from Al Qaeda and its associates, whose membership numbers in the thousands.

The Weather Underground worked in three to four-man groups called "focals." (Note that each terrorist group has its own language, which also helps to separate the organization from the herd.)

The Irish National Liberation Army's cell structure was small and well screened. The rule was that to join you must have killed someone in the British security forces. Needless to say, this was a difficult organization to infiltrate or leave.

The People's Revolutionary Army in Argentina was divided into three types of cells: military cells, "cells of the masses" (responsible for organizing demonstrations, civil disobedience, and propaganda), and "apparatus cells" (the direct support of the military arm).

The second-generation FLQ operated in three- to six-person cells that worked independently of each other. According to an RCMP report dated July 1970, there was "evidence also of cells being formed by a sort of spontaneous generation in that when needed, cells spring up that do not belong to any clearly structured or ascertained organization and which act quite unpredictably." Some of the FLQ cells included Viger, Dieppe, Louis Riel, Nelson, Saint-Denis, Liberation, and Chenier. The last two were the ones involved in the October Crisis.

The hardest terrorist organization to destroy in the West was the Prima Linea, operating in Italy. There was no contact between cells, no commanders at a higher level, and orders were passed two times a year by propaganda material that could be found only at specific magazine stores, if you knew what to look for. The material would give only a general idea of what to attack, such as American corporations or NATO installations. Individual cells would strike targets of their choosing, in any way they were capable of doing at the time. Members did not keep weapons or publications at home, and bombs were constructed only as needed from improvised materials. Delivery was done by public transport, negating the need for theft or a support infrastructure, and all members had ordinary day jobs and used these as cover. This was a movement of like-minded individuals that could be motivated by just a few to start operations.

INTELLIGENCE COMMENTS

This file can give you only a rudimentary understanding of terrorist organization. While every group is different, the principles of organization covered herein are adhered to by every terrorist organization in the world, past and present. Large support infrastructures for all groups still exist and are at least partially used by every current group in the world

Contact with organized crime, black market operators, smugglers, and gunrunners has been a tactic for all terrorist groups over the last half-century. Payments in cash and/or barter have transpired in the past, and this method is definitely a staple of Al Qaeda. Sometimes contact occurs just to show solidarity. Joint operations will become even more common in the future.

Training received by a terrorist group often is passed on to other groups in time, adding to the lethality and professionalism of well-established organizations. A terrorist group's infrastructure can be as large as that of a multinational corporation — virtually a state without borders. Organized in a cell structure, these terrorist groups are extremely difficult to counter and impossible to destroy quickly, especially if they are large organizations such as the Al Qaeda network.

In time, Al Qaeda will definitely follow in the same footsteps and start building up a stronger political arm than it currently has: this will be required to form the future caliphate that is planned. Religion is only one tool that Osama bin Laden can use within Al Qaeda's political division, and more fronts will be established in time to serve this purpose. Now think about this: If forty to one hundred hardcore terrorists could cause havoc across a European nation like Germany for thirty years, what do you think Al Qaeda can eventually do?

11: Losing our Heads

INTELLIGENCE FILE 009/2007 — ASSASSINATIONS IN — TERRORISM

INTRODUCTION

One of the Crown's allegations concerning the Toronto 17 is the nail that sticks up, as the infamous Yakuza would say. Although the idea was dismissed after early brainstorming sessions, some of the suspects considered storming Parliament Hill in a commando-like raid, holding members of the House of Commons hostage and beheading the prime minister unless Canada withdrew its troops from Afghanistan. Had the plot outlined in the Crown's eight-page synopsis been tactically feasible and successfully carried out, it would have been a brilliant propaganda coup.

This was not lost on the press. At initial hearings, a circus of television crews and print reporters from around the world swarmed burka-clad supporters outside the court under the watchful eye of black-clad rooftop snipers, whose presence was evocative of a scene from *The Sentinel* when a U.S. Secret Service agent played by Michael Douglas foils an assassination attempt in Toronto.

Assassination has been a popular form of terrorism for centuries in the Middle East. After the death of the Muslim prophet Muhammad in

A.D. 632, his successor was assassinated. Then there is the case of Ali, son-in-law of Muhammad. When he was not elected caliph, or leader, of Islam, Ali broke from the Sunni Muslims and formed the minority Shiite ("partisans of Ali") sect, which today makes up about one-fifth of the worldwide Muslim population and is based predominately in Iran, parts of Iraq, Syria, and Lebanon. Ali was eventually assassinated as well.

The word "assassin" comes from the Arabic sect *Hashshashin*, meaning "those who use hashish." According to the legend recounted by Marco Polo, prospective candidates were drugged and taken to a garden with conduits of flowing wine, milk, and honey, just like the one described in the Islamic *hadith*, or story, found in Chapter 21 of the Fourth Book of Sunan. Seventy-two virgins then served the hit-man-to-be so that he would have a taste of the afterlife. Drugs were also used to ease the pain when — more often than not — the target's bodyguard quickly killed the assassin. During its reign from 1090 to 1275, the government of the Ismailis of Persia used the Hashshashin as assassins when expanding their control, paying tributes, and protecting their caliphate. The tactic was not new, however. Centuries before, Jewish Sicarri had fought Roman authorities in the crowded markets and streets of the cities they lived in by stabbing victims with a short sword known as a sica (this is where they got their name).

The Muslim Brotherhood, which arose in 1928 under the leadership of Hassan Bana, assassinated political targets well into the 1960s. Included in the group's tactics were forerunners to many of the current concepts of the Egyptian Islamic Jihad, now an integral part of Al Qaeda. But the Middle East has never had a monopoly on the use of assassinations. During the Renaissance, the Di Medici family of Firenze often used poison to kill their political opponents, and this why we have the Western custom of having the host taste wine before it is served to dinner guests. French President Charles de Gaulle was the intended target of more than twenty-five assassination attempts, and Lord Louis Mountbatten was murdered by the Irish National Liberation Army when his yacht exploded off the coast of Ireland on August 27, 1979. Former British Prime Minister Margaret Thatcher also had a close call with the IRA in Brighton when her hotel was bombed in 1985.

Certain governments around the world could also be accused of establishment terrorism with their use of assassination. This tactic is used in their endeavors to keep power or strengthen their political position in foreign lands. The soviet KGB and the Bulgarian KDS targeted Pope John Paul II on May 13, 1981. Libya's Muammar Qaddafi, the Iranian government, and the U.S. Central Intelligence Agency have all used assassination. The CIA has had several euphemisms for the act over the years, including the famous term "executive action" and the instruction to "terminate with extreme prejudice." Another lesser known term was "medical immunization."

Israel has also used assassination in its war against terrorists. The Mivtzan Elohim ("Wrath of God") unit was used to avenge the deaths of the 1972 Munich athletes in addition to crippling the PFLP. The tactic has also been used by Israel against the current terrorist groups that employ suicide bombers, such as Hamas and the Palestinian Islamic Jihad: assassination is a legitimate tactic of counterterrorism from their perspective.

In addition to the Tamil Tiger strikes described on page 113, there have been some significant political assassinations (and attempted hits) by terrorists.

On August 16, 1972, two Moroccan Air Force F-5 fighter jets fired on a Boeing 727 bringing Moroccan King Hassan II back to Rabat. The two jets proceeded to the palace and strafed it afterward. The attempt was part of a failed coup. People on the Boeing 727 were wounded, but the king was not among them.

On October 6, 1981, Egyptian president Anwar al-Sadat was shot dead by terrorists who machine-gunned and threw grenades at the reviewing stand during a military parade in Cairo. Seven other people were also killed and twenty-eight were wounded. The assassins were later executed, but some of those involved during the subsequent hunt for the terrorists were members of the Egyptian Islamic Jihad, now a part of Al Qaeda.

On August 21, 1983, Philippine President Benigno Aquino Jr. was shot and killed by a lone gunman with an AK-47 when he stepped off a plane at Manila International Airport. The assassin was quickly killed by security forces.

King Hussein Ibn Talah of Jordan was almost assassinated numerous times during his reign, including once when he went to his personal washroom to use a bottle of nose drops. Chance had it that a drop fell from the dropper and hit the sink, and the young king noticed fumes and hissing. A valet was quickly apprehended and admitted his crime.

On July 3, 1995, Islamic extremists in Addis Ababa, Ethiopia, attempted to assassinate the president of Egypt, Hosni Mubarak. Mubarak was on his way to attend a summit of the Organization of African Unity; the terrorists knew his arrival time and the even the route his limousine would take. The terrorists blocked the road with one vehicle and opened fire with AK-47s, killing two police officers. Mubarak survived, likely because his car was armour-plated. Two terrorists were killed and the others fled while the convoy turned around. They are linked to Al Qaeda.

On November 4, 1995, Yigal Amir, a right-wing Jewish radical, assassinated Israeli Prime Minister Yitzhak Rabin after attending a rally promoting the Oslo peace process at Tel Aviv's Kings of Israel Square. Rabin died of massive blood loss and a punctured lung on the operating table at Tel Aviv's Ichilov Hospital.

The assassination targets of Al Qaeda in Afghanistan and Iraq are often political rivals, mayors, military and police leaders, and especially Afghan teachers who provide an education for young girls and women. The technique is the main tool of the terrorist in countering the "hearts and minds" campaign being conducted in these two countries.

MOTIVES TO KILL THROUGHOUT HISTORY

Menace to peace and stability: Perhaps the most famous assassination in history took place on the Ides of March in 44 B.C. in the forum of the Pompeian Chamber. Julius Caesar was killed by multiple knife wounds inflicted by as many as twenty-three members of the Roman Senate, who rose in Caesar's honour when he entered the chamber. All the key conspirators had to strike at Caesar based on prior agreement.

Preaching peace: On his way to a prayer meeting on January 30, 1948, Mahatma Gandhi was shot three times in the chest, stomach, and groin at close range by a Muslim extremist named Vinayak Godse and two accomplices while passing through a crowd. Getting to within five feet of the "great soul" in order to use a .38-calibre Beretta pistol was not difficult, as it was a custom of Gandhi's to allow people to touch his garments.

Nationalism: In what would precipitate the First World War, the heir to the Austro-Hungarian throne, Archduke Franz Ferdinand, was assassinated in Serbia while travelling in a six-car procession on June 28, 1914. After surviving two attempts earlier in the day, the Archduke was shot twice by Gavrilo Princip of the Serbian Black Hand after his car had taken a wrong turn.

Traitor to the cause: Michael Collins, leader of the Irish Republican Army, was ambushed on August 22, 1922, by extremist members of the IRA because he had signed a peace accord with the British dividing the north and the south of Ireland.

Domestic politics: When he left his carriage on March 17, 1881, in St. Petersburg to assist wounded Cossacks after a bomb exploded, Russian Tsar Alexander II was killed by another bomb thrown by a member of the People's Will. The tsar was killed simply because of the position he held, not because of his policies, which were actually progressive compared to previous rulers. Abraham Lincoln was killed on April 14, 1865, by John Wilkes Booth, who initially had a plan to kidnap the American president and exchange him for a hundred thousand Southern prisoners. Five days before, however, General Robert E. Lee had surrendered on behalf of the Confederate government, and so Booth's plan changed to assassination. Prominent Communist Leon Trotsky was assassinated courtesy of Stalin and the forerunner of the KGB, the NKVD. Trotsky was at his home in Mexico on August 20, 1940, when Raymond Mercader drove an ice pick into his cranium.

Working for human rights or social change: On April 4, 1968, civil rights activist Martin Luther King was shot on the balcony of Room 306 of the Lorraine Hotel in Memphis Tennessee by a gunman using a sniper rifle.

Foreign policy disputes: Rumours abound that U.S. President John F. Kennedy was assassinated in 1963 because he had reneged on a promise to send in American carrier-based fighter-bombers to support the Bay of Pigs operation in Cuba.

Routine in wartime: During the battle of Waterloo in 1815, the Duke of Wellington turned down the offer to have the Emperor Napoleon shot by a rifleman when he showed himself close to the British battle lines. Reinhard Heydrich, reichsprotector of Czechoslovakia, was assassinated by a grenade that exploded in his open car on May 27, 1942. Heydrich later died in hospital of septicemia, and reprisals followed on June 4, when Hitler wiped an entire Czech town off the map. Hitler himself would later have a close shave with an assassin. Churchill was a target too.

There can be other reasons for assassination as well. The target may be a symbol of some sort, representing a political roadblock, or the tactic can be justified as a means of relief from the misery imposed by a brutal dictator. The killing can be inspired by a need for change based on values and ideas, to slow down a political process, to put a halt to change, or to initiate witch hunts against political opponents. Assassinations may be initiated by someone who has a mental illness or is emotionally disturbed, as was the case with John Hinkley Jr., who attempted to kill American President Ronald Reagan, or Charles Manson's pal "Squeaky," who tried the same game with Gerald Ford. They may have a desire to commit "suicide by cop" and in the process get attention or glory for killing a VIP.

CANADIAN DEATHS AND THREATS

In addition to plotting to kill Prime Minister Pierre Trudeau, the FLQ attempted to assassinate Prime Minister John Diefenbaker while he travelled on a train and Prime Minister Lester B. Pearson when he was about to travel on his private airplane.

In April 1982, Kemelettin Kani Gungor, a commercial

attaché at the Turkish Embassy in Ottawa, was shot twice as he was entering his car in the parking lot of his apartment building and left severely paralyzed. The culprits were members of the Armenian ASALA group.

On August 27, 1989, Colonel Al Attila Altikats, a Turkish military attaché, was assassinated on his way to work in Ottawa. This attack was claimed by the Justice Commandos of the Armenian Genocide, the same organization that was responsible for the 1985 hostage taking at the Turkish Embassy in Ottawa.

When British author Salman Rushdie released *The Satanic Verses* in September 1988, the Ayatollah Ruhollah Khomeni of Iran and many Muslims around the world faulted him for an irreverent depiction of the Prophet Muhammad. Rushdie's book was banned in many countries as a result, and on February 14, 1989, a fatwa was broadcast over Tehran Radio read by the ayatollah himself that set a bounty on Rushdie's head. The death threat resulted in Great Britain severing diplomatic relations with Iran (Rushdie has been in hiding for years under the protection of MI5). What followed was a series of firebombings of bookstores and publishers as well as the murder and injury of some people involved in the book's translation. In Toronto, the Canadian edition's publisher and printer received special assistance by agents (including one of the authors) who set up bomb search procedures and arranged for the purchase of specialized security equipment. Mobile patrols of facilities and other security measures were increased, and contact was established with the police and intelligence services to give quick warning of a possible attack on their facilities close to the downtown area. Luckily, no incidents took place.

Tara Singh Hayer, the publisher of the *Indo-Canadian Times*, survived one assassination attempt in 1988 but was fatally shot in November 1998 by Sikh extremists. Hayer had written sharp words on the activities of the Babbar Khalsa and the International Sikh Youth Federation.

A senior Foreign Affairs diplomat was killed and three Canadian soldiers were wounded after a suicide car bomb struck their convoy in Afghanistan on January 15, 2006. Glyn Berry had been serving as the political director of the 250-member provincial reconstruction team in Kandahar and had previously been the political section chief of Canada's UN mission in New York. Berry and the soldiers were about one kilometre from the city when a nearby vehicle-borne bomb exploded as it approached a crowded bus stop on the main road to the Canadian camp. A man claiming to speak on behalf of the Taliban claimed responsibility for the attack. Qari Mohammed Yousaf warned there are many more suicide attackers ready to go. "We will continue this strategy until all foreign forces leave Afghanistan," he told the press.

At about one in the morning on July 23, 2006, Vancouver-based carpenter Michael Frastacky was tied up and shot three times in the chest, most likely by members of the group Hezb-e Islami, according to investigators from Afghanistan's Ministry of Interior. Frastacky was in Afghanistan using his own money to build a school for both girls and boys as well as to repair an orphanage. "This murder was a political one," concluded the investigators' report.

AL QAEDA ASSASSINATIONS

Al Qaeda will continue to use assassination as a key terror tool in Afghanistan, Iraq, and across the world. In late 1994, World Trade Center bomber Mohamed Atta planned the assassination of Pope John Paul II in Manila. Early the following year, Al Qaeda also planned the assassination of President Bill Clinton in the Philippines.

AFGHANISTAN

Two days before the attacks on 9/11, the resistance leader in northern Afghanistan, Ahmed Shah Massoud, was assassinated by two suicide terrorists posing as Belgian journalists. Rumours circulated about two possible methods used: in the first, the video camera carried the explosives; and in the second, the terrorist who died initially in the blast was wearing a suicide bomb vest. The first is likely the truth, as anyone approaching Massoud was generally thoroughly searched. The blast immediately killed one assassin and Massoud's press secretary. Massoud died a few hours later, and the other terrorist was killed trying to escape. Suicide attacks were not common in Afghanistan at that time, and it had all the trademarks of Al Qaeda, who, according to the *Wall Street Journal*, committed the attack as a favour to the Taliban. This may have led to the kidnapping and eventual murder of *Wall Street Journal* reporter Daniel Pearl in Pakistan as revenge for publishing the story. There is proof that Ramzi Binalshibh, one of the top organizers of 9/11, played a role in Pearl's kidnapping and his murder after the writer's attempt to escape.

An attempted assassination of Afghan Defence Minister Mohammad Qassim Fahim was claimed by Al Qaeda in April 2002. Four people were killed and fifty injured in this Jalalabad car bomb attack. On September 18, 2004, a rocket attack on an American helicopter was made while Afghan President Hamid Karzi was aboard by three Taliban terrorists who were caught within hours. Insider information was suspected due to the attack's accuracy.

The selective assassination of schoolteachers in Afghanistan is also a grave concern. This is not an innovative Al Qaeda tactic: communist terrorists did the same in Malaysia, as did the Viet Cong in Vietnam, for the simple reason that education leads to eventual understanding and trust. With the exception of security and economics, education is the most important building block of a nation-state.

PAKISTAN

The commander of Al Qaeda's Military Committee, Khalid Sheikh Mohammed, is being held responsible for the assassination of two American officials in Karachi in March 1995, and the killing of four American oil workers there in November 1997. Both were in retaliation for the extradition to the United States of Mir Aimal Kansi, who was responsible for an attack on CIA employees at its Langley headquarters in 1993. Kansi was later executed by lethal injection in November 2002; interestingly, he had no links to Al Qaeda. Mohammed is also held responsible for the kidnapping and murder of Daniel Pearl, conducted with the assistance of the Jayash-e-Muhammad group.

On December 30, 2003, Pakistan's president General Musharraf narrowly escaped the second attempt on his life by Al Qaeda in eleven days. In this effort, two bombs went off in the city of Rawalpindi, just a minute after his motorcade had passed by, killing fifteen people and injuring forty-six others. In another case Musharraf escaped when suicide bombers rammed his motorcade with two bomb-laden cars at a gas station two kilometres from his residence in Rawalpindi, an area controlled by the Pakistani military. The general, who seized power in a bloodless coup in 1999, seems to have nine lives. An April 2002 attempt in Karachi failed because a remote-controlled device meant to detonate explosives in a car malfunctioned.

Musharraf himself has said that the latest attacks could be in response to Pakistan's role in the U.S.-led war against terrorism. He's likely right. Suicide bombings were not common in Pakistan before the increased influx of Al Qaeda terrorists there in late 2002. And since joining the fight, Pakistani security forces have captured more than five hundred suspected Al Qaeda members (including three allies close to Osama bin Laden) and handed the majority of them over to American authorities. Moreover, Al Qaeda's second-in-command, Ayman al-Zawahiri, called on Muslims in Pakistan to overthrow Musharraf for "betraying Islam" in an October 2003 broadcast on the Arab television network Al Jazeera.

IRAQ

Al Qaeda certainly has lots of help in Iraq. In early February 2003, General Shawkat Haji Mushir was assassinated with five other members of the Patriotic Union of Kurdistan. The assassins were three members of Ansar Al Islam who posed as defectors from their group. Ansar Al Islam was definitely linked to both Al Qaeda and the Mukkarrat intelligence agency of Saddam Hussein, and many of the group's members received training in Afghanistan. A former Canadian resident is a key leader with the group. Abdul Jaber (a.k.a. Abu Ossama Jaber) is deputy commander of its Yahia Ayash Battalion (named after a Hamas bomb maker known as the "Engineer" who was killed by Israeli intelligence in 1996). Just before the American intervention in Iraq, the battalion consisted of eighty terrorists including a six-man suicide squad. According to an arrested informer, Abu Abdullah Shafeh is the overall commander of Ansar Al Islam, and Mullah Krekar (who is now in the process of being deported from Norway) is the spiritual leader.

Two more of Ansar Al Islam's leaders — Abu Zurbeh, who once referred to "Uncle Saddam," and Abu Wahil — are former Iraqi intelligence officers, and the group now controls some seventeen villages near Halabja in the Shineray Mountains along the Iranian border on the Iraqi side. The leadership of this group of anywhere from five to eight hundred fighters has maintained close contact with the Al Qaeda–Zaqawi network, which includes many Egyptian Islamic Jihad members.

Targets in Iraq are similar to those in Afghanistan. On August 17, 2003, the Mosul police chief was wounded by two bullets in the leg, and attempts on the lives of Iraqi security force leaders are common. Even Iraq's American administrator, Paul Bremer, said that he escaped an assassination attempt on December 6, 2006, when his convoy hit an explosive device and came under small arms fire as it drove from Baghdad's airport. The incident occurred on the same day American Defense Secretary Donald Rumsfeld arrived there, and it was not reported to the press by Bremer's Coalition Provisional Authority.

JORDAN

On October 28, 2002, American diplomat Lawrence Foley was shot dead in front of his residence by two terrorists of the Al Qaeda front group Shurafaa Al-Urdun ("the Honourables") in Amman, Jordan. The two assassins and a third suspect were arrested. The mastermind behind the hit is believed to have been Al Qaeda's operational commander in Iraq, Abu Musab al-Zarqawi, a chemical warfare specialist who was also accused by Jordanian authorities of organizing the foiled January 2000 plot to bomb luxury hotels and bridges in Amman. Al-Zarqawi was killed in 2006 by American security forces.

GREAT BRITAIN

In the city of Birmingham, British authorities arrested nine men on January 31, 2007, for purportedly plotting an Iraqi-style assassination in their green and pleasant land. The terrorists are alleged to have intended to kidnap a British soldier of the Muslim faith and behead him with a sword for our viewing pleasure on the World Wide Web. The first British Muslim soldier to die in Afghanistan was also from Birmingham. A website run by a group known as al-Ghurabaa later posted a picture of the "traitor," Corporal Jabron Hashmi, encompassed in flames.

A section of an Al Qaeda training manual has detailed information on presidential-level bodyguarding, so the group has done its homework. In addition to its propaganda value, the assassination of key political figures could also temporarily affect the world's stock markets, causing substantial turmoil. So in the future, assassination can be viewed as a means of both political and economic attack.

Suicide assassinations were a trademark of the Tamil terrorist groups, who have seen substantial successes since 1987. Oddly, amongst the Islamic groups (with the exception of Al Qaeda), Hamas, the Palestinian Islamic Jihad, the Al-Aqsa Martyrs' Brigade, and Hezbollah have not yet used suicide bombers for assassinations, but rather have targeted the human infrastructure of Israel and its allies. But this could change. Al-Zarqawi and Al Qaeda in Iraq were the first to introduce terrorist suicide attacks and bombings to that country, and now other Islamic extremists, both Sunni and Shiite, have adopted this tactic. The methods used in either Iraq or Afghanistan soon find their ways to the other country, but it would be incorrect to say that all the suicide tactics used in Afghanistan were developed in Iraq. If anything, they are a progression of those used against the Soviet military when they occupied that country and were the targets of many of these same mujahideen. A further argument could be made that all tactics currently in use have been employed by other terrorists at some point in the past.

A former Pakistani lieutenant-general has said militants want to make that country a fortress for Jihad. One of the steps that would have to be taken would be for Al Qaeda to either scare Musharraf into inaction or kill him. Al Qaeda and their supporters are probably hoping that his replacement will be too frightened to stop them. As this may be a protracted conflict, the authors hope that this is not the case. Assassination can be an extremely effective weapon of terror. During a roundup of some Al Qaeda cells in Europe, kidnap and assassination target lists were found that included between three and four hundred names from the public and private sectors.

12: Seventy-two Virgins

INTELLIGENCE FILE 010/2007 — SUICIDE TERRORISTS —

INTRODUCTION

Will suicide terrorists strike Canada? Let's just wait and see. Such volunteers can be imported, as they were for 9/11, and it is not inconceivable that a Canadian citizen could become one, as has happened in France, Holland, Germany, and Great Britain. Past experience has shown that some would-be mujahideen from the West who have tried to enlist in the services of Al Qaeda have been urged to return to their countries of citizenship to form cells. Not all recruits will be arrested in Afghanistan like our young man from Calgary mentioned in Chapter 6. Some may return.

The tactic's use certainly predates 9/11. In the eighteenth century the Muslim communities along the Malabar Coast in India, the Atjeh in Sumatra, and the Mindanao and Sulu sects in the southern Philippines resorted to suicide attacks when faced with European colonial repression. None of these shaheed ever perceived their deaths as suicide: they saw them as acts of martyrdom in the name of their *ummah* ("people") and for the glory of God.

But suicide terrorism has never been merely the product of strong religious beliefs, Islamic or otherwise. The Kurdistan Workers' Party, the Syrian Socialist Nationalist Party, and the Tamil Tigers are groups that are not religious but have used the tactic extensively. The mindset of a suicide bomber is no different from those of Tibetan self-immolators, Irish political prisoners ready to die in a hunger strike, or dedicated terrorists worldwide who wish to live after an operation but know their chances of survival are limited. When the Japanese Red Army assaulted Ben Gurion International Airport with AK-47s and grenades on May 30, 1970, there was little chance of survival for the terrorists carrying out the attack, and that group's ideology was Marxist/Leninist.

If looked upon in this way, suicide terrorism loses its mystic power to intimidate its target audience. It is merely one type of martyrdom venerated by certain cultures or religious traditions, but rejected by others who favour different modes of the supreme sacrifice. Some are satisfied with the sacrifice of Lent; others see it as soft-core. What separates a suicide terrorist from the majority of human animals that naturally attempt to breathe under any circumstances is that the survival instinct of the individual has been suppressed.

A suicide terrorist is only the last link in a long organizational chain. Once the decision to launch a suicide attack has been made, its implementation requires at least six separate phases, including target selection, intelligence gathering, recruitment, physical and psychological training, acquisition of explosives, and transportation of the suicide bombers to the target area. Such a mission often involves dozens in direct support who have no desire to die for any cause.

All suicide bombers and their controllers know that any one incident will not lead to victory or a change in the system they are fighting. However, it will greatly assist the effort psychologically and, based on the target selected, cause serious economic or military damage in comparison to the losses suffered by the terrorist group. Suicide bombing should be considered to be an expression of resistance, one of many tactics that will be used against us. The individual bomber or group of terrorists on the one-way mission realize that martyrdom is even more important than victory because they will reach paradise or be seen as heroes who died for the cause.

Kamikaze, or "the divine wind," was the name given to a typhoon that destroyed an invading Mongol fleet attempting to cross the Sea of Japan in 1281, and it later became the name of a group of suicide pilots in the Second World War. And long after the Battle of the Pacific, the mention of the word invokes not only fear but also thoughts of heroism in the minds of even Japan's former enemies. Loyalty and obedience are significant facets of the Bushido code, the ancient laws of the Japanese warrior, and it was considered an honour to give your life for the emperor and for the country. Parts of the Bushido tradition and the Japanese Shinto faith also emphasize the importance of meeting ancestors in heaven and of setting a good example to others who will follow. Shame and guilt awaited the kamikaze pilot if he did not die for some reason, and from October 25, 1944, to the Japanese surrender less than a year later, approximately two thousand of them did. There were shortages of planes to fly, but not of volunteers.

The kamikaze pilots were organized into units known as *tokubetsu kogeki tai* ("special attack groups") who flew supported by non-suicide fighters. When Vice Admiral Takijiro Onishi, commander of the Japanese garrison in the Philippines, first employed the strategy the purpose was twofold: to destroy the U.S. Pacific fleet and to weaken American morale by demonstrating determination. They were successful in the latter. Suicide tactics demonstrate determination of the weak, and it does weaken the morale of its target. Some kamikaze pilots were only fourteen years old, and this fact was not lost on American sailors.

While there are many examples of suicide in both conventional and unconventional warfare, here are some more from the twentieth century:

- In the 1904–05 Russo-Japanese War, Japanese sword fighters attacked machine gun emplacements, much to the surprise of the Russian gunners.
- Polish cavalry charged headlong into German Panzer tanks during the outbreak of the Second World War.
- During the height of the Cold War, many partisans in Eastern European countries engaged in extremely high-risk operations against the security forces of the former Soviet Union, in which they stood little or no chance of surviving.

There are three key factors that are the same in these examples and in the concepts of jihad and shaheed of Islamic extremists. First, death was accepted by the combatants as pretty much their fate upon entering the battle. Second, they held very strongly to principle of sacrificing one's life for the community. Third, the events occurred during a time of declared war or during unconventional war where one side does not accept the declaration of the underdog for fear of giving them a sense of legitimacy in the eyes of others. The key to remember is that jihad can take conventional or unconventional forms; it appears that our enemy understands this, but many in the West do not.

The Iran-Iraq war in the early 1980s produced the first Iranian suicide soldiers, some as young as ten years old, who in turn convinced the Iranian religious leadership of the tactic's value. The Iranian Revolutionary Guard passed on the concept and practical training to different terrorist groups operating in the Bekka Valley of Lebanon. This manifested itself into the series of suicide bombings mentioned in Chapter 3 that ushered in the modern era of complex terrorism. At about the same time, the Tamil Tigers pioneered the use of a lone bomber in a suicide vest and passed on their expertise to the Hezbollah group in Lebanon. It was there that suicide tactics were refined throughout the 1980s, and about fifty such bombings were carried out in the next two decades, mostly by Hezbollah.

It's an idea that really caught on. As of 2003 there had been well over three hundred suicide attacks carried out in fourteen countries by seventeen terrorist organizations. Hezbollah's success in this sphere was mostly in achieving respect: the "martyrs" of the group became symbols of sacrifice and a source of inspiration for terrorists all over the world. In addition to Al Qaeda, there are many groups in the Middle East that use suicide tactics today, including the PFLP, Hamas, the Egyptian Islamic Jihad, the Palestinian Islamic Jihad, and the Al-Aqsa Martyrs' Brigade, to mention just a few. On January 27, 2002, the first female Palestinian suicide bomber to strike within Israel killed one and wounded forty others in Jerusalem. The tactic's popularity continues to spread.

REASONS AND MOTIVATIONS

In many cases, the justifications for suicide acts by terrorist organizations are based not on fact but on perceptions of current realities, and mistakes in perception can happen with the introduction of an ideology, including religion. This is what makes religious-based suicide terrorism so hard to counter. Provided there are enough recruits, the pragmatic reasons for most groups adopting this method of attack are when the organization has a need for increased media attention or when it feels that conventional methods are not working.

The big motivators in suicide terrorism are shame, monetary gain for the recruit's family, a strong belief in the cause (possibly combined with other religious beliefs), and revenge. Of all these motivations the last two are generally the strongest. In some cases it is possible to threaten a potential recruit's family or other loved ones, and there can be such a thing as a suicide terrorist who is mentally disturbed, but it would be rare. In some cases, parents counsel their sons to become martyrs. On April 20, 2004, it was reported in the press that the Canadian Children's Aid Society was looking into whether Maha Khadr and her late husband, Ahmed Khadr, inflicted child abuse by counselling their youngest son, Abdul Karim, to be a terrorist. His brother Abdurahman has admitted to having been sat down by his father on at least three occasions for that purpose.

PREPARATION OF THE MIND DURING RECRUITMENT

The recruitment process includes specific psychological preparation before selection. For most groups this can include exposing the recruits to posters of dead suicide bombers, participating in funeral processions for them, and mourning their deaths for three days. Inspiration is also found from praise for such endeavours in certain mosques, shrines, and museums dedicated to the fallen and in promotional graffiti painted on walls. University campuses in Gaza are often decorated with pictures of suicide terrorists who have died, and videotapes of suicide attacks and roadside bombs are common. Other seeds are planted in the recruit as well: once you join you have one foot in the grave and the other in prison. Grey propaganda also plays a key role. The media are informed that there are hundreds already prepared to die — which may be true, but they are not yet psychologically prepared to carry out the act.

Surreptitious questioning to confirm the candidate's characteristics is conducted before an approach is ever made. The recruit is often encouraged to join the terrorists; when told that he has already been personally selected for a suicide mission, it is then harder to say no. Surprisingly, brainwashing (or mental programming, as it is sometimes called) is not employed in the development of suicide terrorists.

Brainwashing involves sleep deprivation, extreme food rationing, the use of specific drugs, sensory stimulation and deprivation, and the manipulation of feelings of guilt and fear in the target. This is combined with the possible use of humiliation and the destruction of self-esteem and a form of surreptitious hypnosis to alter a belief system before giving the target a new identity. While there are different paths a suicide terrorist can take within different groups, all of them reinforce what the volunteer already has, as opposed to creating a different identity.

REPETITIOUS LAST RITES

Rituals are a part of the traditions that tie a suicide terrorist to not only those who have gone before him but also those who will follow. The kamikaze fighters had what was called a pre-battle drill before dying for their emperor and country. This consisted of a very repetitious daily routine and certain customs just before the final send-off. Pilots would don a white headscarf emblazoned with an image of the rising sun and have a "belt of a thousand stitches" wound around their waists. (A different woman had woven each stitch of these belts.) This was followed by the drinking of a cup of sake and the composition and recital of a "death" poem — similar to Samurai traditions prior to hara-kiri.

Terrorist groups' mental preparation for suicide attacks may differ in technique, but not in spirit. Palestinian "martyrs" often wear white silk death shrouds and sleep in cemeteries, and they are told that death is a privilege. They are only upholding the ideals of the dead by joining in the same fate. The idea of meeting fate instead of waiting for it (and perhaps not getting into heaven) sounds reasonable. Note that the term "suicide bomber" is never used by any Muslim terrorist group; the suicide terrorist is a shaheed or "martyr." Shaheed are also shown videos of those that have gone before, and they must be filmed in a swearing-in ceremony as well as a last will video that states their personal, as well as the group's, reasons for the attack. A photo of the shaheed is taken that will be used at his funeral and for posters that will be distributed and plastered on walls in the streets and inside mosques. For the most part, the recruit is never ordered to do anything; he is a volunteer and therefore is treated as one. Money may be promised for the suicide bomber's family or to pay off debts beforehand. The candidate is also given practical training with weapons in order to protect himself if intercepted before he can strike.

While the practice is not allowed by all terrorist groups, Al Qaeda bombers spend their last night before an attack with other suicide operatives. Final letters to loved ones may also be prepared the night before, and quotes from the Koran are altered or used to suit terrorist purposes and reinforce the beliefs of the shaheed. The idea that a martyr is not dead but is alive with Allah is common and an easy concept to reinforce. When the time comes, the suicide attack is videotaped to use as propaganda, not only for the media but also for new recruits.

BLACK WIDOWS

In June 2000, Chechen militants fighting against the Russian army joined the current circle of suicide bombers. To date, the Chechens have carried out at least seven suicide attacks, in which more than one hundred Russian soldiers and police officers have been killed and scores more wounded. Many of these Chechen operations have included females known by a macabre moniker: the Black Widows.

In a theatre just several blocks from the Kremlin in downtown Moscow, approximately 50 terrorists held more than 850 people hostage for three days beginning on October 23, 2002. Eighteen of the terrorists were female suicide bombers — widows who had lost their husbands during the Russian-Chechen conflict. It was time for some payback. Their key demand was that the Russian military leave Chechen territory. Note that it is not permitted by Islam for a woman to participate in armed conflict, let alone be a martyr in the traditional sense. These women were driven by a blood feud of revenge sharpened by conditions of economic desolation. It should be remembered that Adat, the Chechen code of revenge for the sake of honour, is more important to this people than any religious motivation. In fact, Adat has been in existence longer than Islam.

The Moscow theatre siege ended with the tragic deaths of 129 hostages. Ironically, these were not caused by the detonation of bombs that the Chechen women were carrying, but rather from the toxic effects of the nerve gas that was used by Russian security forces to "knock out" the terrorists. In the chaotic aftermath, doctors did not know what kind of gas was used and could not treat the injured appropriately. Strangely, the Chechens had several minutes in which to detonate their bombs, but did not do so. Here are some more examples of the Black Widows in action.

- On May 12, 2003, a truck with a woman and two other Chechens aboard smashed through the barrier in front of the State Administrative Building in the city of Znamenskoye, near Grozny. The truck was carrying five tonnes of explosives, and the target was the headquarters of Russian counter-intelligence unit FSB. Fifty-nine people were killed in this attack.
- In an attempt to kill the chairman of the pro-Moscow United Russia Party on May 14, 2003, two female suicide bombers with bombs hidden under their clothes mixed with people at a celebration for the Prophet Muhammad's birthday in Ilaskham-Yurt, east of Grozny. Fourteen people were killed, but not the chairman, who failed to show up.
- On June 5, 2003, a female suicide bomber killed eighteen members of the Russian Air Force in Mosdock, North Ossetia, while they were on their way to work. The Black Widow was disguised as a nurse and signalled a passing bus to stop. Once aboard, she detonated her explosives.

It's important to keep in mind that Al Qaeda is still participating in the fighting against Russian troops in Chechnya. Both they and other Arabs from the Gulf States fighting there are known as the Wahhabites by local Chechens. And while they are only several hundred strong, due to their level of experience many have achieved key positions in the command structure of the Chechen rebel forces.

INSIDE AL QAEDA OPS

The suicide terrorists of 9/11 came from four different countries and were not hermits, deranged, or poor. They led normal lives and were well-educated, many of them in the West. None were personally subjugated by a foreign power. They also had another thing in common besides being Muslim. They believed that they were stronger than their enemy because in their eyes the people of modern Western society seem to value their own lives above anything else. This they considered our greatest weakness and the reason for the eventual victory of their struggle. The 9/11 terrorists were prepared to die for what they believed in.

As is well known, Al Qaeda conducts recruiting for suicide terrorist operations in the madrassas and in their own military camps and organization. Al Qaeda also accepts "volunteers of opportunity," people who often come from the West to volunteer for jihad but then are talked into volunteering for suicide attacks in their land of origin instead. Suicide terrorists are often selected because they have not been registered on any black list. If genuine documents are used for operations, it cuts down the chances of discovery, but if old passports are stamped and indicate former places of travel (and possibly of training), they are exchanged for new ones. If several suicide terrorists are to be used, each has his own bank account for the operation. A legitimate bank card allows for cash withdrawals, and accounts in the target country or one that will be used as a transit point are opened up from overseas. Credit and ATM cards are obtained from overseas and can be mailed or sent by courier.

These operatives travel in a roundabout way to get to the target country, mixing their means of transport, which makes any investigation after an incident more difficult. They are ordered to keep a low profile and to build up their physical strength. They are even allowed to join a gym or a dojo to get in shape as well as to learn or maintain fighting skills. If anything is required for the operation it is bought very shortly beforehand to avoid having any evidence on the terrorists if they are captured: necessary pieces of kit are often very good indicators of the target to be hit. As well, before purchasing anything a pretext for the item's use must be ready if the terrorists are questioned. Web gear to hold explosives comfortably or to allow a bomb to be concealed is always of a special design. Often individuals carry at least a pistol for personal defence to allow them a fighting chance to achieve their objective if challenged. If discovered, their goal is to ensure the death of as many of the security forces or the enemy civilian population as possible.

Shortly before an attack takes place a direct support cell arrives to set things up. This cell provides weapons, transportation, and safe houses if need be. In some cases, Al Qaeda suicide terrorists are self-contained and need no external direct support cell for assistance. The suicide terrorist only arrives at the required time after all arrangements have been completed. Obviously, no exfiltration is required in suicide ops, and there is very little chance of being caught and interrogated.

Suicide terrorists can operate alone, in pairs, or in greater numbers as they did in 9/11, and their popularity is growing. In addition to an assassination attempt on Uzbekistan's President Islam Karimov by an Al Qaeda associate group on April 3, 2004, Al Qaeda also has attempted to assassinate the Pakistani president more than once, as was highlighted in the last chapter. In addition, Turkish security forces arrested nine suspects on May 3, 2004, for plotting a suicide bombing against the leaders of NATO during a summit in Istanbul. Among the items later seized during the raids that rounded up sixty-nine suspects were bomb-making equipment and books, forged identity documents, and CDs that served as training manuals. The terrorists are alleged to belong to Ansar Al Islam, a group suspected of bombing two Istanbul synagogues, a London-based bank, and the British Consulate in Istanbul, killing about sixty people.

In June 2007, *ABC News* in the United States released video footage of an apparent Taliban graduation ceremony of about three hundred jihadists prepared to embark on suicide bombing campaigns in Europe and North America. As he stood congratulating each team assigned to different countries, their leader, Mansoor Dadullah, said, "These Americans, Canadians, British, and Germans come here to Afghanistan from faraway places. Why shouldn't we go after them?"

When questioned, the Canadian minister of Public Safety told reporters, "The Taliban are aware that our troops cannot be intimidated ... so they are trying, through public relations means, to worry the hearts of Canadians at home." He is right. At this time, the event delivers not much beyond propaganda value for Al Qaeda. If the jihadists have been recruited locally, they best serve the cause on the killing fields of Afghanistan. But if the group contained any Westerners, why would Al Qaeda waste them over there?

Terrorist infiltration is a slow process that can take up to three years to complete, so we can't say what the gravity of this threat is at the present time. But it confirms that we are still in their thoughts. According to *ABC News*, a few days earlier Pakistani authorities had arrested three foreign nationals attempting to leave the country. In addition to radios, documents, and equipment, two of them were carrying German passports.

INTELLIGENCE COMMENTS

"Martyrdom" operations are spreading. The recruiting of suicide terrorists is easier than you may think — the worldwide Muslim ummah numbers more than 1.3 billion people. In places like Afghanistan and Iraq, Al Qaeda has adopted a similar strategy to Hamas in that they build five to nine bombs per week, one for each part of the country they operate in. These bombs are often inexpensive, especially if the explosives can be scrounged from the military surplus of previous conflicts, which is often the case in both these countries. The average cost to Al Qaeda or the Taliban is estimated at only $150 for each device; the major expense in suicide terrorism is actually providing for the family of the "martyr," and for posters, ceremonies, and propaganda video production.

On October 1, 2001, a suicide bombing occurred in the state legislative assembly in Srinagar, India. The purpose was mass assassination, and responsibility was claimed by the Jaish-e-Mohammed group. At least twenty-nine people were killed and more than sixty wounded in what one Indian official stated was "an attack on democracy." Then on December 13 of that year, the Indian Parliament was hit in a similar fashion with the same intent. A forty-five-minute gun battle left nine victims dead before the five terrorists were killed. The terrorists' vehicle had all the proper security passes, and they entered through the VIP gates. More than two hundred politicians were inside the building at the time.

We must prepare for such attacks in Canada. The belief that it cannot possibly happen here is about as useful a notion as a faith that New York's twin towers could never collapse and that the Pentagon is impregnable. Instead, we have Canadian academics attending conferences that theorize that the United States was complicit in the events of 9/11, or indeed that the whole day was orchestrated by that country as a pretext to remake the world in its own image.

It's time to for such Canadians to get a grip on real life. There are three main reasons for suicide terrorist operations. First, they make strikes like 9/11 possible; for the attack to succeed terrorists must die in the process. Second, this twist makes the terrorist act more spectacular for the media, and that in turn generates more publicity, which means increased recruitment and support from the political arm. Third, they show the determination and commitment of the terrorist to their enemies and others that do not support their cause.

Perhaps most importantly when looking at this problem, there has been a disturbing trend overseas of a multitude of attempted and successful suicide assassinations of lesser government officials in Afghanistan and in Iraq. Such incidents have mostly gone under-reported due to the fact that they did not involve NATO or American troops. In 2004, there were only six suicide bombings in Afghanistan. A year later there were 21, and last year there were 136 attacks that killed 344 and wounded more than 500 more. The most troubling trend is the use of children in this method.

Over the past two decades, Western governments have often used the term "peacekeeping" to mask the realities of UN operations in zones of full-fledged combat between adversaries in order to tone down the conflicts so their citizens will give support for limited participation. This inability of political will to state the truth has led to major fiascos such as Somalia and Rwanda, as well as great hardships on other UN missions. Understating the threat of terrorism to the Canadian public follows this trend, as security efforts are constantly undermined by trying to make the problem appear to be less serious than it really is.

13: The Threat

"Our society is Al Qaeda's ultimate target."

For some time now there has been, to use noted libertarian author William F. Buckley Jr.'s phrase, "an upwardly mobile cliché going the rounds" in the pages of certain Canadian newspapers that take themselves too seriously when ensconced in the war on terror's big-think department. As posited in our country's largest daily, a "Canadian way forward" from today's dilemma would be based upon "the rule of law and an effective multilateral system, with the UN system at its core." Such attitudinal sunshine was proposed after the editorial page editor emeritus had told his readers that because most of the rationales offered for today's threat — such as austere interpretations of the Islamic faith, the influence of madrassas, and the lure of seventy-two virgins — have been found wanting, we need a "reality check on terrorism."

How's this for reality: shortly after Black September's Munich massacre, Buckley was on a rare learning curve when working as an American delegate to the UN's General Assembly. Together with a few allies, the United States was trying to pass a resolution condemning terrorism and had decided upon a definition of what the term actually means. But the ambassador from Saudi Arabia desired the following amendment to its title: "Measures to prevent terrorism and other forms of violence which endanger or take innocent lives or jeopardize fundamental freedoms, and study of the underlying causes of those forms of terrorism and acts of violence which lie in misery, frustration, grievance and despair and which cause some people to sacrifice human lives, including their own in an attempt to effect radical changes."

We're not finished yet. After that hasty note was added, the ambassador from Algeria (yet another bastion of democracy) demanded that the resolution also include the following qualifying sentence: "When people engage in violent action against colonialist, racist, alien regimes as part of a struggle to retain its legitimate rights or to redress an injustice of which it is a victim, the international community, when it has recognized the validity of these actions, cannot take repressive measures against any action which it ought, on the contrary, to encourage support, and defend."

With all due respect to the aforementioned editorial page editor, it doesn't look like the United Nations can help us very much with terrorism. (For more on austere religious interpretations assisting terrorists and on the influence of maddresses in spreading Islamic extremism, see Chapter 6. For more on the motivations of suicide bombers, see Chapter 12.)

Terrorism may be an incredibly difficult concept to understand, but our society is Al Qaeda's ultimate target, and our problems won't go away by simply abandoning Afghanistan to sort itself out on its own. The North American mainland was hit by Al Qaeda long before Canada had boots on the ground in Asia, and despite what some of the elite say, that sort of pusillanimous political behaviour emboldens terrorists and others who play in the real world. A civic Canadian way forward in the war on terror must include the sword as well as the rule of law.

To briefly recap, Al Qaeda was established in the late 1980s to bring together Arabs who fought in Afghanistan against the Soviet Union. As a result, its members have had years of preparation and experience in both terrorism and guerrilla warfare. The leadership consists of war-tested veterans whose combat experience has been gained since 1980 in places such as Chechnya, Bosnia, Kosovo, Uzbekistan, Azerbaijan, Turkmenistan, Georgia, Somalia, Sudan, Eritrea, the Philippines, Indonesia, Kashmir, and Iraq. These locales cover not only widely differing terrain but also various enemies fought and tactics used, making Al Qaeda's membership not only experienced but also very flexible.

Al Qaeda is also much more dangerous than previous terrorist groups because while operating as MAK, the organization had received training at a very high level from Pakistani intelligence. In addition, defectors to Al Qaeda from the intelligence services of the Afghan puppet state following the Soviet withdrawal all had training from the KGB. This added more expertise to the group's intelligence collection and analysis capabilities. These two facts alone make Al Qaeda an extremely sophisticated threat.

The bank accounts of well-established terrorist groups have always run into the millions of dollars. Organizations' financing includes illegally obtained funds as well as monies from legitimate financial investments and businesses. Al Qaeda's financial support operations are currently being reorganized to include more criminal activity, especially as a means of financing tactical operations. Any remaining assets that haven't been frozen by various governments are also being transferred and reorganized.

Due to the cyclical nature of terrorism, there will be lulls between violent incidents, but that hardly means Al Qaeda has turned the other cheek. Al Qaeda is focused. There will also be mergers of terrorist groups around the world as operations by Western governments, especially by the U.S., take effect. The principles of terrorist generations, merger, and spread are part of the reason the Americans have said that any war on terror will be lengthy. Al Qaeda has already merged with other groups to form an umbrella organization, giving it more resources and a better ability to operate between countries.

Countries that sponsor terrorism provide money; places for training, operating bases, and R&R; intelligence information; documents for travel; and weapons and explosives. States such as Iran and the Sudan are key facilitators to the survival and operation of terrorist groups. They provide specialist training otherwise not available and the facilities to do this training properly. Terrorist groups also train each other, the connecting factor usually being the intelligence service of a sponsor state. Select terrorists receive the same level of training as would a government agent, making them extremely difficult to locate and apprehend.

Bases in chaotic states like Afghanistan, Iraq, and Somalia, or in terrorist-tolerant states like Syria and Lebanon, give safe haven and are a part of state sponsorship that must be addressed by Western governments. Regimes that currently tolerate terrorism against our society — toward its citizens, its property, or its value systems — must be forced to choose sides.

Terrorist sponsor states can play a large part in providing propaganda to garner political, financial, material, and technical support. The strongest propaganda is the direct action of a terrorist attack. The second strongest is a video or tape recording. Sponsor states and their intelligence services often teach sophisticated propaganda techniques to the terrorists they shelter. All terrorist groups, no matter what their level of maturity, use propaganda techniques, but many members of the media who report on the subject unfortunately do not seem to realize this.

Al Qaeda is currently regrouping into new cells, and recruitment and training is now being concentrated in urban centres around the world. Urban safe houses are being organized to provide terrorist training schools, and new final selection criteria may be developed for Al Qaeda recruits as a result. These criteria will be based on the area of operation and time available and will make infiltration of the groups even more difficult.

Cells in more rural environments continue to be organized, especially in Southeast Asia and the Horn of Africa, and based on the large Muslim population along Africa's east coast, more cells and training bases will likely be organized there for future operations

Broad-based support infrastructures for terrorists still exist and can be at least partially used by any group. Terrorists often maintain contact with organized crime, black market operators, smugglers, and gunrunners; their infrastructure can be as large as that of a multinational corporation. Links with new criminal gangs will be established as Al Qaeda cells push out into new territory and countries. In Western countries especially, Al Qaeda will likely not identify themselves when conducting such dealings. In the past, organized crime has often assisted their respective governments in their security efforts so that activity could return to "normal." Prolonged police crackdowns are generally not appreciated by criminal organizations: they can be as bad for business as the aftermath of a terrorist attack.

Al Qaeda continues to plan and prepare for more terrorist acts against the West and to support operations in Afghanistan and Iraq. While dead terrorists are being replaced with new but less experienced ones, a wider regeneration is in progress as Muslims throughout the world become more politicized. Experts call this the cockroach factor, due to the seemingly impossible task of eliminating those pests. Al Qaeda continues to have a broad-based ideological appeal and a diverse membership that blurs both class and ethnic boundaries.

Even though the military arm of Al Qaeda has been severely damaged in the past five years, the political arm of this pseudo-Islamic movement has not been influenced by a strong "hearts and minds" campaign from the West or from moderate Islam. So with continued strikes or even unsuccessful attempts, Al Qaeda will have no problems with continued recruitment.

In North America, the recruitment of Muslims in the prison community by sympathetic mullahs will probably show results in the next several years, and it would be wise to remember lessons learned from the IRA and Red Brigade campaigns, in which these groups used their environment while incarcerated to recruit and train new members. Black American Muslims who join the jihad will have even stronger racial reasons for doing so than those from an Arab or Middle Eastern ethnic background. Watch for Al Qaeda interaction with fringe African-American groups on the horizon. The continued recruitment of Caucasians to the Al Qaeda cause can also be expected: the ability to melt into the milieu of Europe or North America has many obvious advantages.

Western media often forget that Al Qaeda is just one group in an international network, so links with new terrorist entities due to religious appeal should be anticipated. Due to the number of contacts still to be made and the resources required to influence all of them, it will be a slow process, however, and not everyone will want to partner with Al Qaeda. But the organization is capable of establishing contact with even a non-Islamic terrorist group if mutual benefit is seen, and especially if their respective enemies are perceived to be the same to some degree.

Note that future growth will also entail greater risk of infiltration into Al Qaeda through new member groups, but the effort could be worthwhile. Historically, security forces have often infiltrated and decimated terrorist groups that expanded too quickly. Associate and allied groups will probably continue to mount lesser regional and local operations to maintain pressure on targeted governments. It is expected that these groups will be able to mount large operations in the near future, as independent action by network membership is encouraged at the lower levels of Al Qaeda.

The possibility of sleeper cells in North America and Europe — through the infiltration of trained terrorists in the guise of refugees arriving as complete family units — has already been raised by different intelligence services. With enough time, multinational cells based on common languages will probably develop. Sleeper cells have been created in the past in the United States and Canada by terrorist groups such as ASALA and by intelligence agencies such as the Cuban DGI, the Soviet KGB, and the Czech STB. The most important asset for such cells is simply patience. On February 11, 2003, while presenting an unclassified report to the Senate Intelligence Committee, the CIA stated that several hundred Al Qaeda terrorists had the required backgrounds to be capable of conducting terrorism in North America. In addition, independent terrorist actions by individuals or small groups that believe in the ideology of Al Qaeda have already happened in California and Jordan. These so-called copycat crimes could increase over time — and keep in mind that individual terrorists have struck Canada in the past.

Kidnappings are very common in other parts of the world and are initiated not only as propaganda by deed but sometimes to fund terrorist groups. Tourists, foreign workers, and business people, as well as the corporations they work for, are considered wealthy and legitimate targets for kidnappers. Al Qaeda cells in Europe were found with a kidnap list of more than four hundred names made up of various politicians and CEOs.

Skyjacking has taken a new twist with the arrival of complex terrorism. When a person is skyjacked today, survival may be dependent on the whether the terrorist wants to use the passengers as a bargaining chip or the plane as a weapon. These days physical resistance must be considered part of surviving.

Hostage takings and assassinations of well-known people automatically get wide press coverage, and the killing of a key government figure could affect the world's stock markets, making assassination a means of both political and economic attack. Suicide assassinations (a successful trademark for Tamil terrorists) could also be carried out by Al Qaeda and its affiliates, making spectacular headlines around the world.

Conventional terrorist groups will continue using bombs, which are another key tool in Al Qaeda's arsenal. Threats play a crucial role in any war of nerves and will continue to be used by all Al Qaeda–linked terrorist groups because of the great effect they have and the low cost, low security, and minimal effort required to place them. Al Qaeda will use ambush and sniping attacks to inflict casualties when terrorist cells do not have the training or weapons to conduct larger operations. An atomic bomb is unlikely to be in terrorist hands today, but the manufacture of a dirty bomb is possible over time with enough effort and good cell security. Chemical and biological attacks are also possible, and talk of this is not idle chatter.

Al Qaeda's strategic operations against the West continue to be run in a project management style. Its targets and style of operations have not changed in the past five years, based on the intelligence available. But soon the Al Qaeda network may widen its selection of targets and means: there are numerous choices in both Europe and North America, and many do not have any security measures in place. Future tactics could include the destruction of priceless works of art or historical monuments that represent Western civilization. The Fuerzas Armadas de Liberación Nacional raided an exhibition of art in Venezuela and stole a painting back in 1963. Such attacks could also cause numerous casualties, affect the economy of the targeted country, and be sensational for propaganda purposes.

The infiltration of military, security, and intelligence services is a terrorist tactic used around the world, and it is no different here in Canada. The FLQ infiltrated units of both the regular and reserve ground forces as well as the Royal Canadian Air Force. Before a dishonourable discharge, Brent Taylor of Direct Action trained with the Canadian Armed Forces, as did one of the suspects in Toronto 17 case. This tactic needs close monitoring, especially if security checks on recruits are being waived in an effort to replenish a depleted military, as some press reports have indicated.

Al Qaeda will strike again, and attacks against Canada are inevitable (see Appendix II). The terrorist must maintain momentum or lose credibility. And based on the many military, political, social, and economic grievances currently held by Islamic fundamentalists, as well as the role of ideological extremism, there seems to be no shortage of recruits and suicide bombers. As of July 2007, Al Qaeda was still pursuing weapons of mass destruction and had restored its safe havens in certain areas of Pakistan. It replaced senior leaders eliminated by counterterrorist action and replaced and developed the group's operational lieutenants. Sponsor funding from Saudi Arabia had not been curtailed, and the increased opium production in Afghanistan placed more money into the group's hands. Al Qaeda continues to actively recruit and train, and there is an increased threat of homegrown terrorism in Europe, especially Great Britain. In addition, there is a growing extremist brand of Islam in North America, and some feel the group appears to be positioning operatives for strikes overseas.

We are faced with perhaps our greatest enemy since the Second World War: it will take all of our resources, stamina, and discipline to face it. We will all be at war against terrorism for the rest of our lives. It is perfectly clear that eventually Al Qaeda or its break-off groups will in time employ improvised NBC weapons, as well as more violent types of complex terrorism. The Canadian military must therefore be prepared to provide massive aid to the civil power when the time comes.

As a country, we must psychologically prepare ourselves to expect casualties overseas and at home for many years. As Al Qaeda and other terrorist organizations transform, they will become even more ruthless. We must prepare to defend ourselves. The Canadian pyjama party is over.

Appendix I:
Outlawed Terrorist Groups in Canada

Source: *Ministry of Public Safety, November 1996*

Abu Nidal Organization (ANO)

Also Known As

Fatah Revolutionary Council, Revolutionary Council, Revolutionary Council of Fatah, Al-Fatah Revolutionary Council, Fatah — the Revolutionary Council, Black June, Arab Revolutionary Brigades, Revolutionary Organization of Socialist Muslims, Black September, Egyptian Revolution, Arab Fedayeen Cells, Palestine Revolutionary Council, Organization of Jund al Haq

Description

The Abu Nidal Organization is an international terrorist organization founded by Sabri al-Banna (a.k.a. Abu Nidal) that has a demonstrated ability to carry out terrorist attacks throughout the Middle East, Asia, South America, and Europe. The main goal of the ANO is the destruction of Israel and the creation of an independent Palestinian state. The ANO has utilized many methods to further its cause, including bombings, hijackings, assassinations, and armed attacks against civilians. In total, it has carried out more than ninety terrorist attacks in twenty countries, killing approximately three hundred people. Its philosophy is purely rejectionist in that it refuses to countenance any type of compromise with Israel. The ANO is known for the brutality and indiscriminate nature of its attacks, as well as careful planning and execution.

Date Listed
February 12, 2003

Date Reviewed*
November 9, 2006

Abu Sayyaf Group (ASG)

Also Known As
Al Harakat Al Islamiyya (AHAI), Al Harakat-ul Al Islamiyya, Al-Harakatul-Islamia, Al Harakat Al Aslamiya, Abou Sayaf Armed Band (ASAB), Abu Sayaff Group, Abu Sayyef Group, Mujahideen Commando Freedom Fighters (MCFF)

Description
The Abu Sayyaf Group is the smallest and most radical of the Islamist separatist groups fighting to establish an Iranian-style Islamic state in Mindanao, an island in the southern Philippines. ASG activities include bombings, assassinations, kidnappings, and extortion from companies and wealthy businessmen in order to attain their aims. Its targets are primarily security forces, foreign priests and religious figures, and Christian populations. The ASG has gained international notoriety for kidnapping foreigners. Abu Sayyaf declared it would continue kidnapping American nationals if the government refused to grant the ASG a separate homeland and the U.S. did not withdraw support for Israel. ASG ideology is not predicated simply on demands for regional autonomy or independence for Mindanao; instead, it espouses Al Qaeda's line on the need for relentless struggle to achieve the global domination of radical Islam.

Date Listed
February 12, 2003

Date Reviewed
November 9, 2006

Al Jihad (AJ)
Also Known As
Egyptian Islamic Jihad (EIJ)

Description
The Al Jihad, founded during the 1970s, claims to offer a remedy for Egypt's social, economic, and political problems by challenging the current Egyptian government. The group employs terrorism in an attempt to overthrow the current government and replace it with an Islamic state. The AJ has been actively involved in terrorism since its inception, including the assassination of then Egyptian President Anwar Sadat in 1981. AJ activity outside of Egypt has included involvement in the two 1998 U.S. Embassy bombings in Africa in which some AJ members were indicted by the U.S. The group has links with Osama bin Laden and Al Qaeda, and is also a signatory to the 1998 fatwa against the U.S. and Israel.

Date Listed
November 2002

Date Reviewed*
November 9, 2006

Al Qaeda
Description
Al Qaeda is the central component of a network of Sunni Islamic extremist groups associated with Osama bin Laden, which functions as an umbrella organization, with branches in the Middle East, Africa, Central Asia, and North America. Al Qaeda is committed to overthrowing secular governments in Islamic countries and using force to eliminate all Western influences in such countries. Bin Laden, and those within his network, believe that the only way these goals can be achieved is through violence and terrorist activities up to and including martyrdom. The bin Laden network has been directly or indirectly associated with the 1998 bombings of two U.S. embassies, the 2000 bombing of the USS *Cole*, and the 2001 World Trade Center and Pentagon attacks.

Date Listed
November 2002

*Date Reviewed**
November 9, 2006

Al-Aqsa Martyrs' Brigade (AAMB)

Also Known As
Al-Aqsa Intifada Martyrs' Group, Al-Aqsa Brigades, Martyrs of al-Aqsa group, Al-Aqsa Martyrs Battalion, Armed Militias of the Al-Aqsa Martyr Battalions

Description
The Al-Aqsa Martyrs' Brigade is an armed faction comprised of an unknown number of small cells of Fatah-affiliated Islamic nationalists. It emerged following the outbreak of the Palestinian-Israeli clashes in September 2000 and consists of local clusters of armed activists. The AAMB aims to drive the Israeli military and settlers from the West Bank, Gaza Strip, and Jerusalem, to end the Israeli occupation, and to establish an independent and sovereign Palestinian state. During the period from September 30, 2000, to August 31, 2002, the AAMB claimed responsibility for some sixteen attacks, twelve of which were against civilian targets. In these twelve attacks, 38 people were killed, including 36 civilians, and the number of wounded was estimated, at a minimum, at 435. The AAMB has also claimed responsibility for at least twelve of the thirty-eight suicide bombing attacks against Israeli civilians during the January to August 2002 period. Early in January 2003, a foreign agency concluded that the AAMB was becoming more organized, resilient, and co-ordinated. Later in January 2003, the AAMB indicated that they had decided to pursue the intifada and would continue suicide operations.

Date Listed
April 2, 2003

*Date Reviewed**
November 9, 2006

Al-Gama'a al-Islamiyya (AGAI)

Also Known As
Islamic Group (IG)

Description

The AGAI strives to violently overthrow the current Egyptian government and replace it with a state governed by Islamic law. It is one of the largest and most extreme Egyptian terrorist groups. The AGAI specializes in armed attacks against government and security officials, Western tourists, and any others believed to be opponents of an Islamic state in Egypt. The group has been described as having links to the network of Osama bin Laden and signed his February 23, 1998, fatwa against the United States and Israel saying it was the individual duty of all Muslims to kill American citizens and their allies, civilian or military, wherever possible.

Date Listed
November 2002

Date Reviewed*
November 9, 2006

Al-Ittihad Al-Islam (AIAI)

Description

The AIAI is an internationally established Islamist organization that engages in terrorism in Somalia and Ethiopia. Guided by the goal of creating an Islamist theocracy based on Islamic law, the AIAI's objective is the unification of all Muslims in the region under the banner of creating a "greater Somalia." To achieve this goal, the AIAI is committed to using indiscriminate terror tactics, including the targeting of foreigners and political leaders of foreign states. The AIAI has ties with states that are known to support terrorism and is believed to have operational links with Al Qaeda.

Date Listed
November 2002

Date Reviewed*
November 9, 2006

Ansar al-Islam (AI)

Also Known As
Partisans of Islam, Helpers of Islam, Supporters of Islam, Soldiers of God, Kurdistan Taliban, Soldiers of Islam, Kurdistan Supporters of Islam, Supporters of Islam in Kurdistan, Followers of Islam in Kurdistan

Description
Ansar al-Islam is a radical, Sunni Islamist, para-military terrorist group composed of Iraqi Kurds, Arabs, and others. The group was established in September 2001 as a result of a merger of several Kurdish Sunni groups, and follows the same extremist interpretation of Islam as does Al Qaeda. It is closely affiliated with the Al Qaeda and forms part of the Al Qaeda network.

Date Listed
May 17, 2004

Date Reviewed*
November 9, 2006

Armed Islamic Group (GIA)

Also Known As
Groupe islamique armé

Description
The Armed Islamic Group is a radical anti-government, anti-intellectual, anti-secularist, and anti-Western Sunni Muslim group based in Algeria. The GIA is known to have targeted intellectuals, journalists, and foreigners, and is known to operate outside Algeria. The group has links with terrorist organizations throughout the Middle East and Central/Southern Asia, including Al Qaeda and Osama bin Laden.

Date Listed
November 2002

Date Reviewed*
November 9, 2006

Asbat Al-Ansar ("The League of Partisans")

Also known as
Osbat Al Ansar, Usbat Al Ansar, Esbat Al-Ansar, Isbat Al Ansar, Usbat-ul-Ansar

Description
Asbat Al-Ansar is a Lebanon-based, Sunni extremist organization, composed primarily of Palestinians. Asbat Al-Ansar builds upon the ideology of fighting the U.S. and Israel, and seeks to establish a radical Islamic regime in Lebanon. In order to achieve its goals, Asbat Al-Ansar participated in and facilitated several terrorist attacks in Lebanon, which have included targeting some Western and other embassy personnel, killing Lebanese officials, bombing public and religious places, and killing senior members from rival groups.

Date Listed
November 27, 2002

Date Reviewed*
November 9, 2006

Aum Shinrikyo

Also Known As
Aum Shinri Kyo, Aum, Aum Supreme Truth, A.I.C. Comprehensive Research Institute, A.I.C. Sogo Kenkyusho, Aleph

Description
Aum Shinrikyo/Aleph is a religious terrorist organization that was founded by Shoko Asahara in Japan in 1987. Apart from the teachings of Asahara, the sect's beliefs are based on an eclectic selection of Tibetan Buddhism, the apocalyptic aspects of Shiva, the Hindu god of destruction, the Zen masters, Isaac Asimov's science fiction, and the Judeo-Christian concept of Armageddon. Its organizational structure mimics that of the nation-state, and its 2001 membership was estimated at fifteen hundred to two thousand people, most of whom were located in Japan. Despite its status as a religious organization, Aum Shinrikyo/Aleph was run like a business, and at one point, the Japanese government estimated its net worth at approximately $1 billion. Aum Shinrikyo/Aleph was responsible

for twelve deaths and the hospitalization of more than five thousand people as a result of its sarin gas attack on the Tokyo subway system on March 20, 1995. It was also responsible for several other mysterious chemical incidents in Japan in 1994, and has been accused of detaining members against their will, extortion, kidnapping members who decided to leave, and even murdering members who either refused to turn over all their possessions or to return to the sect. Despite the arrest and convictions of many of its members, in March 2002 the Japanese Justice Minister was quoted as saying that "the cult group still maintains its essential dangerousness and we need to keep watching its moves."

Date Listed
December 11, 2002

Date Reviewed*
November 9, 2006

Autodefensas Unidas de Colombia (AUC)

Also Known As
Autodéfenses unies de Colombie, United Self-Defense Forces of Colombia

Description
The Autodefensas Unidas de Colombia is a right-wing terrorist organization which acts as an umbrella organization for like-minded paramilitary groups. Guided by its objective of countering the influence and activity of left-wing guerrilla organizations in Colombia, the AUC has come into conflict with rival terrorist groups the ELN and FARC. Growing out of the right-wing death squads assembled by drug cartels in the 1980s, the core of the AUC was founded in 1997 by Carlos Castaño. Closely linked to the drug trade, revenue from illegal narcotics smuggling is the lifeblood of the AUC. In order to achieve its goals, the AUC has employed a variety of tactics including the intimidation, torture, assassination, and kidnapping of individuals, in addition to its practice of massacring communities that the paramilitaries have labelled as opposing it and its goals.

Date Listed
April 2, 2003

Date Reviewed*
November 9, 2006

Babbar Khalsa (BK) and Babbar Khalsa International (BKI)
Description
Babbar Khalsa and Babbar Khalsa International are entities of a Sikh terrorist organization whose aim is to establish a fundamentalist, independent Sikh state called Khalistan ("land of the pure") in the area that is presently the Indian state of Punjab. BK and BKI continue to be one of the most vicious and powerful of the militant Sikh groups. Ideologically, members of BK and BKI follow in the path of its historical namesake Babbar Akalis, and thus vow to avenge the deaths of Sikhs killed in defence of the faith. Puritan in its conception of Sikhism, BK and BKI do not compromise on religious issues and thus spirituality is central to the groups' goal, which is to establish a fundamentalist, independent Sikh state.

Date Listed
June 18, 2003

Date Reviewed*
November 9, 2006

Ejército de Liberación Nacional (ELN)
Also Known As
National Liberation Army, the Army of National Liberation

Description
The Ejército de Liberación Nacional, founded in 1964, is the second-largest leftist rebel group in Colombia, after FARC. The group strongly opposes foreign involvement in Colombia's oil industry, saying it violates the country's sovereignty and that foreign companies are unfairly exploiting Colombia's natural resources. The ELN's principal aim is to "seize power for the people" and establish a revolutionary government. For the ELN, guerrilla warfare is the indispensable means with which to solve all of Colombia's problems. It is estimated to have between three and five thousand active members. There are close ties between the ELN

and FARC. One of the more important links is common membership in the Simon Bolivar Guerrilla Coordination Board. The ELN is known for kidnapping, hijacking, bombing, extortion, and guerrilla warfare. The ELN hits strategic economic targets, particularly the oil pipeline owned by the Colombian Petroleum Enterprise (Ecopetrol), causing disruption and loss of revenue to the state oil company. While its activities have been limited to Colombia, it has acted against Canadian interests by kidnapping a Canadian employee of Occidental Petroleum and attempting to assassinate the Canadian manager of a Texas oil company in Bogotá.

Date Listed
April 2, 2003

Date Reviewed*
November 9, 2006

Euskadi Ta Askatasuna (ETA)

Also Known As
Basque Homeland and Liberty, Euzkadi Ta Azkatasuna, Euzkadi Ta Askatasanu, Basque Nation and Liberty, Basque Fatherland and Liberty, Basque Homeland and Freedom

Description
The Euskadi Ta Askatasuna is the most powerful of the Basque terrorist groups and has been called the most dangerous terrorist organization in Europe. It is said to have killed over eight hundred people and carried out about sixteen hundred terrorist attacks since it was formed. It is headquartered in the Basque provinces of Spain and France, but has bombed Spanish and French interests elsewhere. Its stated goal is the creation of an independent Basque state that would contain the six Basque provinces of Spain and France, as well as the Navarra province of Spain. It has further demonstrated a muted commitment to Marxism such that its created state would likely be based on Marxist principles. The ETA has engaged in bombings, assassinations, and kidnappings to further its political and ideological goals. These activities are intended to intimidate the public (or a segment of the public) and force the Spanish government to accede to its demands.

Date Listed
April 2, 2003

Date Reviewed*
November 9, 2006

Fuerzas Armadas Revolucionarias de Colombia (FARC)

Also Known As
Revolutionary Armed Forces of Colombia, Revolutionary Armed Forces of Colombia — People's Army (Fuerzas Armadas Revolucionarias de Colombia-Ejército del Pueblo, FARC-EP), National Finance Commission (Comisión Nacional de Finanzas), Coordinadora Nacional Guerrillera Simon Bolivar (CNGSB)

Description
Established in 1964, FARC is Colombia's oldest, largest, most capable, and best-equipped Marxist insurgency. Representing a dangerous threat to the government and integrity of Colombia, as well as to regional stability, FARC poses a significant danger to political leaders, villagers, expatriates, and the military, as it operates with no regard for the law. FARC is guided by its goal of overthrowing the current government in Colombia and replacing it with a leftist, anti-American regime that would force all U.S. interests out of Colombia and Latin America. FARC has been responsible for terrorist activities such as bombings, hijackings, assassinations, and the kidnapping of Colombian officials and Westerners.

Date Listed
April 2, 2003

Date Reviewed*
November 9, 2006

Gulbuddin Hekmatyar

Also Known As
Gulabudin Hekmatyar, Gulbuddin Khekmatiyar, Gulbuddin Hekmatiar, Gulbuddin Hekmartyar, Gulbudin Hekmetyar; Golboddin Hikmetyar, Gulbuddin Hekmetyar

Description

Gulbuddin Hekmatyar, leader of the group Hezb-e Islami Gulbuddin (HIG), espouse an Islamist anti-Western ideology whose political or religious objective is the overthrow of the administration of Afghan President Hamid Karzai, the elimination of all Western influence in Afghanistan, and the creation of an Islamist fundamentalist state. On July 23, 2002, Al Qaeda became a listed entity pursuant to section 83.05 of the Criminal Code. Since late 2002, and to achieve its political and religious objectives, Hekmatyar has joined forces with Al Qaeda and the Taliban to form an anti-Western, anti-U.S., anti-Afghan government alliance which would continue targeted jihad against the "anti-Islam and anti-Muslim elements." Since 2002, Hekmatyar has reportedly established a base, recruited new members, and initiated mobile training camps with Al Qaeda and the Taliban in Afghanistan and Pakistan, with the goal of carrying out terrorist activity in Afghanistan.

Date Listed
May 24, 2005

Date Reviewed*
November 9, 2006

Hamas (Harakat Al-Muqawama Al-Islamiya) ("Islamic Resistance Movement")

Description

Hamas, the Arabic acronym of which means "zeal," is a radical Sunni Muslim terrorist organization which developed from the Palestinian branch of the Muslim Brotherhood (MB) in 1987. It uses political and violent means, including terrorism, to pursue the goal of establishing an Islamic Palestinian state in Israel. Hamas has stated that "it is in a war with the Jewish people, as well as the state of Israel. The purpose of every operation is to kill Jews; for by killing Jews, all the Zionist settlers and their allies will be driven from the area." Hamas is well financed and organized, with its funding coming from an array of sources. In March 1996, Israeli intelligence officials estimated that roughly 95 percent of the estimated $70 million a year that it collected went into such charities as hospitals, clinics, and schools, with only a small portion siphoned off to pay for weapons and military operations. While some funds supposedly raised for charity go directly to the military wing, some of the charity funds intended for activists, families, and institutions are "leaked" to the terrorist apparatus and are used for terrorist activities. The charity associations pay fines and assist the families of the arrested activists or the activists themselves. In other words, funds need not be utilized exclusively for weapons, explosives, or logistical support to facilitate terrorist activities. Since 1990, Hamas has been responsible for several hundred terrorist attacks against both civilian and military targets. Hamas has been one of the primary groups involved in suicide bombings aimed at Israelis in the course of the intifada that started in September 2000.

Date Listed
November 27, 2002

Date Reviewed*
November 9, 2006

Harakat ul-Mudjahidin (HuM)

Also Known As
Al-Faran, Al-Hadid, Al-Hadith, Harkat-ul-Mujahideen, Harakat ul-Mujahideen, Harakat al-Mujahideen, Harkat-ul-Ansar, Harakat ul-Ansar, Harakat al-Ansar, Harkat-ul-Jehad-e-Islami, Harkat Mujahideen, Harakat-ul-Mujahideen al-Almi, Holy Warriors Movement, Movement of the Mujahideen, Movement of the Helpers, Movement of Islamic Fighters, Al Qanoon

Description
Harakat ul-Mudjahidin is a Pakistan-based radical Kashmiri Islamist organization which advocates the liberation and subsequent integration of Kashmir from Indian control into Pakistan, in addition to calling for a jihad against America and India. Within this context, the HuM advocates, is devoted to, and has called for the creation of an Islamist theocracy in Pakistan based on *shariah* (Islamic law), as well as a jihad to "liberate oppressed Muslims worldwide"; denounces pluralist parliamentary democracy, religious tolerance, and equal rights for women as corrupting influences on Islam; and views the United Nations as an institution supporting the genocide of Kashmiris. Guided by these goals and ideology, the HuM employs various methods to achieve

its goals, which have included, but are not limited to, the targeting, kidnapping, and execution of foreigners; hijacking; and the targeting of Indian government officials, their representatives, and symbols of the Indian government, as well as foreigners and political representatives of other foreign states. The HuM signed the 1998 fatwa put out by Al Qaeda and Osama bin Laden and is therefore allied with, or part of, the Al Qaeda coalition.

Date Listed
November 27, 2002

Date Reviewed*
November 9, 2006

Hezb-e Islami Gulbuddin (HIG)

Description
Gulbuddin Hekmatyar's faction of the Hezb-e Islami, Hezb-e Islami Gulbuddin (HIG), espouses an Islamist anti-Western ideology whose objectives are the overthrow of the administration of Afghan President Hamid Karzai, the elimination of all Western influence in Afghanistan and the creation of an Islamist fundamentalist state. In furtherance of its objectives, HIG has formed an alliance with Al Qaeda and the Taliban. On July 23, 2002, Al Qaeda became a listed entity pursuant to section 83.05 of the Criminal Code and on May 24, 2005, HIG leader Gulbuddin Hekmatyar became a listed entity pursuant to section 83.05 of the Criminal Code. HIG has a history of engaging in terrorist activities inside Afghanistan in order to achieve its goals, including killings, torture, kidnappings, attacking political targets, as well as targeting civilians, journalists, foreigners, and foreign aid workers.

Date Listed
October 23, 2006

Hizballah

Also Known As
Hizbullah, Hizbollah, Hezbollah, Hezballah, Hizbu'llah, the Party of God, Islamic Jihad (Islamic Holy War), Islamic Jihad Organization,

Islamic Resistance, Islamic Jihad for the Liberation of Palestine, Ansar al-Allah (Followers of God/Partisans of God/God's Helpers), Ansarollah (Followers of God/Partisans of God/God's Helpers), Ansar Allah (Followers of God/Partisans of God/God's Helpers), Al-Muqawamah al-Islamiyyah (Islamic Resistance), Organization of the Oppressed, Organization of the Oppressed on Earth, Revolutionary Justice Organization, Organization of Right Against Wrong, Followers of the Prophet Muhammed

Description
Hizballah, meaning "party of God," is an Islamist terrorist organization based in Lebanon. Hizballah seeks to restore Islam to a position of supremacy in the political, social, and economic life of the Muslim world. The objectives of Hizballah, as derived from its February 16, 1985, political manifesto, include removing all Western influences from Lebanon and from the Middle East, as well as destroying the state of Israel and liberating all Palestinian territories and Jerusalem from what it sees as Israeli occupation, with no option for any negotiated peace. Guided by these goals, Hizballah's ultimate objective is to establish a radical Shi'a Islamist theocracy in Lebanon. Hizballah has been responsible for car bombings, hijackings and kidnapping Western and Israeli/Jewish targets in Israel, Western Europe and South America. Hizballah operates principally in Lebanon, but has also been active in Europe, North and South America, and Africa.

Date Listed
December 11, 2002

Date Reviewed*
November 9, 2006

International Sikh Youth Federation (ISYF)
Description
The International Sikh Youth Federation was founded in 1984 in the United Kingdom as an international branch of the All India Sikh Students' Federation with centres in several countries, including Canada. The ISYF is a Sikh organization whose aim is to promote Sikh philosophy and the establishment of an independent Sikh nation

called Khalistan. In the pursuit of their goal, the ISYF does not hesitate to resort to violence. Since 1984, its members have been engaged in terrorist attacks, assassinations and bombings mostly against Indian political figures, but also against moderate members of the Sikh community opposed to their extremist ways. The ISYF collaborates and/or associates with a number of Sikh terrorist organizations, notably Babbar Khalsa (BK), the Khalistan Liberation Force (KLF), and the Khalistan Commando Force (KCF).

Date Listed
June 18, 2003

Date Reviewed*
November 9, 2006

Islamic Army of Aden (IAA)
Also Known As
Islamic Army of Aden-Abyan (IAAA), the Aden-Abyan Islamic Army (AAIA), Aden Islamic Army, Islamic Aden Army, Muhammad's Army/ Army of Mohammed, the Jaish Adan Al Islami

Description
The Islamic Army of Aden is a Yemen-based radical Islamic organization which advocates the overthrow of the Yemeni government and the creation of an Islamist theocracy in Yemen based on *shariah* (Islamic law). Combating Western influences not only in Yemen but also within the Islamic world, the IAA opposes the use of Yemeni ports and bases by the United States and other Western countries, in addition to its call for the expulsion of Western forces in the gulf and the lifting of international sanctions against Iraq. Guided by these goals, the IAA has used terror tactics in order to achieve their objectives, including the targeting of foreigners and political representatives of foreign states. While the IAA is based in Yemen, its ties with terrorist groups, such as Al Qaeda, and states that are known to support international terrorism make it of broad significance in the region.

Date Listed
November 27, 2002

Date Reviewed*
November 9, 2006

Islamic Movement of Uzbekistan (IMU)
Description
The Islamic Movement of Uzbekistan is a terrorist organization that emerged in Central Asia in the late 1990s. The primary goal of the IMU is to overthrow the government of Uzbekistan. The IMU has employed kidnapping, armed attacks against government installations, cross-border incursions, coordinated efforts with other terrorist groups (such as Osama bin Laden's Al Qaeda network), and other methods to achieve its goals. The IMU has attacked Westerners and declared its intention to strike at Western interests in Central Asia.

Date Listed
April 2, 2003

Date Reviewed*
November 9, 2006

Jaish-e-Mohammed (JeM)
Also Known As
Jaish-i-Mohammed (Mohammad, Muhammad, Muhammed), Jaish-e-Mohammad (Muhammed), Jaish-e-Mohammad Mujahideen E-Tanzeem, Jeish-e-Mahammed, Army of Mohammed, Mohammed's Army, Tehrik Ul-Furqaan, National Movement for the Restoration of Pakistani Sovereignty, Army of the Prophet

Description
Jaish-e-Mohammed is a Pakistan-based radical Islamist organization which advocates the liberation and subsequent integration of Jammu and Kashmir from Indian control into Pakistan, in addition to calling for the destruction of America, India, and all infidels worldwide. Seeking the creation of an Islamist theocracy in Pakistan based on *shariah* (Islamic law), JeM has sought to unite the various militant groups fighting in Kashmir so as to be better able to establish an Islamic State of Kashmir through armed struggle, and thereby extend their jihad throughout

India, south Asia, and the rest of the world to wherever they believe Muslims are oppressed. Guided by these goals and ideology, JeM is committed to using indiscriminate terror tactics in order to achieve their objectives, including targeting foreigners and political representatives of foreign states.

Date Listed
November 27, 2002

*Date Reviewed**
November 9, 2006

Jemaah Islamiyyah (JI)

Also Known As
Jemaa Islamiyah, Jema'a Islamiyya, Jema'a Islamiyyah, Jema'ah Islamiyah, Jema'ah Islamiyyah, Jemaa Islamiya, Jemaa Islamiyya, Jemaah Islamiyya, Jemaa Islamiyyah, Jemaah Islamiah, Jemaah Islamiyah, Jemaah Islamiyyah, Jemaah Islamiya, Jamaah Islamiyah, Jamaa Islamiya, Jemaah Islam, Jemahh Islamiyah, Jama'ah Islamiyah, Al-Jama'ah Al Islamiyyah, Islamic Group, Islamic Community

Description
The Jemaah Islamiyyah is an Islamist terrorist organization that has developed economic and military assets, through the use of *fiahs* (cells) operating throughout Southeast Asia. Guided by its objective of creating an Islamic state ruled by *shariah* (Islamic law), the JI wishes to create an Islamist theocracy (JI's conception of Dawlah Islamiyyah or Islamic state) that would unify Muslims in Thailand, Malaysia, Indonesia, Brunei, and the southern Philippines. Sharing a common philosophy with the groups in the Al Qaeda network, the JI and its leadership have been linked to Al Qaeda, both before and after the attacks of September 11, 2001. The JI has emerged as the most extensive transnational radical Islamist group in Southeast Asia. Since its inception, the JI has been responsible for a series of bank robberies, hijackings, and the bombing of civilian targets.

Date listed
April 2, 2003

Date reviewed*
November 9, 2006

Kahane Chai (KACH)

Also Known As

Repression of Traitors, the State of Yehuda, the Sword of David, Dikuy Bogdim, DOV, the Judea Police, Kahane Lives, the Kfar Tapuah Fund, State of Judea, the Judean Legion, the Judean Voice, the Qomemiyut Movement, the Way of the Torah, the Yeshiva of the Jewish Idea

Description

The Kahane Chai is a group of right-wing, politico-religious, anti-Arab Jewish terrorists, whose overall aim is to restore the biblical state of Israel, i.e. to expand the borders of Israel to include the occupied territories and parts of Jordan. To this end, the group aims to intimidate and threaten Palestinian families and mount sustained political pressure on the Israeli government. In the past, Jewish extremist groups, like Kahane Chai, have been willing to engage in terrorism to derail the Arab-Israeli peace process. The Kahane Chai is known to have links both to other members of the "Kahanist Movement" and to other Jewish extremist splinter groups.

The Kahane Chai organizes protests against the Israeli government, and harasses, threatens and assaults Arabs and Palestinians in the West Bank. Its tactics include shouting down opponents, disturbing public speeches and engaging in physical confrontations with law enforcement officials. It has also threatened to attack Israeli government officials. Like the approach taken by the Jewish Defence League (JDL), the targets of the Kach Party (KP), and Kahane Chai have also included leading figures in Israel, as well as Jews and Jewish organizations that support policies of the Israeli government, or those who disagree with their violent tactics and philosophy. Kahanists have shot, stabbed and thrown grenades at Palestinians in Jerusalem and the West Bank. In instances where the KP and KACH have not themselves claimed responsibility for anti-Arab attacks, they have declined to condemn such violence and have often glorified it.

Date Listed
May 24, 2005

*Date Reviewed**
November 9, 2006

Kurdistan Workers Party (PKK)

Also Known As
Kurdistan Workers Party, Partya Karkeren Kurdistan, Kurdistan Labor Party, Kurdistan Freedom and Democracy Congress, KADEK, Kurdistan People's Congress, Kurdistan Halk Kongresi (KHK), People's Congress of Kurdistan, Kongra-Gel

Description
Founded in 1974 by Abdullah Ocalan, the PKK/KADEK is a Kurdish political party that follows a Marxist-Leninist ideology and whose main goal is the creation of an independent Kurdish state in southeast Turkey and in northern Iraq (a region that is part of the traditional territory of the Kurdish people and called Kurdistan). To arrive at its goal, the PKK/ KADEK has led a campaign of guerrilla warfare and terrorism, especially in Turkey and in northern Iraq, by attacking the Turkish government's armed forces and diplomats and Turkish businesses in some western European cities and by attempting to destabilize tourism in Turkey by bombing resorts and kidnapping tourists.

Date Listed
December 11, 2002

*Date Reviewed**
November 9, 2006

Lashkar-e-Jhangvi (LJ)

Also known as Lashkar-i-Jhangvi, Lashkar-e-Jhangvie, Laskar-e-Jhangvi, Lashkare Jhangvi, Lashkar-e-Jhangwi, Lashkar-i-Jhangwi, Jhangvi Army, Lashkar-e Jhangvi, Lashkar Jhangvi, Lashkar-e-Jhanvi (LeJ), Lashkar-i-Jangvi, Lashkar e Jhangvi, Lashkar Jangvi, Laskar e Jahangvi

Description
The Lashkar-e-Jhangvi (LJ), or the Army of Jhang (from the name of a region in Pakistan), is a Sunni Islamic organization that commits

terrorist acts, including bombings and assassinations, traditionally against individuals or groups belonging to the Shiite Islamic community in Pakistan. The LJ's goal is the creation of a Sunni Muslim state. The LJ believes that Shiites whom it considers to be heretics or infidels of Islam, are the main obstacle to the establishment of an orthodox caliphate. Since September 11, 2001, and the American coalition's attack on the Taliban in Afghanistan, members of the LJ have also been involved in attacks against Christians and foreigners in Pakistan, in whole or in part for a political, religious, or ideological purpose, objective, or cause.

Date Listed
June 18, 2003

Date Reviewed*
November 9, 2006

Lashkar-e-Tayyiba (LeT)

Also Known As
Lashkar-e-Toiba, Lashkar-i-Toiba (LiT), Lashkar-i-Taiba (Holy Regiment), Lashkar-e-Tayyiba (LT) (Army of the Righteous), Lashkar-e-Taibyya, Lashkar-e-Taiba, Lashkar-e-Tayyiba (Army of the Pure and Righteous), Lashkar-e-Taiba (Righteous Army), Lashkar-Taiba (Army of the Good), Lashkar e Toiba, Lashkar e Taiba, Lashkar-E-Tayyaba, Lashkar e Tayyiba

Description
Lashkar-e-Tayyiba ("Army of the Pure") is a Pakistan-based, radical Islamist organization operating in the Indian state of Kashmir and Jammu, one of the main centres of extremist activity in South Asia. The LeT is the militant wing of the Markaz Da'wa wal-Irshad (MDI), a fundamentalist centre for religious learning and social welfare established in the late 1980s. The LeT has targeted both civilians (including prominent politicians) and the Indian security forces (including local police forces), and has become infamous for carrying out massacres of non-Muslims. Attacks on the security forces generally take the form of suicide assaults. In addition to links to Al Qaeda, the LeT also has links with the Taliban and other Islamic extremist groups throughout the Middle East, Chechnya, and the Philippines. Al Qaeda's

close links to the LeT can be traced to their common training in Afghan camps and in the 1980s jihad against the Soviets. Osama bin Laden is reportedly one of the LeT's leading financiers.

Date Listed
June 18, 2003

Date Reviewed*
November 9, 2006

Liberation Tigers of Tamil Eelam (LTTE)

Also Known As
The Tamil Tigers, the Eellalan Force, the Ellalan Force, the Tiger Movement, the Sangilian Force, the Air Tigers, the Black Tigers (Karum Puligal), the Sea Tigers, the Tiger Organization Security Intelligence Service (TOSIS), the Women's Combat Force of Liberation Tigers (WCFLT)

Description
The Liberation Tigers of Tamil Eelam) is a Sri Lankan–based organization which advocates the creation of an independent homeland in the north and northeastern part of Sri Lanka, which it has called "Tamil Eelam." Its war against the government of Sri Lanka has been fought on three fronts: a political campaign, guerrilla warfare, and a terrorist campaign. The LTTE is committed to using a variety of terror tactics in order to achieve its objectives, including attacking political, economic, religious, and cultural targets, as well as targeting civilians. The LTTE's campaign has included plans to create Tamil-only northern and eastern provinces, and to this end it has aggressively expelled non-Tamils from these regions. The LTTE also endeavours to eliminate moderate Tamils and other Tamil militant groups that compete with it for influence and power within the Sri Lankan Tamil community.

Date Listed
April 8, 2006

Date Reviewed*
November 9, 2006

Mujahedin e Khalq (MEK)

Also Known As
From its original Persian name: Sãzimãn-i Mujãhidn-i Khalq-i Irãn (Holy Warrior Organization of the Iranian People) / Sazman-i Mojahedin-i Khalq-i Iran (Organization of the Freedom Fighters of the Iranian People) / Sazeman-e Mojahedin-e Khalq-e Iran (Organization of People's Holy Warriors of Iran) / Sazeman-e-Mujahideen-e-Khalq-e-Iran. The group's name was shortened to Mujahedin-e-Khalq (MEK) or Mojahedin-e Khalq Organization (MKO). Other spellings: Mujahiddin e Khahq, al-Khalq Mujahideen Organization, Mujahedeen Khalq, Modjaheddins khalg, Moudjahiddin-é Khalq. Also known as: National Liberation Army of Iran (NLA) / Armée de Libération nationale iranienne (ALNI) (the military wing of the MEK); People's Mujahidin Organization of Iran (PMOI) / People's Mujahedin of Iran (PMOI) / Organisation des moudjahiddin du peuple d'Iran (OMPI) / Organisation des moudjahidines du peuple

Description
The Mujahedin-e-Khalq is an Iranian terrorist organization that was based in Iraq until recently. It subscribes to an eclectic ideology that combines its own interpretation of Shiite Islamism with Marxist principles. The group aspires to overthrow the current regime in Iran and to establish a democratic, socialist Islamic republic. This Islamic socialism can only be attained through the destruction of the existing regime and the elimination of Western influence, described as "Westoxication." To achieve this Islamic ideology, the use of physical force, armed struggle, or jihad is necessary. Besides having had an alliance with Saddam Hussein, the organization has or had ties with: Amal, the Kurdish Democratic Party of Iran (KDPI), the Palestine Liberation Organization (PLO), Al Fatah, and other Palestinian factions. The MEK is even suspected of past collusion with the regime of the Taliban in Afghanistan.

Date Listed
May 24, 2005

Date Reviewed*
November 9, 2006

Palestine Liberation Front (PLF)

Also Known As
Abu Abbas Faction, Front for the Liberation of Palestine (FLP)

Description
The Palestine Liberation Front is a small, armed splinter group allied to the Palestinian Liberation Organization (PLO). It professes an ideology that is both leftist and nationalist, and has as its objective the destruction of the state of Israel and the establishment of an independent Palestinian state, with Jerusalem as its capital. First founded in 1961 by Ahmad Jibril, the group operates primarily in Europe as well as Israel, Lebanon, and other areas in the Middle East. During its most active period, it is known to have conducted several high-profile attacks, including the operation for which it is best known, the October 1985 hijacking of the Achille Lauro.

Date Listed
November 13, 2003

Date Reviewed*
November 9, 2006

Palestinian Islamic Jihad (PIJ)

Also Known As
Islamic Jihad Palestine (IJP), Islamic Jihad — Palestine Faction, Islamic Holy War

Description
The Palestinian Islamic Jihad is a terrorist organization that operates primarily in Israel, the West Bank, the Gaza Strip, and other areas of the Middle East, including Lebanon and Syria. It is committed to the destruction of Israel and the establishment of an Islamic state in Palestine. Islamic Jihad countenances no settlement to the Arab-Israeli, Muslim-Israeli, Muslim-Jewish conflict in the region other than the complete destruction of the State of Israel. It is also opposed to moderate secular Arab regimes because they see them as corrupt and contaminated by Western secular values. From 1986 to the present, the PIJ has been responsible for numerous terrorist attacks against

Israeli targets within Israel, southern Lebanon, and the occupied territories; has been responsible for the deaths of several dozen Israelis and Palestinians; and has carried out a number of dramatic bombings. PIJ attacks have included, but are not limited to, assaults with knives, daggers, axes, grenades, car bombs, and, particularly after 1994, the use of suicide bombers. For example, on May 5, 2002, a suicide bomber pulled his explosive-laden vehicle alongside a bus near Megiddo Junction in northern Israel and then detonated the explosives, killing at least seventeen Israelis and injuring dozens of others. Several of the passengers on the bus were Israeli soldiers travelling to posts in northern Israel. The military wing of the Palestinian Islamic Jihad claimed responsibility for the attack.

Date Listed
November 27, 2002

Date Reviewed*
November 9, 2006

Popular Front for the Liberation of Palestine — General Command (PFLP-GC)
Also Known As
Al-Jibha Sha'biya lil-Tahrir Filistin-al-Qadiya al-Ama

Description
The Popular Front for the Liberation of Palestine — General Command is a nationalist, Marxist Palestinian organization whose aim is the destruction of the state of Israel and the establishment of a Palestinian state. The PFLP-GC has conducted some of its most imaginative attacks inside Israeli territory using hot-air balloons and motorized hang-gliders. In 1970, PFLP-GC operatives blew up a Swissair jet flying to Tel Aviv. In the 1980s, they were responsible for injuring U.S. Marines participating in the international peacekeeping force in Beirut. In January 2003, the PFLP-GC claimed its gunmen were responsible for wounding two residents of a Jewish settlement in the West Bank, one of whom was an eight-year-old boy. The PFLP-GC said that its armed branch acted in "response to the daily massacres committed against the Palestinian people" in the occupied territories. It reaffirmed its intention

of "pursuing the resistance and the intifada until all the [Palestinian] objectives are achieved."

Date Listed
November 13, 2003

Date Reviewed*
November 9, 2006

Popular Front for the Liberation of Palestine (PFLP)

Also Known As
Al-Jibha al-Sha'biya lil-Tahrir Filistin

Description
The Popular Front for the Liberation of Palestine is a secular Palestinian group purportedly guided by a Marxist interpretation. The PFLP's terrorist activities began on July 23, 1968, with the hijacking to Algeria of an El Al flight en route from Rome to Tel Aviv. The PFLP's armed wing — almost completely inactive in the four years preceding the start of the latest Palestinian uprising (the Al Aqsa intifada) on September 29, 2000 — raised its profile in 2001. It conducted car bombings and some suicide bombings in Israel (including in the city of Jerusalem), an assassination of an Israeli Cabinet minister, Tourism Minister Rehavam Ze'evi, and other attacks on Israelis. The first reported PFLP killing of a civilian in Israel since the start of the latest intifada was on August 27, 2001. The PFLP has claimed several other attacks, including a suicide bombing in a pizzeria in Karnei Shomron, Israel, on February 16, 2002, killing three civilians.

Date Listed
November 13, 2003

Date Reviewed*
November 9, 2006

Salafist Group for Call and Combat (GSPC)

Also Known As
Groupe salafiste pour la prédication et le combat

Description
The GSPC is a radical Sunni Muslim group seeking to establish an Islamist government in Algeria. It is a breakaway faction of the GIA. The GSPC has adopted a policy that violence should be targeted on security or military targets, foreigners, intellectuals, and administrative staff. The GSPC is believed to have been active outside Algeria. The group has been affiliated with Osama bin Laden and groups financed by him.

Date Listed
July 23, 2002

Date Reviewed*
November 9, 2006

Sendero Luminoso (SL)

Also Known As
Shining Path, Partido Comunista del Peru en el Sendero Luminoso de Jose Carlos Mariategui, Communist Party of Peru on the Shining Path of Jose Carlos Mariategui, Partido Comunista del Peru, Communist Party of Peru, the Communist Party of Peru by the Shining Path of Jose Carlos Mariategui and Marxism, Leninism, Maoism and the Thoughts of Chairman Gonzalo, Revolutionary Student Front for the Shining Path of Mariategui, Communist Party of Peru — By Way of the Shining Path of Mariategui, PCP — por el Sendero Luminoso de Mariategui, PCP, PCP-SL

Description
Sendero Luminoso has been stated to be among the world's most ruthless guerrilla organizations whose goal it is to destroy existing Peruvian institutions and replace them with a communist peasant revolutionary regime which would rid the country of foreign influences. Its area of operations is limited to Peru, with most of its activities in rural areas, but some of its attacks have taken place in the capital, Lima. It is estimated that over thirty thousand people have died by political violence in Peru since SL took up arms in 1980 and that their activities have caused US$20 billion in property damage. SL was founded by Abimael Guzman, a university professor, in the late 1960s but began its armed struggle, or "People's War," in or about May 1980. SL is known for its indiscriminate bombing campaigns, selective assassinations,

and killing of innocents. While none of its activities have taken place in Canada, the group has targeted some Canadian citizens and interests such as the bombing of a Bata shoe warehouse in Lima, the bombing of the Canadian Embassy, an ambush of trucks associated with a Canadian alpaca operation that killed eight people, and the murder of a Canadian aid worker.

Date Listed
February 12, 2003

Date Reviewed*
November 9, 2006

Vanguards of Conquest (VOC)

Description
The VOC is a radical armed wing of, but closely aligned with, the AJ that has actively been involved in terrorism, including attempted assassinations against the Egyptian Interior Minister, Prime Minister, and President. The VOC has released "assassination lists," which have included civilians.

Date Listed
November 2002

Date Reviewed*
November 9, 2006

*Note: The two-year review of the list was completed pursuant to subsections 83.05(9) and 83.05(10) of the Criminal Code. Last updated: 2006-11-10.

Appendix II:
Osama bin Laden Talks to Canadians

On November 12, 2002, the Arabic television channel Al Jazeera broadcast the following message, believed by experts to be from Osama bin Laden.

(Translated by BBC Monitoring)

In the name of God, the merciful, the compassionate, from the slave of God, Osama bin Laden, to the peoples of the countries allied with the tyrannical U.S. Government:

May God's peace be upon those who follow the right path. The road to safety begins by ending the aggression.

Reciprocal treatment is part of justice.

The incidents that have taken place since the raids on New York and Washington up until now — like the killing of Germans in Tunisia and the French in Karachi, the bombing of the giant French tanker in Yemen, the killing of marines in Failaka [in Kuwait] and the British and Australians in the Bali explosions, the recent operation in Moscow, and some sporadic operations here and there — are only reactions and reciprocal actions.

These actions were carried out by the zealous sons of Islam in defence of their religion and in response to the order of their God and prophet, may God's peace and blessings be upon him.

What [U.S. President George W.] Bush, the pharaoh of this age, was doing in terms of killing our sons in Iraq, and what Israel, the United States' ally, was doing in terms of bombing houses that shelter old people, women, and children with U.S.-made aircraft in Palestine were sufficient to prompt the sane among your rulers to distance themselves from this criminal gang.

Our kinfolk in Palestine have been slain and severely tortured for nearly a century.

If we defend our people in Palestine, the world becomes agitated and allies itself against Muslims, unjustly and falsely, under the pretence of fighting terrorism.

What do your governments want by allying themselves with the criminal gang in the White House against Muslims?

Do your governments not know that the White House gangsters are the biggest butchers of this age?

[U.S. Defense Secretary Donald] Rumsfeld, the butcher of Vietnam, killed more than two million people, not to mention those he wounded.

[U.S. Vice-President Dick] Cheney and [U.S. Secretary of State Colin] Powell killed and destroyed in Baghdad more than Hulegu of the Mongols.

What do your governments want from their alliance with America in attacking us in Afghanistan?

I mention in particular Britain, France, Italy, Canada, Germany, and Australia.

We warned Australia before not to join in [the war] in Afghanistan, and [against] its despicable effort to separate East Timor.

It ignored the warning until it woke up to the sounds of explosions in Bali.

Its government falsely claimed that they [the Australians] were not targeted.

If you were distressed by the deaths of your men and the men of your allies in Tunisia, Karachi, Failaka, Bali, and Amman, remember our children who are killed in Palestine and Iraq every day, remember our deaths in Khowst mosques, and remember the premeditated killing of our people in weddings in Afghanistan.

If you were distressed by the killing of your nationals in Moscow, remember ours in Chechnya.

Why should fear, killing, destruction, displacement, orphaning, and widowing continue to be our lot, while security, stability, and happiness be your lot?

This is unfair.

It is time that we get even.

You will be killed just as you kill, and will be bombed just as you bomb.

And expect more that will further distress you.

The Islamic nation, thanks to God, has started to attack you at the hands of its beloved sons, who pledged to God to continue jihad, as long as they are alive, through words and weapons to establish right and expose falsehood.

In conclusion, I ask God to help us champion His religion and continue jihad for His sake until we meet Him while He is satisfied with us. And He can do so.

Praise be to Almighty God.

Appendix III:
Direct Action Communiqué

Statement Regarding the October 14 Litton Bombing

We claim responsibility for the bombing of a Litton Systems of Canada Ltd. Industrial plant in Toronto, Ontario where the guidance system for the Cruise Missile nuclear weapons is being produced.

We sincerely regret that any injuries occurred as a result of this action. We never intended any harm to come to anyone — especially the workers at Litton — but instead, we took great care in preparing what we seriously assumed were adequate precautions to insure the safety of all people in the area. Unfortunately, this did not turn out to be the case.

We do not regret, however, our decision to attempt to sabotage the production of the Cruise Missile's guidance "brain." We only claim in all honesty that this action was never meant to be an act of terrorism.

We were not trying to threaten or kill the workers or executives of Litton Systems. We were attempting to destroy part of an industrial facility that produces machinery for mass murder. We wanted to blow up as much of that technology of death as possible.

Accidents happen; no systems or people are infallible. For us, however, this fact of life in no way excuses us for the mistakes that we made which contributed to causing injury in this action. We only pose these simple questions to put this tragedy into proper perspective.

How many thousands will suffer from cancer-related diseases because of breakdowns at nuclear power plants? How many thousands are maimed and killed every year in industrial accidents? And isn't it a fact that millions of people starve to death annually because so much money and human effort is put into systems of war rather than developing the means to feed the people of the world?

Although we still firmly believe that it is right to attack the technologies of death, we identify our mistakes in this action as the following:

1. The bomb exploded 12 minutes before it was supposed to, assuming that it did detonate at 11:31 p.m. as stated in the media. The bomb was set to go off at 11:43 p.m. If it had exploded at this time, we feel that it was reasonable to have assumed that the Litton plant and the surrounding area would have been safely secured. It is a mystery to us why it exploded early, as we had checked and double-checked the accuracy of the timing system many times.

2. The warning call was not repeated. The van was left on the lawn in front of the Litton building at 11:17 p.m. We telephoned a warning to Litton Security just one minute after the van was parked. This was to ensure a quick reaction by authorities, even though we felt certain that the van would have been seen as it was being driven across the lawn and parked.

    The van was parked 100 meters directly in front of an exposed glass-walled security guard's booth. In fact, the driver of the van could see 3 guards in the booth at all times during the approach and, as a result, knew that the van had not been noticed.

    Unfortunately, the Litton guard did not completely understand the instructions of the telephone warning. When he asked that the instructions be repeated, he was only told to go out front and look at the van. We see now that the telephone warning should have been carefully repeated.

    However, if the warning had been understood, and even the police have said it was "meticulous," then the authorities would have had approximately 25 minutes to clear the plant, the area, and surrounding roads — if the bomb had detonated on time.

This was certainly a reasonable length of time to have left the authorities to evacuate the plant and secure the area. Even though the bomb went off early, it seems obvious that even 13 minutes was enough time for the plant to have been safely emptied had the instructions been understood.

3. We made errors in judgement about the "orange box" which was left in front of the van. This box was meant to be a back-up warning system to the telephone warning — again to help authorities understand the situation and ensure prompt and knowledgable action on their part.

The box was painted fluorescent orange so it could be easily seen and taped to all four sides of it was a sheet of paper with information and instructions. On top of the box was taped a stick of unarmed dynamite.

We felt certain that the Litton guards, either by seeing the van being parked or by being alerted to it by the telephone warning, would quickly come upon the box — thus having written information in their possession to guide them. Unfortunately, we wrote "Danger Explosives" on top of the sheets of instructions.

As well, it was not a good idea to leave an unarmed stick of dynamite visable on top of the box.

Although these two things were done to prove that this was a real bombing, they actually frightened the Litton guards and police away from the box so that the instructions were never read.

Because we left evidence of real explosives, and because the instructions contained the information that there were 550 pounds of explosives inside the van, we assumed that the authorities would have undertaken a massive emergency response and evacuation. This is what we were hoping would happen to make sure that no one was hurt.

It was specifically stated in the telephone warning that the box contained important instructions and that the dynamite attached to it was harmless, in both the written instructions and the telephone warning, we stated that the van would explode in approxiately 15–25 minutes. We said this to insure that everyone, including bomb squad members, would clear away from the van well before it exploded.

4. We were mistaken in believing that the Litton guards and police would be on top of things. The image of cops and guards as "super heroes" caused us to believe that they would have security and safety matters underway very quickly.

This obviously did not turn out to be what happened. The Litton guards did not observe the van being parked even though it occurred essentially right before their eyes.

A Litton guard did not understand the phone warning even though it was given clearly. It seems that the Litton guards did little or nothing to evacuate the workers until after the police arrived. As the workers have said, they were only told to leave the building seconds before the explosion.

The police took a very long time to arrive after they were alerted — approximately 10 minutes — and even then they only sent one car at first to investigate.

Finally, neither the police, but especially Litton security, even took a close look at the orange box. We did not expect this kind of slow and indecisive response from the authorities.

We are very disturbed and saddened that injuries occurred as a result of this action. We have gone over what went wrong time and time again. Most significantly, the bomb exploded 12 minutes too early. But nevertheless, we feel we must strongly critisize the Litton security guards for the way in which they "handled" this incident.

We know that there were at least 3 guards in the security booth where the van was parked and when the phone warning occurred. We feel it is undeniable that all injury to the workers could have been avoided if the guards had promptly evacuated the Litton plant, as they obviously should have.

Although we had no knowledge of the previous false bomb threats (in fact, we oppose the use of fake bomb threats precisely because they do cause the authorities to be sceptical of the authenticity of real bomb attacks), we put effort into making sure that the authorities would quickly understand that this threat was real.

It is not as if we said that a pipe-bomb was hidden somewhere within the entire Litton complex, so evacuate everything. We informed Litton security of where the van and box were. They were both completely visible to the guards simply by looking straight out through their booth's window, and the fact that they were there at all obviously indicated that something was definately amiss.

We would like to know why a Litton guard went running into the plant to evacuate the workers only seconds before the explosion — instead of at least 10 minutes earlier? And we would like to know why the two other Litton guards were standing around on the front lawn, instead of informing workers in the other plants?

As well, it is irresponsible of Litton to have never informed the workers of past bomb threats, and to not have a loudspeaker system combined with evacuation plans so that workers could be quickly moved to safety in the event of any danger, be it a bombing or otherwise.

The position where the van was parked was chosen for two reasons. One, so that it could be easily and quickly seen from the guard's booth. It would have been much less conspicuous, and therefore far less risky for the driver of the van, if it had been parked in front of the other two Litton buildings, as neither of these are within direct view of the guard's booth.

Secondly, the van was parked in a corner of the building in order that the two walls of this corner would prevent debris from being cast in a southerly or south-westerly direction where the two nearby hotels are located. This position was the only such corner at the front of the three Litton buildings.

Again it was at the risk of being apprehended on the spot that we chose to park the van in a location which provided the least risk to public safety.

We have written the above not to redeem ourselves, as we did commit inexusable errors, but simply as an explanation of our motives and intentions for those people who may feel threatened that there are crazed terrorists on the loose against the Canadian people.

Again, we repeat, that we took great care in preparing what we seriously assumed were adequate precautions to insure the safety of all people in the area.

Understand and remember, the terrorists are those who have set the world on the brink of nuclear war, not those who are fighting this insanity and inhuman madness!

Finally, we wish to state that in no way was this bombing the work of the Cruise Missile Conversion Project, or any other public peace movement organization in Toronto.

Direct Action
October 17, 1982

Front de Libération du Québec Manifesto, April 16, 1963

Patriots:

Since the Second World War, the diverse dominated peoples of the world have broken their chains in order to acquire the freedom to which they have a right. The immense majority of these peoples have defeated the oppressor and today live freely.

After so many others, the Québécois people have had enough of submitting to the domination of Anglo-Saxon capitalism.

In Quebec, as in all colonized countries, the oppressor furiously denies his imperialism, and is supported in this by our so-called national elite, which is more interested in serving its personal economic interests than in serving the vital interests of the Québécois nation. It persists in denying the evidence and works at creating multiple false problems, wanting to turn the subject people away from the only one that is essential: INDEPENDENCE.

Despite this, the workers' eyes every day open a little bit more concerning reality: Quebec is a colony.

We are politically, socially, and economically colonized. Politically because we don't possess the political levers vital to our survival. The colonialist government in Ottawa in fact has all jurisdiction in the following domains: economy, foreign trade, defence, bank credit, immigration, criminal law, etc. In addition, any provincial law can be refused if Ottawa wills to do so.

The federal government, being totally owned by the interests of Anglo-Saxon imperialists, and who have an overwhelming constitutional and practical majority in it, serves to constantly maintain and accentuate Québécois inferiority. Whenever Anglo-Saxon and Québécois interests come in conflict, Quebec's interests are invariably put at a disadvantage. Be it militarily as in the case of conscription; demographically in the case of the favoritism in assimilation shown to Anglo-Saxons; internationally, with the total supremacy of Anglophones in the diverse diplomatic domains, always, without exception, the government in Ottawa has imposed Anglo-Saxon interests to the detriment of those of Quebec. On certain occasions, the resort to force has not been disdained. Our peoples' blood has flowed for the benefit of colonial capital. Politically, the people of Quebec are thus a colonized people.

It is also so economically. One sentence alone is enough to prove it: more than 80% of our economy is controlled by foreign interests. We furnish the labor, they pocket the profits.

Even socially Quebec is a colonized country. We are 80% of the population, yet the English language dominates in the most diverse domains. Little by little French is relegated to the rank of folklore, while English becomes the language of the workplace. The contempt of the Anglo-Saxons towards our people remains constant. The "Speak white, Stupid French Canadian", and other epithets of this kind, are very frequent. In Quebec itself, thousands of cases of English unilingualism are arrogantly displayed. The colonialists consider us inferior beings, and let us know this without any shame.

The historical background of the problem: When on September 8, 1760 Monsieur de Vaudreuil, Governor of New France, signs the act of capitulation of Montreal, the die is cast. A short while later, England was to officially take possession of the French colony, as well as the 60,000 French Canadians who were there. It is then that the history of Anglo-Saxon domination in Quebec began. Our country was rich, and the financiers of London were already casting an eye on the future profits.

In order for Anglo-Saxon supremacy over Quebec to become uncontested, it was necessary — at whatever cost — to assimilate these 60,000 colonials in one way or another. This then seemed to them quite simple. In fact, what was this handful of men before the overwhelming strength that England then represented? Suddenly, the American

Revolution took place. It was necessary, for a certain time, to treat the French Canadians with care. But the process of assimilation wasn't abandoned. One day the Anglo-Canadians overstepped their limits: then there was the Rebellion of 1837. They crushed it in blood.

Then there was the Durham Report. Since it has shown to be impossible to assimilate the Québécois by force, the latter said, let's set out to do it differently; progressive elimination demands more time, but remains every bit as effective. The Act of union having been a failure, the Confederation was created, a perfect means of assimilation, whose very name was a falsehood. Since the advent of this latter, all the efforts of the people of Quebec to obtain its fundamental rights have been blocked by colonialism.

In 1963, though we are more than five million, assimilation still pushes forward in its insidious progress. While in 1940 we were 40% of the Canadian population, we are now only 28%. This alone interests them. Time is in their favor, and they know it.

Even so, the colonialists have forgotten one thing, something that is nevertheless essential. It is currently happening. Patriots have realized that they are colonized, dominated, exploited. The have also realized that only immediate and total action can break their chains. An action where the petty personal profits, the rotten mentality of utopian compromise at any price, the national inferiority complexes are thrown overboard.

The Québécois patriots have had enough of fighting for almost a century for things of no importance, of expending their vital energy in obtaining illusory profits that are always put in doubt.

It's enough to think of the hundreds of thousands of unemployed, of the wretched poverty of the fishermen of the Gaspe Peninsula, of the thousands of farmers across Quebec whose revenue is barely more than $1000 a year, of the thousands of young people who can't pursue their studies due to lack of funds, of the thousands of people who have no recourse to the most elementary medical care, of the poverty of our miners, of the general insecurity of all those who have a job: This is what colonialism has given us.

In Quebec we also have the unjust and paradoxical situation that is exemplified in the comparison between the neighborhoods of St Henri and Westmount. On one side we find a mass typically Québécois, poor and miserable, while on the other side an English minority shows-off the most shameful of riches. Our progressive economic defeat, a foreign domination more and more complete, don't demand provisional and short-term solutions. The Patriots say NO TO COLONIALISM, NO TO EXPLOITATION.

But it's not enough to refuse a situation; it must be remedied. Our situation is one of national urgency. It is now that it must be remedied.

Let us acquire the vital political levers; let us take control of our economy; let us radically purify our social framework; let us tear off colonialist restraints; let's throw out the imperialists who live by the exploitation of the workers of Quebec. The immense natural riches of Quebec must belong to the Québécois!

In order to do this there is one solution and one solution alone: the national revolution in the midst of INDEPENDENCE. Otherwise the people of Quebec cannot hope to live free.

But it's not enough to want independence, to work within the existing indepedantiste political parties. The colonialists will not so easily let go such a tasty morsel. The independantiste political parties can never have the power needed to defeat colonial political and economic power. What is more, independence alone will resolve nothing. It must at all costs be completed by the social revolution.

The Québécois Patriots aren't fighting for a title, but for facts. The Revolution doesn't happen in salons. Only a total revolution can have the strength necessary to carry out the vital changes that will impose themselves in an independent Quebec. The national revolution, in its essence, doesn't allow any compromise. There is only one way to defeat colonialism, and that's to be stronger than it! Only the most aberrant naïveté can lead one to believe the contrary. The time of slavery is over.

PATRIOTS OF QUEBEC, TO ARMS! THE HOUR OF NATIONAL REVOLUTION HAS COME!

INDEPENDENCE OR DEATH!

Front de Libération du Québec Manifesto, June 23, 1970

I. OBJECTIVES

We want to respond to the provocation that the established order constitutes. We want to respond to the blackmail of businessmen who think they can maintain the current political and economic system by inculcating fear of change in the populace. To the bombs of the Royal Trust type we oppose real ones.

We do nothing but respond to their violence with counter-violence. We defend ourselves against the permanent attacks of the anti-worker and anti-Québécois forces that are the financial syndicates, the big companies, the chamber of commerce, and others, all of which are supported by the Liberal Party of Trudeau-Bourassa.

We attack the economic organisms that the puppet French-speaking politicians (in the style of Trudeau-Bourassa-Drapeau) use to protect their interests, and with which the people believe they periodically enter into dialogue thorough a fake electoral democracy.

We fight that clique of exploiters that the big capitalist bourgeoisie dominated by Anglo-American financiers constitute, and with which several Francophone parvenus collaborate

We fight all forms of exploitation, the most glaring of which is linguistic segregation: the need to speak two languages because we are Québécois. The colonialist bosses are those most responsible in this area.

We fight all forms of racism, discrimination and segregation. We are in solidarity with all the struggles carried out by peoples victim of American imperialism. We support the struggle carried out by the first exploited of the continent: the Amerindians. We are in solidarity with Black Americans and Puerto Ricans who fight Yankee capitalism.

We are with all the immigrant workers in Quebec, and it is alongside them that we want to fight the common enemy: Anglo-American capitalism. It's with all workers that we want to lead to success the struggle for national liberation.

In solidarity with union struggles, the FLQ wants unionized workers to throw themselves more vigorously into the second front. It's necessary that as soon as possible the representatives of the workers replace the false representatives of the people in Parliament. When the worker's party will have been created, the Front de Libération du Québec will no longer have a reason to exist.

The FLQ fights the big companies who are owners of the means of information and who attempt to make people believe that the current government is in the service of all of society. The current government can only be in the service of those who finance it. We fight those capitalists who monopolize all the great means of communication of the people of Quebec. It's up to free intellectuals to denounce this monopoly of information.

The FLQ is in solidarity with all Québécois movements that act for the true economic liberation of the workers of Quebec, and who work for the political emancipation of Quebec. There will be either independence or destruction.

II. MEANS OF ACTION

To effectively fight the reactionary forces that work against the Québécois people it is urgent that we form a COMMON FRONT of all the progressive forces of Quebec. An end must be put to our isolation, which only aids the establishment. It is together that we must carry on the fight: our enemy's enemies are our friends.

This COMMON FRONT will unite the many movements, committees, and popular associations that currently work for a true democracy, a true economic liberation, a cultural revolution, or openly for an independent and socialist Quebec.

The leaders of all these movements, in coordination with the political committees of the unions, must meet to establish together a consensus at the base, to participate in the writing of a Manifesto, and to elaborate a global strategy that will respect the particular character of each of its movements.

The COMMITTEE of the Common Front that will unite delegates of different movements, associations, or "groupuscules" must GUIDE action, COORDINATE AND MOBILIZE IT; it can:

- Work at the distribution of documentation; furnish analyses and propaganda
- Organize peaceful demonstrations with the goal of "politicizing" the greatest number
- Bring together union militants, and resolutely put itself at the service of worker's struggles
- Explain the political action of the FLQ (for example, through tracts, petitions, formation of a political committee for the defence of political prisoners, communiqués in the newspapers, demanding

of newspapers the reading of communiqués by the information service of the FLQ that are currently boycotted, denouncing the monopoly of information by occupations and other means, cultural demonstrations of the "guerrilla theatre" type, training of militants, etc.)

Front de Libération du Québec

Front de Libération du Québec Manifesto, October 8, 1970

The people in the Front de Libération du Québec are neither Messiahs nor modern-day Robin Hoods. They are a group of Quebec workers who have decided to do everything they can to assure that the people of Quebec take their destiny into their own hands, once and for all.

The Front de Libération du Québec wants total independence for Quebeckers; it wants to see them united in a free society, a society purged for good of its gang of rapacious sharks, the big bosses who dish out patronage and their henchmen, who have turned Quebec into a private preserve of cheap labour and unscrupulous exploitation.

The Front de Libération du Québec is not an aggressive movement, but a response to the aggression organized by high finance through its puppets, the federal and provincial governments (the Brinks farce, Bill 69, the electoral map, the so-called "social progress" [sic] tax, the Power Corporation, medical insurance — for the doctors, the guys at Lapalme ...)

The Front de Libération du Québec finances itself — through voluntary [sic] taxes levied on the enterprises that exploit the workers (banks, finance companies, etc. ...).

"The money powers of the status quo, the majority of the traditional tutors of our people, have obtained from the voters the reaction they hoped for, a step backwards rather than the changes we have worked for as never before, the changes we will continue to work for." (René Lévesque, April 29, 1970)

Once, we believed it worthwhile to channel our energy and our impatience, in the apt words of René Lévesque, into the Parti Québécois, but the Liberal victory shows that what is called democracy in Quebec has always been, and still is, nothing but the "democracy" of the rich. In this sense the victory of the Liberal party is in fact nothing but the victory of the Simard-Cotroni election-fixers. Consequently, we wash our hands of the British parliamentary system; the Front de Libération du Québec will never let itself be distracted by the electoral crumbs that the Anglo-Saxon capitalists toss into the Quebec barnyard every four years. Many Quebeckers have realized the truth and are ready to take action. In the coming year Bourassa is going to get what's coming to him: 100,000 revolutionary workers, armed and organized!

Yes, there are reasons for the Liberal victory. Yes, there are reasons for poverty, unemployment, slums, for the fact that you, Mr. Bergeron of Visitation Street, and you too, Mr. Legendre of Ville de Laval, who make

$10,000 a year, do not feel free in our country, Quebec.

Yes, there are reasons, the guys who work for Lord know them, and so do the fishermen of the Gash, the workers on the North Shore; the miners who work for Iron Ore, for Québec Cartier Mining, for Noranda know these reasons too. The honest workingmen at Cabano, the guys they tried to screw still one more time, they know lots of reasons.

Yes, there are reasons why you, Mr. Tremblay of Panet Street and you, Mr. Cloutier who work in construction in St. Jérôme, can't afford "Golden Vessels" with all the jazzy music and the sharp decor, like Drapeau the aristocrat, the guy who was so concerned about slums that he had coloured billboards stuck up in front of them so that the rich tourists couldn't see us in our misery.

Yes, Madame Lemay of St. Hyacinthe, there are reasons why you can't afford a little junket to Florida like the rotten judges and members of Parliament who travel on our money. The good workers at Vickers and at Davie Shipbuilding, the ones who were given no reason for being thrown out, know these reasons; so do the guys at Murdochville that were smashed only because they wanted to form a union, and whom the rotten judges forced to pay over two million dollars because they had wanted to exercise this elementary right. The guys of Murdochville are familiar with this justice; they know lots of reasons. Yes, there are reasons why you, Mr. Lachance of St. Marguerite Street, go drowning your despair, your bitterness, and your rage in Molson's horse piss. And you, the Lachance boy, with your marijuana cigarettes ...

Yes, there are reasons why you, the welfare cases, are kept from generation to generation on public assistance. There are lots of reasons, the workers for Domtar at Windsor and East Angus know them; the workers for Squibb and Ayers, for the Quebec Liquor Commission and for Seven-up and for Victoria Precision, and the blue collar workers of Laval and of Montreal and the guys at Lapalme know lots of reasons.

The workers at Dupont of Canada know some reasons too, even if they will soon be able to express them only in English (thus assimilated, they will swell the number of New Quebeckers, the immigrants who are the darlings of Bill 69).

These reasons ought to have been understood by the policemen of Montreal, the system's muscle; they ought to have realized that we live in a terrorized society, because without their force and their violence, everything fell apart on October 7.

We've had enough of a Canadian federalism which penalizes the dairy farmers of Quebec to satisfy the requirements of the Anglo-Saxons of the Commonwealth; which keeps the honest taxi drivers of Montreal in a state of semi-slavery by shamefully protecting the exclusive monopoly of the nauseating Murray Hill, and its owner — the murderer Charles Hershorn and his son Paul who, the night of October 7, repeatedly tore a .22 rifle out of the hands of his employees to fire on the taxi drivers and thereby mortally wounded Corporal Dumas, killed as a demonstrator. Canadian federalism pursues a reckless import policy, thereby throwing out of work the people who earn low wages in the textile and shoe industries, the most downtrodden people in Quebec, and all to line the pockets of a handful of filthy "money-makers" in Cadillacs. We are fed up with a federalism which classes the Quebec nation among the ethnic minorities of Canada.

We, and more and more Quebeckers too, have had it with a government of pussy-footers who perform a hundred and one tricks to charm the American millionaires, begging them to come and invest in Quebec, the Beautiful Province where thousands of square miles of forests full of game and of lakes full of fish are the exclusive property of these all-powerful lords of the twentieth century. We are sick of a government in the hands of a hypocrite like Bourassa who depends on Brinks armoured trucks, an authentic symbol of the foreign occupation of Quebec, to keep the poor Quebec "natives" fearful of that poverty and unemployment to which we are so accustomed.

We are fed up with the taxes we pay that Ottawa's agent in Quebec would give to the English-speaking bosses as an "incentive" for them to speak French, to negotiate in French. Repeat after me: "Cheap labour is main d'oeuvre à bon marché in French."

We have had enough of promises of work and of prosperity, when in fact we will always be the diligent servants and bootlickers of the big shots, as long as there is a Westmount, a Town of Mount Royal, a Hampstead, an Outremont, all these veritable fortresses of the high finance of St. James Street and Wall Street; we will be slaves until Quebeckers, all of us, have used every means, including dynamite and guns, to drive out these big bosses of the economy and of politics, who will stoop to any action however base, the better to screw us.

We live in a society of terrorized slaves, terrorized by the big bosses, Steinberg, Clark, Bronfman, Smith, Neopole, Timmins, Geoffrion, J.L. Lévesque, Hershorn, Thompson, Nesbitt, Desmarais, Kierans (next to these, Rémi Popol the Nightstick, Drapeau the Dog, the Simards' Simple Simon and Trudeau the Pansy are peanuts!).

We are terrorized by the Roman Capitalist Church, though this is less and less true today (who owns the square where the Stock Exchange was built?); terrorized by the payments owing to Household Finance, by the advertising of the grand masters of consumption, Eaton's, Simpson's, Morgan's, Steinberg's, General Motors — terrorized by those exclusive clubs of science and culture, the universities, and by their boss-directors Gaudry and Dorais, and by the vice-boss Robert Shaw.

There are more and more of us who know and suffer under this terrorist society, and the day is coming when all the Westmounts of Quebec will disappear from the map.

Workers in industry, in mines and in the forests! Workers in the service industries, teachers, students and unemployed! Take what belongs to you, your jobs, your determination and your freedom. And you, the workers at General Electric, you make your factories run; you are the only ones able to produce; without you, General Electric is nothing!

Workers of Quebec, begin from this day forward to take back what is yours; take yourselves what belongs to you. Only you know your factories, your machines, your hotels, your universities, your unions; do not wait for some organization to produce a miracle.

Make your revolution yourselves in your neighbourhoods, in your places of work. If you don't do it yourselves, other usurpers, technocrats or someone else, will replace the handful of cigar-smokers we know today and everything will have to be done all over again. Only you are capable of building a free society.

We must struggle not individually but together, till victory is obtained, with every means at our disposal, like the Patriots of 1897–1898 (those whom Our Holy Mother Church hastened to excommunicate, the better to sell out to British interests).

In the four corners of Quebec, may those who have been disdainfully called lousy Frenchmen and alcoholics begin a vigorous battle against those who have muzzled liberty and justice; may they put out of commission all the professional holdup artists and swindlers: bankers, businessmen, judges and corrupt political wheeler-dealers ...

We are Quebec workers and we are prepared to go all the way. With the help of the entire population, we want to replace this society of slaves by a free society, operating by itself and for itself, a society open on the world. Our struggle can only be victorious. A people that has awakened cannot long be kept in misery and contempt.

Long live Free Quebec!
Long live our comrades the political prisoners!
Long live the Quebec Revolution!
Long live the Front de Liberation du Quebec!

Appendix V:
Prime Minister of Canada's Televised Statement on the *War Measures Act*, October 16, 1970

I am speaking to you at a moment of grave crisis, when violent and fanatical men are attempting to destroy the unity and the freedom of Canada. One aspect of that crisis is the threat which has been made on the lives of two innocent men. These are matters of the utmost gravity and I want to tell you what the government is doing to deal with them.

What has taken place in Montreal in the past two weeks is not unprecedented. It has happened elsewhere in the world on several recent occasions: it could happen elsewhere within Canada. But Canadians have always assumed that it could not happen here and as a result we are doubly shocked that it has.

Our assumption may have been naive, but it was understandable: understandable because democracy flourishes in Canada; understandable because individual liberty is cherished in Canada.

Notwithstanding these conditions, partly because of them, it has been demonstrated now to us by a few misguided persons just how fragile a democratic society can be if democracy is not prepared to defend itself, and just how vulnerable to blackmail are tolerant, compassionate people.

Because the kidnappings and the blackmail are most familiar to you, I shall deal with them first.

The governments of Canada and Quebec have been told by groups of self-styled revolutionaries that they intend to murder in cold blood two innocent men unless their demands are met. The kidnappers claim they act as they do in order to draw attention to instances of social injustice.

But I ask them whose attention are they seeking to attract. The Government of Canada? The Government of Quebec?

Every government in this country is well aware of the existence of deep and important social problems. And every government to the limit of its resources and ability is deeply committed to their solution. But not by kidnappings and bombings. By hard work.

And if any doubt exists about the good faith or the ability of any government, there are opposition parties ready and willing to be given an opportunity to govern. In short there is available everywhere in Canada an effective mechanism to change governments by peaceful means. It has been employed by disenchanted voters again and again.

Who are the kidnap victims'? To the victims' families they are husbands and fathers. To the kidnappers their identity is immaterial. The kidnappers' purposes would be served equally well by having in their grip you or me, or perhaps some child.

Their purpose is to exploit the normal, human feelings of Canadians and to bend those feelings of sympathy into instruments for their own violent and revolutionary ends.

What are the kidnappers demanding in return for the lives of these men? Several things. For one, they want their grievances aired by force in public on the assumption no doubt that all right-thinking persons would be persuaded that the problems of the world can be solved by shouting slogans and insults.

They want more. They want the police to offer up as a sacrificial lamb a person whom they assume assisted in the lawful arrest and proper conviction of certain of their criminal friends.

They also want money. Ransom money.

They want still more. They demand the release from prison of 17 criminals and the dropping of charges against six other men, all of whom they refer to as "political prisoners."

Who are these men who are held out as latter-day patriots and martyrs? Let me describe them to you.

Three are convicted murderers; five others were jailed for manslaughter; one is serving a life imprisonment after having pleaded guilty to numerous charges related to bombings; another has been convicted of 17 armed robberies; two were once parolled but are now back in jail awaiting trial on charges of robberies.

Yet we are being asked to believe that these persons have been unjustly dealt with, that they have been imprisoned as a result of their political opinions, and that they deserve to be freed immediately, without recourse to due process of law.

The responsibility of deciding whether to release one or another of these criminals is that of the federal government. It is a responsibility that the government will discharge according to law.

To bow to the pressures of these kidnappers who demand that the prisoners be released would be not only an abdication of responsibility, it would lead to an increase in terrorist activities in Quebec.

It would be as well an invitation to terrorism and kidnapping across the country. We might well find ourselves facing an endless series of demands for the release of criminals from jails, from coast to coast, and we would find that the hostages could be innocent members of your family or of your neighborhood.

At the moment the FLQ is holding hostage two men in the Montreal area, one a British diplomat, the other a Quebec cabinet minister. They are threatened with murder.

Should governments give in to this crude blackmail, we would be facing the breakdown of the legal system and its replacement by the law of the jungle. The government's decision to prevent this from happening is not taken just to defend an important principle.

It is taken to protect the lives of Canadians from dangers of the sort I have mentioned. Freedom and personal security are safeguarded by laws; those laws must be respected in order to be effective.

If it is the responsibility of government to deny the demands of the kidnappers, the safety of the hostages is without question the responsibility of the kidnappers. Only the most twisted form of logic could conclude otherwise.

Nothing that either the government of Canada or the government of Quebec has done or failed to do, now or in the future, could possibly excuse any injury to either of these two innocent men.

The guns pointed at their heads have FLQ fingers on the triggers. Should any injury result, there is no explanation that could condone the acts. Should there be harm done to these men, the government promises unceasing pursuit of those responsible.

During the past 12 days, the governments of Canada and Quebec have been engaged in constant consultations. The course followed in this matter had the full support of both governments, and of the Montreal municipal authorities. In order to save the lives of Mr. Cross and Mr. Laporte, we have engaged in indirect communications with the kidnappers.

The offer of the federal government to the kidnappers of safe conduct out of Canada to a country of their choice, in return for the delivery of the hostages, has not yet been taken up. neither has the offer of the government of Quebec to recommend parole for the five prisoners eligible for parole.

This offer of safe conduct was made only because Mr. Cross and Mr. Laporte might be able to identify their kidnappers and to assist in their prosecution. By offering the kidnappers safe exit from Canada, we removed from them any possible motivation for murdering their hostages.

Let me turn now to the broader implications of the threat represented by the FLQ and similar organizations.

If a democratic society is to continue to exist, it must be able to root out the cancer of an armed, revolutionary movement that is bent on destroying the very basis of our freedom. For that reason the government, following an analysis of the facts, including requests of the government of Quebec and the city of Montreal for urgent action, decided to proclaim the War Measures Act.

It did so at 4:00 a.m. this morning, in order to permit the full weight of government to be brought quickly to bear on all those persons advocating or practising violence as a means of achieving political ends.

The War Measures Act gives sweeping powers to the government. It also suspends the operation of the Canadian Bill of Rights. I can assure you that the government is most reluctant to seek such powers, and did so only when it became crystal clear that the situation could not be controlled unless some extraordinary assistance was made available on an urgent basis.

The authority contained in the act will permit governments to deal effectively with the nebulous yet dangerous challenge to society represented by terrorist organizations. The criminal law as it stands is simply not adequate to deal with systematic terrorism.

The police have therefore been given certain extraordinary powers necessary for the effective detection and elimination of conspiratorial organizations which advocate the use of violence. These organizations, and membership in them, have been declared illegal.

The powers include the right to search and arrest without warrant, to detain suspected persons without the necessity of laying specific charges immediately, and to detain persons without bail.

These are strong powers and I find them as distasteful as I am sure you do. They are necessary, however, to permit the police to deal with persons who advocate or promote the violent overthrow of our democratic system.

In short, I assure you that the government recognizes its grave responsibilities in interfering in certain cases with civil liberties, and that it remains answerable to the people of Canada for its actions.

The government will revoke this proclamation as soon as possible.

As I said in the House of Commons this morning, the government will allow sufficient time to pass to give it the necessary experience to assess the type of statute which may be required in the present circumstances.

It is my firm intention to discuss then with the leaders of the opposition parties the desirability of introducing legislation of a less comprehensive nature. In this respect I earnestly solicited from the leaders and from all honourable members constructive suggestions for the amendment of the regulations.

Such suggestions will be given careful consideration for possible inclusion in any new statute.

I recognize, as I hope do others, that this extreme position which governments have been forced into is in some respects a trap. It is a well-known technique of revolutionary groups who attempt to destroy society by unjustified violence, to goad the authorities into inflexible attitudes. The revolutionaries then employ this evidence of alleged authoritarianism as justification for the need to use violence in their renewed attacks on the social structure.

I appeal to all Canadians not to become so obsessed by what the government has done today in response to terrorism that they forget the opening play in this vicious game. That play was taken by the revolutionaries; they chose to use bombing, murder and kidnapping.

The threat posed by the FLQ terrorists and their supporters is out of all proportion to their numbers. This follows from the fact that they act stealthily and because they are known to have in their possession a considerable amount of dynamite.

To guard against the very real possibility of bombings directed at public buildings or utilities in the immediate future the government of Quebec has requested the assistance of the Canadian Armed Forces to support the police in several places in the province of Quebec. These forces took up their positions yesterday.

Violence, unhappily, is no stranger to this decade. The Speech from the Throne opening the current session of Parliament a few days ago said that "we live in a period of tenseness and unease." We must not overlook the fact, moreover, that violence is often a symptom of deep social unrest.

This government has pledged that it will introduce legislation which deals not only with symptoms but with the social causes which often underlie or serve as an excuse for crime and disorder.

It was in that context that I stated in the House of Commons a year ago that there was no need anywhere in Canada for misguided or misinformed zealots to resort to acts of violence in the belief that only in this fashion could they accomplish change.

There may be some places in the world where the law is so inflexible and so insensitive as to prompt such beliefs.

But Canada is not such a place. I said then, and I repeat now, that those who would defy the law and ignore the opportunities available to them to right their wrongs and satisfy their claims will receive no hearing from this government

We shall ensure that the laws passed by Parliament are worthy of respect. We shall also ensure that those laws are respected.

We have seen in many parts of Canada all too much evidence of violence in the name of revolution in the past 12 months. We are now able to see some of the consequences of violence.

Persons who invoke violence are raising deliberately the level of hate in Canada. They do so at a time when the country must eliminate hate, and must exhibit tolerance and compassion in order to create the kind of society which we all desire.

Yet those who disrespect legal processes create a danger that law-abiding elements of the community, out of anger and out of fear, will harden their attitudes and refuse to accommodate any change or remedy any shortcomings. They refuse because fear deprives persons of their normal sense of compassion and their normal sense of justice.

This government is not acting out of fear. It is acting to prevent fear from spreading. It is acting to maintain the rule of law without which freedom is impossible.

It is acting to make clear to kidnappers, revolutionaries and assassins that in this country laws are made and changed by the elected representatives of all Canadians — not by a handful of self-selected dictators. Those who gain power through terror rule through terror. The government is acting, therefore, to protect your life and your liberty.

The government is acting as well to ensure the safe return of Mr. James Cross and Mr. Pierre Laporte. I speak for millions of Canadians when I say to their courageous wives and families how much we sympathize with them for the nightmare to which they have been subjected, and how much we all hope and pray that it will soon conclude.

Canada remains one of the most wholesome and humane lands on this earth. If we stand firm, this current situation will soon pass. We will be able to say proudly, as we have for decades, that within Canada there is ample room for opposition and dissent, but none for intimidation and terror.

There are very few times in the history of any country when all persons must take a stand on critical issues. This is one of those times; this is one of those issues.

I am confident that those persons who unleashed this tragic sequence of events with the aim of destroying our society and dividing our country will find that the opposite will occur. The result of their acts will be a stronger society in a unified country. Those who would have divided us will have united us.

I sense the unease which grips many Canadians today. Some of you are upset, and this is understandable. I want to reassure you that the authorities have the situation well in hand.

Everything that needs to be done is being done; every level of government in this country is well prepared to act in your interests.

About the Authors

A former member of Canadian military intelligence, Dwight Hamilton worked at *Influence* and *Toronto Life* magazines before beginning to write for the *Toronto Sun* and *Financial Post Magazine*. He has been a staff editor at two of Canada's largest professional journals, has served on the board of directors of the Canadian Society of Magazine Editors, and his work has appeared in over a dozen publications in the last twenty years. He is a graduate of Trinity College School, the Ontario College of Art and Design, the University of Toronto (international relations), and Ryerson University. Hamilton was the principal author and editor of *Inside Canadian Intelligence*.

Kostas Rimsa, CD, served for many years as an officer in Canadian military intelligence and once instructed a program on international terrorism at Humber College in Toronto, the first of its kind in North America. He is a graduate of Ottawa's Ashbury College as well as the University of Toronto. He later worked in a variety of roles in the former Soviet Union for over a decade, teaching crisis management and assisting in the formation of Lithuania's new secret service. Rimsa was a key contributor to *Inside Canadian Intelligence*.